THE PRACTICE OF
CONTINUING EDUCATION
IN THE HUMAN SERVICES

THE PRACTICE OF CONTINUING EDUCATION IN THE HUMAN SERVICES

Armand Lauffer
The University of Michigan

with contributions by
Kenneth Kenney
Roger Manela
Celeste Sturdevant

Published in conjunction with the Continuing Education Program for the Human Services of The University of Michigan School of Social Work

McGRAW-HILL BOOK COMPANY
*New York   St. Louis   San Francisco   Auckland   Bogotá   Düsseldorf
Johannesburg   London   Madrid   Mexico   Montreal   New Delhi   Panama
Paris   São Paulo   Singapore   Sydney   Tokyo   Toronto*

362.071
L373p

Library of Congress Cataloging in Publication Data

Lauffer, Armand.
 The practice of continuing education in the human services.

 Includes index.
 1. Mental hygiene—Study and teaching (Continuing education)
I. Title.
RA790.8.L38   362'.07'1   76-58391
ISBN 0-07-036625-X

THE PRACTICE OF CONTINUING EDUCATION IN THE HUMAN SERVICES

1 2 3 4 5 6 7 8 9 0   D O D O   7 8 3 2 1 0 9 8 7

This book was set in Times Roman by Creative Book Services, subsidiary of McGregor & Werner, Inc. The editor was Robert G. Manley; the designer was Creative Book Services, subsidiary of McGregor & Werner, Inc.; the production supervisor was Milton J. Heiberg. The cover was designed by Toni Goldmark.

Contents

v

Introduction

THE IDEA FOR THIS STUDY

This study was conceived in a tornado shelter. The scene was the Kellogg Center for Continuing Education in Norman, Oklahoma. It was May 1971, five years before this book was completed. Some sixty persons had been convened by the National Institute of Mental Health (NIMH) in order to identify the principles upon which the practice of continuing education (CE) in mental health could be based. Most of us were directors of CE projects supported by NIMH.[1]

The group was composed of psychiatrists, nurses, social workers, psychologists, and adult educators. About half were employed by professional schools and by university extension services. The others included directors of manpower and training divisions in state

[1] National Institute of Mental Health Continuing Education Branch, Department of Health, Education and Welfare, Washington, D.C.

departments of mental health, staff development specialists from mental hospitals, administrators of community mental health centers, private practitioners, and representatives of national and professional associations. Some directed large projects, nation- or statewide in scope. Others were concerned with staff development in relatively small agencies. A half-dozen federal officials and consultants were also present.

Despite the diversity of our backgrounds, we had three things in common. We were all directly involved in or concerned with the development and expansion of continuing education, most of us were new to continuing education, and few of us had any training in it. Continuing education had only recently received concerted attention in our respective professions and occupational settings.

Much of the first two days was spent in trying to identify a set of underlying practice principles. We looked primarily to the developing field of adult education for concepts that we could borrow or adapt. The effort soon broke down.

By the third day we scuttled the planned sessions in order to uncover the practices from which principles might be derived. We broke into small groups to talk about what we did on our jobs that might be identified as continuing education. It was during one of those exchange sessions that the twister hit. It was a propitious occurrence.

Two or three project directors, a consultant, and two staff members of the NIMH Continuing Education Branch found themselves in the same shelter. I noticed some beer in a refrigerator. We passed it around and continued on the theme of one of the discussions begun aboveground.

As we talked, it became increasingly clear that the boundaries of continuing education practice in the mental health professions were undergoing a continuous process of testing and expansion. Even the purposes of CE were unclear. For example, some continuing educators were concerned primarily with increasing the skill, expanding the knowledge, enhancing the sensitivity, or modifying the attitudes of mental health practitioners. Their CE activities tended to be oriented toward helping the practitioner do a job better, advance within a chosen occupation, or move into new occupational roles.

Other continuing educators directed most of their efforts at systems change. Explicitly concerned with the way in which mental health services were delivered, resources allocated, or new programs established, they used educational activities as only one of a number of means toward improving service delivery. Although all of us tended to identify with the field of mental health, many of us were involved in other fields as well. We found that no discussion of staff development and continuing education in mental health could be complete without a broader human services concern.

In the context of this diversity, any efforts to develop a unifying set of principles seemed premature. It threatened early closure on what is considered effective practice. Our practices, we felt, had to shake themselves out through a process of trial and error before staff development CE in the human services could be defined and its underlying principles identified.

We agreed on the need for better descriptions of practice. We needed to know what continuing educators and staff developers do, how they do it, and why. Two years later this project was funded; and the study began.

STUDY METHODS

Interviews with continuing educators and staff developers in mental health and other human services were the primary source of our data. Initially, we did not find the literature particularly useful. Very little written material was available in continuing education in the human services and even less in mental health. Professional articles tended to be ideological in nature, specifying what the writer thought continuing educators *should* be doing rather than describing what they were *in fact* doing.

Other than project reports, there were virtually no histories, no case materials, and no critical analyses of practice. But project reports were also inadequate for our purposes. Although they might summarize a project's objectives and results, they generally ignored the processes and means used or the reasons why one or another choice was made. Program evaluations tended to focus on inputs (what went into a program, such as quality of staff, facilities, instructional content) or on outputs (what changes, if any, occurred). Few described what we were after—the "throughput."

Finally we decided to interview practitioners in order to elicit the information we sought.

In order to decide whom to interview, we examined the summaries of all CE projects funded by the Continuing Education Branch of NIMH. We requested the names of additional project directors from the appropriate professional organizations: the National Association of Social Workers, the Council on Social Work Education, the

American Medical Association, the American Psychiatric Association, the American Nurses' Association, and the American
Psychological Association. We also selected a number of projects in
the manpower and staff development units of state human service
agencies. We then sent questionnaires to some 230 project and program directors, asking them to describe their programs briefly and to
send us project reports and descriptions they felt were representative of their work. On the basis of these returns, we phoned
approximately 100 continuing educators, staff developers, and administrators to get further information and to make tentative interview appointments. In some cases these conversations led to additional contacts.

Finally, some sixty project and program directors were selected
for interviews, and appointments were made. In order to be as geo-
graphically inclusive as possible, we located interview sites in differ-
ent· sections of the country: New England, the New York–New
Jersey–Philadelphia area, the South and Southwest, the Midwest, the
Northwest, and the West Coast. We spoke to people who considered
themselves to be professional continuing educators or staff developers and to others who thought of themselves as administrators or
practitioners who "did CE on the side." We included paraprofessionals and volunteers. We interviewed people from each of the
mental health professions, although many interviewees, especially
social workers and nurses, were involved in human service agencies
not generally categorized as mental health settings (e.g., nursing
homes, general hospitals, social service departments, drug clinics).We spoke with people in university settings, in national agencies,
in state and local agencies, and in private practice. (A list of interview
sites and interviewees is found in Appendix 8.)

It was only after completing half the interviews and some preliminary analysis of the resulting data that we decided to conduct a
more structured and projective Delphi study. The use of Delphi for
assessment purposes is discussed in a separate report to NIMH.[2]
Delphi is a highly structured technique in which a series of questionnaires are used to elicit informed opinions on probability, feasibility,
desirability, and so on. Thirty-five nationally known experts on
mental health practices, administration, and education were selected

[2]Charles Garvin, "Training and the Future of the Mental Health Services: Steps
towards the Service Society," in Armand Lauffer, *Mental Health Continuing Education for the Future: Report and Recommendations*, University of Michigan, Ann
Arbor, 1976.

to serve as panelists. They identified trends in mental health practice and in education for that practice.

At about this point in our research, we returned to the literature, weaving our readings into our interviewing and our analysis. Although we wanted this volume to reflect what practitioners told us they do and how they do it, we also felt the need to use social science concepts to better understand some of the rationales educators use to advance their ideas.

This is not to say that we initially approached our interviews with *tabulae rasae* or without a set of instrumental concepts. On the contrary, we began with an open, theoretical scheme built upon social science concepts and practice-based experiences. Our project team included a psychologist, a sociologist, a social worker, and an adult educator. Our previous experiences had included CE and staff development, direct practice in varied mental health settings, administration, community work, research on occupations and careers, and research on curriculum and instructional technology. We drew heavily on these experiences, just as we drew heavily and eclectically on concepts from the social sciences.

The approach we used was heuristic. In essence, we used existing theory, concepts, and conceptual schemes whenever they seemed useful in furthering the investigation or in the analysis of our initial findings. For example, in order to determine the reasons that people become continuing educators, we drew heavily on the works of Everett Hughes, Howard Becker, Anselm Strauss, Donald Super, and others who have written on the psychology and sociology of careers.

In examining the organizational structure of continuing education programs and their relationships to their environments, we selected from the works of organizational theorists such as J. D. Thompson, Sol Levine, and Phillip Selznick. We looked to economists, staffing experts, and educators for a better understanding of the functions of continuing education for both the society and the individual. The writings of such adult educators as Cyril Houle and Malcolm Knowles offered concepts on how adults learn and how they are taught. Other issues led us to the writings of George Herbert Mead, Kurt Lewin, B. F. Skinner, Jean Piaget, and John Dewey.

Each time our staff came back from a series of interviews, new questions were raised that led us to examine additional concepts and theories in the literature. These concepts were tested against observed reality until they no longer suggested new interpretations or questions for subsequent interviews. Both theory and experience were used to sharpen the questions asked and to give added meaning to the answers received.

Theory, then, became the cause and effect of a constant chain of reformulation of observations and evaluations of the data from the field. Although this approach may have resulted in some spotty or unsystematic gathering of data, it nevertheless helped us to refine and expand our notions of what was important. By neither imposing a set of rigid hypotheses on the data prior to collection nor doing a *post-factum* analysis on all the data after they were gathered, we left the door open to discovery throughout the project. This permitted us to proceed with a fairly flexible statement of the problems. In a sense, we pursued a strategy of "planned serendipity."

Unfortunately the process had to end when we began writing this volume in the summer of 1974. Although we've added more recent observations in the final rewrite, events have probably outdistanced many of our findings. It could not be otherwise in describing a new occupation in its early stages of development.

METHOD OF PRESENTATION

To avoid painting a static picture of an occupational group that is undergoing rapid change, we have chosen both to describe what we actually saw happening and to discuss the trends we saw developing. At times we found ourselves slipping off our objective perch, strongly tempted to substitute our own opinions for our observations. This is perhaps inevitable in a study that tries to describe the boundaries of practice. Someone, after all, has to decide where those boundaries should be drawn, so that they are not so broad as to be meaningless or so narrow as to be constrictive.

Although our own biases and the limits of our observational and analytical capacities have certainly influenced our reporting, we have tried to balance these influences by extensively quoting other staff developers and continuing educators. Throughout these pages continuing educators speak directly of their own work and their own experiences. Thus, in many ways, the reader is provided with the raw data, albeit those selected by the investigators. Persons quoted and situations described have been disguised to protect the anonymity of respondents and to avoid identifying any practitioners as special or outstanding. Because quotes have been lifted out of rather extensive interviews, the actual words spoken have sometimes required editing for purposes of comprehensibility and brevity. We have found many continuing educators to be eloquent in describing who they are, what they do, and how they do it.

This method of presentation was chosen because we are convinced that doing otherwise might lead to the premature closure we sought to avoid at the outset. The diversity of the CE programs and projects that we examine here should be viewed as indicative rather than descriptive of the diversity that exists in reality.

THE IMPORTANCE OF CONTINUING EDUCATION

Perhaps, for these reasons, what we have examined and described is only the tip of an iceberg. This diversity is no accident; it is a response to what one of our interviewees described as "a new reality in which there is no longer such a thing as a terminal degree." We agree. Professional education and the professional degree are no longer coterminous. No "once forever" education can prepare human services personnel for the complexities of their work. The more technical the requirements of professional practice, the more technical are the qualifications for participation and employment within it.

Requirements change as knowledge grows and as changes occur in occupational tasks to be accomplished or in societal problems to be solved. Individuals who do not keep up often find themselves increasingly isolated from the mainstream of their occupational groups and in some cases pushed out of meaningful work. Their competence decreases as their knowledge and skills become obsolete. The implications for the individual are loss of meaningful occupational choice. The implications for a profession or other grouping include reductions in efficiency and drop in effectiveness, challenges to its role and mandate, and reduction in client demand and in available resources.

Knowledge has become the key to individual and societal success. The society that is incapable of systematically acquiring and applying knowledge cannot succeed economically, nor can it deal adequately with its social problems. Individuals who do not keep up will find themselves progressively isolated and obsolete. The same may be said of a profession or subgroup within that profession and of any organization providing professional services.

Cure and containment are possible through new forms of schooling and knowledge dissemination available through an expanding network. The network includes universities and professional schools, professional associations, social and mental health service agencies, private firms, individual consultants, and materials production centers. This network is supported through changing standards of professional practice, periodic recertification, and awareness of the need coupled with new sources of support for programs of continuing education and lifelong learning. The network and its support system are described in the chapters that follow.

ORGANIZATION OF THIS VOLUME

We have organized the volume into three sections, followed by several appendixes. Part One provides an overview of CE practice in three major arenas: (1) higher education in the university or professional school and its constituents, (2) the professional association and its members, and (3) the service agency and its employees. Staff development is discussed as part of the service-agency arena rather than as a distinct form of CE practice. The term "continuing education program" (CEP) is used generically to refer to that organizational unit or complex of activities within any of the arenas of practice that conducts or coordinates CE activities as one of its major functions. Thus, for example, a staff development or manpower and training unit in a state department of mental health will be referred to as a CEP.

Part Two examines the growth of the CEP within the context of its institutional relationships. Individual chapters focus on relationships with elements in the CE's host institution or task environment, growth and institutionalization, the management of exchange, patterns of financing CE and staff development activities, and strategies employed for marketing these activities.

Part Three examines the processes of programming and program development from the point of view of the CE practitioner. Analytic and interactional tasks performed in each of five stages of the planning process are described. Special attention is given to assessment and program evaluation. Relatively typical program formats are identified. We conclude with an exploration of the future of continuing education in the human services in which we discuss the emergence of a new occupational specialist within the human services—the continuing educator whose identity is no longer shrouded in ambiguity and whose functions are increasingly central to the entire enterprise.

Although we have limited our examination of practice primarily to CE and staff development in the professions identified with the field of mental health, we have looked at a number of other settings as well. We believe our findings may be of interest to other occupational groups within the human services and to adult educators. Accordingly, we have attempted to organize the material in a fashion that permits easy identification of issues. The result is a cross between a study report, a textbook, and a series of newspaper Sunday supplement items. This may leave some readers wishing for more consistency, but it provided us with comfortable latitude in reporting what we saw and in sharing what we found.

The reader is directed to a companion volume by Armand Lauffer and Celeste Sturdevant, *Doing Continuing Education and Staff Development*, which provides a nuts-and-bolts approach to practice. It includes a number of how-to-do-it guides and program design tips.

Acknowledgments

First, I must express my personal gratitude to Celeste Sturdevant, Roger Manela, and Ken Kenney, whose clear thinking, energy, and interviewing skills made it possible for me to put together the first draft of this volume. The four of us owe a collective debt to the continuing educators, staff developers, and administrators who were honest and thoroughly open with us when we asked tough and probing questions. It is their work, after all, that fills these pages and makes them come alive. Their names are listed in Appendix 8.

I am especially grateful to those continuing educators who took the time to read a preliminary draft and to comment extensively in writing, in person, and by telephone. They are Elda Popiel (nursing), Margaret Hoffman (social work), Donald Brown (psychiatry), Harold McPheeters (psychology), and Lawrence Berlin (adult education). Other faculty and staff of the University of Michigan Continuing Education Program for the Human Services made significant contributions. Carole Berlin cleaned up our language, taught us to write concisely, and asked the kind of questions only a perceptive lay person could. Sara Gorodezky consulted on the suggested readings that follow the chapters. Carla Overberger, Jan Stark, Charles Jones, and Charles Garvin participated in many of the think sessions that led to the conceptualizations found on the following pages. The pages themselves were typed, retyped, and typed again by Pat Morris, Joan Eadie, Marion Sernick, Bill Mahder, Walter Carroll, Selma Sussman, and Howard Williams. I hope they consider their efforts worthwhile.

For their support and indulgence, I am indebted to Dean Philip Fellin of the University of Michigan School of Social Work and to Shlomo Sharlin of the School of Social Work at Haifa University, where I spent a sabbatical year.

Finally, I wish to mention the staff of the Continuing Education branch at the National Institute of Mental Health. Without NIMH's support, neither this volume nor many of the CE activities we describe would ever have come about. The growth of CE in the mental health professions and in the human services owes a great deal to the conceptual leadership and devotion given by NIMH staff. They helped many of us get started, supported us when we felt discouraged, defeated, or uncertain of where to go, and shared their knowledge and vision generously. Four persons in particular—Thomas Webster, Margaret Hoffman, Jeanette Chamberlain, and Warren Lamson—saw the project through the various stages of research.

The contributions of those persons mentioned are so intertwined with the final product that I am left with a final thought, which applies to both this volume and to CE in general: *A hen is an egg's way of creating another egg.* Puzzle on that as you peruse the following pages. I think you'll know what I mean.

Armand Lauffer

THE PRACTICE OF
CONTINUING EDUCATION
IN THE HUMAN SERVICES

Part One

Three Arenas of Practice

Chapter 1

The Arenas of Practice in Continuing Education and Staff Development

The center of gravity in professional education has shifted from the formal, time-limited, on-campus course of instruction toward more informal community or on-the-job, work-oriented learning activities. In the human services these activities have become increasingly important as vehicles for providing individual learners with means for expanding knowledge and skill, increasing opportunities for career and occupational mobility and improving job satisfaction, raising professional standards, protecting or expanding the domains of existing occupational groups, and bringing nonprofessional and subprofessional personnel into the system of service delivery.

Although CE activities are conducted in a variety of settings, three principal arenas of practice were identified by our research team: the service agency and its employees, the university or professional school and its constituents, and the professional association and its members. The continuing educator in each of these arenas operates within a complex sphere of action. It includes the organization or host institution within which the educator is located, the population or complex of organizations that he or she serves or hopes to change, and the other elements in the environment that support or detract from his or her activities. Continuing education activities are also offered in a variety of other settings and lesser arenas described in this chapter.

THE PRINCIPAL ARENAS OF PRACTICE

CE at the University

Continuing educators working at the university are usually located in a professional school or a universitywide extension division. Perhaps in no other setting are their activities more varied. They plan and conduct summer workshops, coordinate extension course offerings, direct materials development projects, and contract with agencies to provide consultation or to do staff development. They are often directly involved in teaching and "stand-up" training. They perform administrative and management tasks such as recruitment and assignment of faculty, payment of stipends and collection of fees, and needs assessment and program evaluation.

They frequently work with and through a variety of advisory and planning committees that may provide them with the auspices for and the consumers of their services. Collaborative activities with state and local service agencies and with professional associations are common.

The university's involvement in continuing education is very much related to its missions of education, research, and service. These missions are increasingly intertwined with other institutions in the larger community. Research in the human services, for example, is frequently the result of contracts with operating agencies or responses to requests for proposals (RFPs) from government agencies. The findings of service-oriented research are often disseminated through CE activities.

Formal campus-based education is no longer perceived as a vaccine that can prevent ignorance in later life. Obsolescence of current knowledge, together with the rapid development of new knowledge, shifts in national priorities, and multiplication and complication of social problems, suggests that continuing education has already become a necessary rather than an adjunct function of the university and professional school.

Today nearly all professional schools address the need to create special units for the delivery of CE services to their graduates and to allied personnel and for the management of these programs. During the past five years CE programs have tended to be the most rapidly growing components of the instructional programs of these schools. This growth seems to be intertwined closely with other changes in professional education. For example, several AMA officials and medical professors predict growing support for a system of professional education whereby the core of the curricula may be offered over a physician's lifetime instead of during his or her four years in medical school. This core would shift in keeping with advances in knowledge and changes in practice.

The move from the M.S.W. to the B.S.W. as the basic professional degree and to the Ph.D. as an advanced degree may have an even more immediate effect on social work. Schools of social work may soon begin to shift their emphasis from on-campus to off-campus or part-time instruction as a means of upgrading the knowledge and skill of B.S.W. graduates, or of providing M.S.W.s with transitional instruction leading to a Ph.D. Rapidly changing perceptions of the nurse's functions and the opening up of new practice settings may create similar shifts in schools of nursing. For both social work and nursing, management training has taken on increased importance.

By 1986 no university-level professional school will be without an identifiable continuing education structure. In the human service professions some of these units may be so large and so varied as to be highly competitive with their host institution in their ability to attract resources and consumers. In many instances the lines between on-campus degree-related education and off-campus nondegree programs will blur considerably.

Already several schools of public health and almost all schools of education provide students with the opportunity to earn their degrees off campus through extension courses or local, community-based facilities. One school of social work has created a four-year program that permits employed practitioners to complete their degree requirements without ever leaving their places of work. Although they take courses on campus, they do so on a part-time basis and flesh out their degree requirements through enrollment in CE seminars and workshops. Another school of social work is in the process of designing an on-off campus degree program in which enrollees would complete the first year of the M.S.W. degree through extension satellites located in social agencies throughout the state. The second year would be completed in weekend courses, laboratories, and workshops offered on campus.

Although some of these programs are not restricted to continuing education, they utilize formats and delivey mechanisms in common with CE programs: intense instructional activities in concentrated time periods, modular instruction, workshops and laboratories, and so on. The same activities may be utilized for basic as well as for continuing education. Thus, in some locales, participants in a CE activity might elect academic credit for their participation to be applied toward a degree. Others might elect continuing education units (CEUs) to be applied toward certification or relicensure. Still others would enroll for no reason other than the direct benefits accrued from acquiring new knowledge or developing a new skill.

Lines are further blurred when CE activities offered through a university are cosponsored by a professional association or service agency. For example, we increasingly found schools of social work and nursing conducting staff development activities on a contractual basis with an agency or hospital. Although the selection of content for the development of the course was often negotiated with agency administrative personnel, the participants were free to choose whether or not to elect academic credit applicable to an advanced degree.

CE within Professional Associations

Every professional association in the human services has at least one staff member responsible for continuing education. The nature of the responsibilities varies. In some organizations, such as the American Medical Association and the American Nurses' Association, the continuing educator may be involved in the conduct or coordination of CE activities at the national, state, or regional level. In others, such as the Council on Social Work Education and the National Association of Social Workers, the CE person provides program consultation and acts as a resource person to member schools or member chapters. In still others, such as the American Psychiatric Association and the American Psychological Association, the person may engage in activities aimed at developing the competence and skills of continuing educators within their professions.

In each of these associations continuing educators tend to spend much of their time on promotional activities, setting standards, and program development. They do not necessarily limit themselves to promoting their associations' own CE offerings. They do promote the idea of continuing education in general and its relationship to granting professional credentials and the upgrading of knowledge.

In some associations CE personnel are responsible for development of instructional materials: self- and agency-assessment forms, knowledge of inventories, journals, books, pamphlets, and cassette tapes of particular interest to a professional or occupational group.

They may also coordinate national and regional conferences and skill-training sessions or provide consultation on CE to local and state affiliates.

The increasing involvement of the professional association in the conduct or support of continuing education activities stems from two sources of pressure, one outside and one within the association itself. External pressure comes from the general public, which increasingly demands high-quality service from the professions. The association perceives CE as one means of maintaining the occupation's control over certain practice domains. Nationally—or regionally—set standards may be voluntary or compulsory. They tend to be compulsory when related to professional certification programs or state licensing laws. A number of professional associations have lobbied at the state or national level for licensing as a way of protecting the profession's claim to mandate and as one way of increasing or maintaining the competence of its members. Certification and licensing may require periodic examination or evidence of having participated in certain CE activities. Training may be offered as a direct response to any change or upgrading of these standards or licensing requirements.

CE in Agency Staff Development

Perhaps the largest number of human service continuing educators are those charged with responsibility for agency staff development. At the state level they may be located in a department's division of manpower and personnel or department of planning and program development. Some are located more centrally in the state director's office. The location is critical to the prominence given staff development and to the CE program's access to resources and trainees. This is true equally of state departments of mental hygiene, public health, social services, vocational rehabilitation, and others.

Continuing educators and staff development personnel may direct, coordinate, and consult on all learning activities within the department or only on those emanating from the division within which they are located. In general, their activities include materials development, consultation with local, branch, or affiliated agencies, setting standards, the conduct of in-service training, and involvement in organizational or program development.

The work of a staff development specialist in a local mental health or other human service agency may be quite similar. This specialist is also responsible for the conduct of the planning or learning activities related to in-service training, organizational development, or program development. He or she generally will be less involved in materials development but may be heavily involved in work with planning committees from within his or her agency or in managing interagency collaborations.

From the employer's point of view, continuing education can be used to enhance the agency's programmatic or service elements, or for organizational and system maintenance. Agencies often use orientation and training programs to protect both staff members and consumers from inadvertent harm. Staff development activities may be aimed at giving a new staff person preliminary instructions on how to perform on the job. Subsequent activities might be oriented to reinforcing that performance, shifting people to new responsibilities, or filling gaps within the organization as they arise, or might be offered as part of a benefit package.

A number of state agencies have moved beyond the use of staff development for purely in-service or orientation training, to organizational program development concerns. Their CE activities are increasingly problem-focused. These activities may be oriented toward improving services to a population currently underserved or ineffectively served, or they may be directed to improving communication within the agency. Focusing on problems tends to shift responsibility for training from central office personnel to the direct line supervisor, who becomes an integral part of the staff development operation.

Like health insurance and vacations, CE and learning opportunities may be necessary for the maintenance of staff morale and work efficiency. CE is often used as means toward increasing communication and understanding between staffs at different levels for purposes of program and organizational development.

CE is also perceived by some administrators as an efficiency measure. It is sometimes less costly to retrain people internally than to recruit new staff who must be socialized into the agency or whose very recruitment may be costly. Retraining current staff is generally a low-risk activity. New recruits, whatever their backgrounds, are unknown quantities.

Some agencies conduct training activities for workers in other settings to help them better understand how to refer clients to the agency. Others may engage in activities aimed at client populations or community leaders to enable them to make better use of agency services or to increase public support for their programs.

OTHER ARENAS OF PRACTICE

Continuing educators also practice in a number of other arenas which we have designated as auxiliary or secondary. This designation is not intended to imply lack of importance. On the contrary, auxiliary CE programs may offer the only learning opportunities in a particular locale. The director of training in a health and welfare council expressed this aptly:

> We may be doing more training than anybody other than the hospitals and the department of social services in this town, but I still perceive our function as an auxiliary one. A lot of the smaller agencies don't have the staff, the money, or the know-how to conduct their own training. We're doing it for them as a service. Ultimately I'd like to see us work ourselves out of business. Each agency should have its own internal training and staff development capability. We might be helpful in coordinating some resource exchange between agencies, but it would be defeating for us to do the job for them.

In addition to coordinating bodies, other continuing education activities occur in entrepreneurial arenas, research organizations, a "self-help" CE arena, and in mixed arenas.

Coordinating Bodies

Coordinating bodies exist both for institutions of higher education and for service agencies. For higher education there are two regional coordinating bodies: the Southern Regional Education Board (SREB) and the Western Interstate Commission on Higher Education (WICHE). Coordinating bodies for human service agencies include regional mental health service boards, health and welfare councils, human resource commissions, area agencies on aging, and others. Although each may designate continuing education responsibilities to staff members, they generally perceive these responsibilities as auxiliary or secondary in nature. This is so even when few, if any, of the services agencies they coordinate have CE or staff development activities of their own.

Continuing educators working in these coordinating bodies are generally involved in consulting with local affiliates, setting standards, conducting instructional activities aimed at training other trainers, and developing curriculum or other training materials that can be utilized by their affiliates.

Entrepreneurial Arena

The growing demand for continuing education services has spawned a number of entrepreneurs. They generally provide a limited range of services built upon one or two areas of expertise for which they are known. These areas may include consultation, staff development, materials development, and management training. Or they may specialize in specific content areas such as crisis intervention, drug services, guided group interaction, and behavior modification.

The continuing educator as independent entrepreneur may be a single individual who sells his or her services to mental health agencies or who organizes a course, workshop, or seminar for individual consumers. Increasingly, however, these entrepreneurs have discovered the advantages of joining with others to establish consultation, research, service, and/or training firms. The services are then sold for set fees.

In some sections of the country these firms have proliferated at such a rate as to make any attempt to catalog or inventory them an exercise in futility. Although they are important in terms of the numbers of human service practitioners they attract, we have designated them as secondary because of their commercial nature. Because they are rarely affiliated with universities, agencies, or professional associations, they are not generally subject to the same standards of accountability, nor are they always perceived as integral to the larger system of professional education. This is not to suggest that the quality of their services is any less rigorous than that of activities conducted by continuing educators in the three primary arenas. On the contrary, their very dependence on the market sometimes serves to weed out some CE activities of poor quality. Nevertheless, there have been almost no systematic efforts to coordinate these activities or to relate them to those conducted by agencies, universities, or professional associations. Such coordinating efforts may be long overdue, if continuing educators are to reach the consumers, develop effective standards for their work, and hold each other accountable for effective practice.

Self-Help Arena

Many CE activities are not conducted either under institutional auspices or by private practitioners or entrepreneurs. They emerge from interactions between practitioners, administrators, and educators who band together because of common interests.

Some of these self-help groups last only for short periods of time, whereas others maintain themselves over many years. A particularly interesting association of physicians humorously refers to itself as the "Vermont School of Psychiatry."

Most of our members come here every summer for anything from two weeks to two months. At first a couple of guys had the idea of creating a tax dodge by running a weekly workshop. Well, it wasn't much of a tax dodge, but it was a damned good learning experience. So we decided to establish the Vermont School of Psychiatry.

It really is very simple. Once or twice during the summer, we rent an old barn. All the psychiatrists and some other mental health types in the area are invited to enroll. Anybody who wants to teach something can. All he has to do is post the subject matter on one of the beams holding up the barn and indicate what time he'll be there to run the seminar.

People go from beam to beam looking for topics of interest, settle around one beam or one guru, and the school is in session. It's really what the university should be like. I guess it's what some universities were like in medieval times. Too bad we only benefit from it during summer vacation.

The Vermont School represents a natural helping system that is little understood and too often unrecognized by the continuing educator. To find out where human service professionals go for their continuing education, we interviewed a number of people with varied educational backgrounds, from different work settings, and with different work responsibilities. We asked them where they ordinarily went for help with a practice problem, how they learned new skills or techniques, and why they chose to attend certain formally organized and structured CE activities.

Learning from colleagues on or off the job appears to be the most common source of CE. As a member of the training division in a state agency explained:

Learning from your peers is the most crucial aspect of in-service training, one administrators too often ignore. We used to run these orientation sessions for new workers—for everybody from the secretary through the nurses and social workers and up to the psychiatrists.

We found that, although people do want some information from us, they get most of their information from their colleagues right on the job. It didn't make much sense for us to try and socialize them into the goals of the agency or to teach them procedures, when others could do it better on the job, and when what they learn in each hospital sometimes serves to nullify what we teach anyway. In fact, we found that our orientation sessions sometimes did more to discredit the state office and to diminish our authority than to enhance it.

So we decided to leave the orientation to individual hospitals and to departments within each hospital. In some cases it is a formalized process, but in some others there is no formal orientation other than the materials we and the hospital administration make available to people. I really think it works best this way.

He went on to describe how in each hospital, and sometimes in each service or ward, there tended to be one or two people who knew all the rules and regulations. These people acted as the socializers and educators. They did not necessarily have "all the answers," but they usually knew the system in which they worked well enough to make appropriate referrals when questions or problems arose that they couldn't answer or solve.

This role of "information network coordinator" could be filled by anyone: an orderly who keeps his eyes and ears open to such an extent that nurses and psychiatrists frequently become dependent on him, the nursing director of a ward, a psychiatric intern, or a caseworker whose feet are planted in both the hospital and the community, where she has frequent contact with many workers and clients in the mental health system.

There are numerous advantages to this ad hoc colleagueal support system. It is accessible and available. It tends to be personalized, direct, quick, and responsive. It is a good deal less expensive than a more formalized instruction program that requires professional trainers and sometimes specialized facilities and equipment. Moreover, this system does not require that the learner surrender any of his or her independence to the authority of an instructor or training institution.

Conversely, its disadvantages lie precisely in the ad hoc nature of this information exchange and instruction. It is not easily held accountable and frequently breaks down. Inappropriate things may be learned, some of them inhibiting good practice, others subverting institutional goals or good service to patients and clients.

Even an effective ad hoc system may result in a considerable drain upon those called on to give advice or instruction informally, to refer people to others, and so on. It may, in actuality, result in a certain degree of resentment by workers who feel that they are being taken away from their primary responsibilities in order to make up for the fact that formal educational opportunities are not availble to those who seek them out.

This system sometimes extends beyond the boundaries of a particular agency or work setting into a professional association or chapter meeting. Thus some members of a local association may know about new advances or new practices by their fellow professionals in other parts of the country, whereas others may have access to similar information about new therapeutic approaches or successful community strategies employed by mental health workers in other professions. In some cases they may "package" this information by conducting informal workshops or exchange sessions as adjuncts to professional meetings or in their own homes.

We found CE self-help groups of various types in communities throughout the country:

- Tuesday luncheon groups that may have grown out of case conferences and now include short conceptual papers or case materials presented by participants.
- Groups of para- and subprofessionals or volunteers who find they can learn from each other in ways they cannot from professionals. One example is a group of ex-mental patients who had banded together to give each other mutual support for reentry and who over a period of time found themselves serving as adjunct counselors or therapists to professionals. They have now moved to conducting occasional workshops for professionals.
- Caseworkers involved in family practice on a private basis who find they have common concerns both as therapists and as individual entrepreneurs and who support each other through regular meetings that revolve around exchanges of techniques.

Although these self-help groups tend to have instrumental purposes often couched in educational terms, they also serve more expressive functions by providing mutual support and socializing experiences for their members. In addition to regularizing some of the benefits of the ad hoc system described earlier, they perform much the same functions.

They also have many of the same disadvantages. Moreover, they sometimes suffer from a closed perspective, which may discourage the gaining of knowledge and information from sources outside the group. The initiator of one such group explained: "It got so bad that I had to quit or be thrown out for deviant behavior. I couldn't express an unpopular point of view."

Whatever their advantages or disadvantages, the great bulk of mental health CE probably occurs in this natural system, a system that mental health continuing educators are either unaware of or have ignored. Some may now know how to relate to it. One continuing educator, however, uses it as a referral source:

> There's not a town in this state that hasn't got one person who knows more than anybody else about what's happening in the mental health field. If I want to find out what people are interested in, or if I want to spread the word about a workshop or an institute, all I have to do is contact these people by telephone.

In a rural state like ours, that's the way you have to operate. No sense in sending out a broadside message with lots of brochures. All you need is one or two people from each county to pick up a new bit of information or come to a training program. They'll spread the word soon enough, and you'd be surprised at what kind of spread effect you get around here.

One of the more unusual CE project reports we examined built directly on an indigenous helping system. An NIMH-supported project in Arizona made it possible for Navaho medicine men to train apprentices. The project was intended to ensure the perpetuation of the Indians' ancient traditional medicine, which was on the verge of extinction. Both the goals and techniques of traditional medicine were integrated with those of contemporary medicine. The trainees—Indian medicine men—subsequently became the trainers of their client population.

The use of trainees as trainers is common to many other CE activities and settings as well. A physician's education project employs a rather ingenious "budding" system. The bud or germ of an idea is taken by a participant from a workshop session and put into practice in his or her own work place. He or she then reports to colleagues through a newsletter on how things worked out. The report may suggest new ideas so that a particular bud may flower into a tree with many branches and many new buds.

We also came across another novel device for ensuring that others would take responsibility for their own continuing education. The staff of a new CE project in an urban area was searching for a way to train people in grantsmanship and staff development at the same time as they were doing an assessment of needs and interests:

We had about $5,000 in our budget for assessment purposes. We figured nobody could do the assessment better than our consumers themselves. So we hit on an interesting idea that would get things rolling, provide us with some assessment materials, and make us known all at the same time.

We sent out letters to the directors of all the agencies in our area offering each a grant of two hundred and fifty dollars if they were interested in designing a proposal for an internal staff development program that they might fund or that might get funded through some outside source. We pointed out that only twenty planning grants were available. These would be offered to the first twenty agencies that submitted an acceptable outline of how they wanted to proceed. We included some suggestions on procedure in the form of an inventory of needs. This was the start of the assessment process.

We got twenty-seven responses from which we selected the twenty most promising for grants. We notified the twenty that we would help them with their work by conducting two workshops without fee. The first would be on grantsmanship, and we would provide consultation and instruction on proposal design as well as on potential sources of outside funding. This would be followed by a second workshop on the principles of staff development. Here we would be available to consult with them to turn their plans into reality.

We pointed out that agency people might find the workshops useful even if their proposals did not receive funding. The response of the agencies was super. Almost one hundred percent sent staff. They learned something and so did we. They got to know us and we them. Now our working relationships are set.

Practice in Mixed Arenas

Many continuing educators view themselves as practicing in more than one arena. Thus the perceptive staff developer will make effective use of natural helping systems within his or her agency. The university-based continuing educator will develop collaborative relationships with the state or regional professional associations and academies. Private entrepreneurs will sometimes contract to conduct training under a university's auspices. The university and the state agency or local coordinating body may cosponsor consultation efforts, training activities, or the development of training materials.

Just as continuing educators work in different arenas of practice, they may also employ different models of practice. These are described in the next chapter.

Chapter 2

Objectives, Targets, and Program Orientations

Most of the continuing education programs we examined conducted activities that were aimed at (1) improving the capabilities of individual human service personnel in their professional or occupational capacities as practitioners, administrators, supervisors, organizers, and policymakers, or (2) improving the ways in which human services are organized and delivered. The individual and the organization or service system can be defined as either a consumer of service or a target of change.

Those educators with a service orientation treat the individual learner or organization as the consumer. Those with a change orientation perceive the individual or service organization as the target of change. Both orientations may be held simultaneously by the same continuing educator. They are often complementary.

Few continuing education programs operate according to an ideal model; for most, the style of operation tends to follow one or more of the models indicated in Chart 1.

Chart 1 Models of Practice: Consumer or Target vs. Service or Change Orientation

Consumer or target	Orientation	
	Service	Change
The individual learner	1 Consumer choice model	2 Training model
A service agency or service complex	3 Consultation model	4 Systems change model

Consumer Choice Model

When the CEP is service-oriented and perceives the individual as the consumer of that service, it generally pursues a consumer choice model. The model presumes that adult learners are or have the capacity to be autonomous and self-directing.

The consumer is variously perceived as client, "customer," or bona fide partner. Educators who define the consumer as a client are concerned with helping that client make appropriate choices and take increasing responsibility for those choices. The CE service may include counseling and guidance. The continuing educator may perceive himself or herself as an enabler, guide, or facilitator.

When the consumer is defined as a customer, the educator predetermines the choices by designing specific activity options for consumers. The choices will be determined on the basis of an assessment of the needs of a particular class of consumer—such as child welfare workers, family physicians, or psychiatric aides. The continuing educator may then promote those activity choices through a variety of means, such as brochures, leaflets, and announcements at professional meetings. The continuing educator may perceive himself or herself– or be perceived by others—as a promotor, provider, or resource person.

When the educator perceives the consumer as a partner, he or she often involves the individual in setting learning objectives and in the design, conduct, and evaluation of the educational activity. Responsibility for learning is increasingly delegated to the learner.

Training Model

In the training model the individual is the target of change. Persons other than the learner or population of learners (e.g., school counselors, agency board members, crisis-center workers, psychiatric nurses) generally identify training needs or sets instructional objectives. Typically these others might be the employer, a state or federal agency, the leadership of a professional association, or a university faculty group. These others are often viewed as the consumers while trainees are perceived as the targets of change. Their concerns might be focused on the trainees' (1) debilitating or inappropriate attitudes, values, and perspectives; (2) inability to perform certain tasks at an appropriate level of skill; (3) lack of appropriate knowledge of human service issues, problems, and intervention strategies; (4) lack of awareness of services, programs, and facilities that may be important to populations at risk; and (5) need for personal and professional growth.

Acting as an expert in training methods or a particular substantive area, the continuing educator or staff developer is directed to an instructional strategy on the basis of the way in which the problem is defined. If the problem is defined in terms of lack of skills, for example, it may be appropriate to utilize training clinics, tutorials, workshops, or field practice experiences. If the problem is defined as lack of awareness of available facilities and programs, then intervention strategies may include interagency visits and information exchange through newsletters and monthly meetings. If the problem is defined as lack of knowledge, the continuing educator might consider conducting courses, creating self-instructional learning materials, and arranging for lectures or film showings.

In both the consumer choice and training models, the continuing educator may focus on helping the learner perform better in his or her occupational role. At other times the educator may set up learning opportunities that help the worker move laterally from one field of service or one agency to another (e.g., from a child welfare agency to a geriatrics ward in a mental hospital, or from school counseling to the community health center). Finally, the educator may provide learning opportunities that enable the practitioner to move vertically from direct service to supervision or administration.

Consultation Model

As in the consumer choice model, the consultation model also presumes choice on the part of the consumer. In this case, however, the consumer may be a subunit within a service agency, the total agency itself, a complex of service agencies or providers, or a local chapter or affiliate of a professional association. Someone or some group within that unit recognizes a problem that needs to be addressed. This problem is generally defined in terms of poor and inefficient organizational performance, low morale, poor communication, and inappropriate management style.

Once a problem is perceived, even if it is not identified fully, the continuing educator may become involved in the effort to define the problem operationally and to design a plan to overcome it. The educator may be either an outside agent or an insider responsible for staff development and related personnel problems. He or she may be responsible primarily for managing training or learning activities aimed at overcoming the identified problem. The employing agency or other organization becomes the consumer of the service provided by the continuing educator/consultant. It may also perceive itself as the recipient of a service. The individual worker within the agency may be viewed as the target of change.

Systems Change Model

The systems change model is characteristic of many CE programs in the mental health and human service fields. Like other change agents, continuing educators pursuing this model begin by focusing on specific problems in practice. These are generally defined as (1) a lack of appropriate, available, or accessible services for specific population and (2) inadequate coordination, cooperation, and collaboration between service providers in a given geographic area. For example, if mental health services to Chicano populations in the southwest region of the state are relatively unavailable, the continuing educator or staff developer may design instructional activities aimed at preparing workers in traditional agencies to work with new client populations. The workers are the targets of change; their clients are the consumers of the new or changed services the workers are able to provide.

Systems change strategies might include such diverse educational approaches as awareness-raising workshops, problem-focused conferences, seminars, and public-information campaigns. When problems lie in lack of cooperation or basic communication between various service providers, the continuing educator may establish local task forces that identify practice problems of concern to each of them. These task forces may then contract with the educator or the CEP for training in the identified area.

At other times a continuing educator may organize special projects to demonstrate how local providers can redeploy their efforts more effectively. He or she may point out that lack of coordination frequently results not only in gaps or duplications in service but in totally ineffective operations. For example, it is inappropriate for a mental hospital to release geriatric patients into the community if there are no facilities available to reintegrate them into the community. Even if community facilities are available, hospital staff may now be aware of these resources or how to work with them. Similarly, the clinical services of a child guidance center may prove ineffective unless they are supported by complementary activities in the school, the home, the courts, and elsewhere.

The reader may ask what these activities have to do with continuing education. Ought we not leave demonstration projects to planners and researchers and let continuing educators stick to the business of coordinating and conducting instructional programs? Stated otherwise, the question might be: When is an intervention identified as continuing education and when is it not? This is a boundary question for which the answers are tentative. The boundaries of CE and staff development may overlap with community development, social planning, adult education, social action, and community education.

CONTINUING EDUCATION OR STAFF DEVELOPMENT?

The reader will notice that we use the terms "staff developer" or "continuing educator" somewhat interchangeably and do the same with the terms "staff development" and "continuing education." We also use the term "continuing education program" (CEP) generically to refer to the CE unit within any of the practice arenas we discussed earlier: the agency, the university or professional school, or the professional association.

This "fudging," so to speak, is not unintentional. Within our frame of reference, staff development and continuing education are coterminous, if not identical. Although the agency-based continuing educator is almost invariably referred to as a staff developer, continuing educators in other settings are also engaged in staff development.

When the agency-based continuing educator engages in training, consultation, or social planning activities, he or she is doing staff development, a form of CE. When the educator provides opportunities for learner choice (such as going to conferences or attending workshops outside the agency), he or she is serving as a facilitator, much as he or she might do in another setting or practice arena. The university-based continuing educator and the educator located in the professional association are almost invariably involved in staff development when they are called on to consult on training within a service agency or other provider system. They may be engaged in staff development when they pursue change-oriented objectives aimed either at individuals or the service system. In the first case they might be pursuing a training model; in the second, a systems change model.

The distinctions may become somewhat clearer in the chapters that follow. We will examine each of the three principal arenas of practice with a view to identifying how continuing educators pursue service or change orientations in their work with individuals and service systems. We will quote liberally from our interviews with continuing educators. They are more eloquent than we possibly could be in describing that work.

Chapter 3

Continuing Education in the University Arena

No higher education programs have grown as rapidly in the past decade as continuing education. This is as true in professional education as in the arts and sciences. It is as true in the human services as in other occupations. It is particularly true in the mental health professions. These changes can best be understood in the context of other changes in higher and professional education.

CHANGES IN HIGHER EDUCATION

Higher education in the United States has gone through several significant metamorphoses. The first American colleges of the seventeenth century drew heavily on the British tradition of providing quality education to a select group of men. Those who went to college were those who could afford it and who needed to attend in order to maintain their station in life. This tradition was soon modified by drawing on the German university's emphasis on research, specialized graduate training, and advancement of knowledge. The

German influence had its greatest impact in the latter half of the nineteenth century as America moved into rapid industrial, technological, and urban development.

In a parallel development the American university began drawing on a third tradition, that of the medieval university of the twelfth and thirteenth centuries, which was established to train schoolmasters, doctors, lawyers, and theologians. The university's original function as a servant of the aristocracy was modified, thereby opening a gateway to two new elites—the scientist-scholar and the professional.

The Morrill Act of 1862 further challenged earlier notions of aristocracy by maintaining that a college education was an earned right, not a birthright. Its underlying philosophy was one of meritocracy, stressing that the criteria for college admissions should be based upon scholastic ability and the willingness to study hard. The Morrill Act also led to the creation of land-grant colleges that were oriented toward service to society. This meant tailoring at least some courses to the needs or interests of individual students. A credit system was established by which individuals could make choices within limits, thus opening fissures in what had until then been a rigid lockstep curriculum. By the turn of the century many universities were copying Wisconsin and Kansas by offering night classes and extension courses or had established cooperative extension programs.

In the 1920s and 1930s three adult education mechanisms reached mature form: general extension, cooperative extension, and the evening college. General extension took university instruction into the far corners of the state. Subject matter was varied. Some courses were given for credit, others were not. General extension has broadened to include correspondence courses and TV programs for the general public. Some TV courses are aimed at reaching professional and semiprofessional audiences at home (e.g., foster parents and operators of small-group homes) and professional audiences on the job (e.g., mental health–agency personnel, engineers, and business executives.)

New cooperative extension services were disseminated by county agents who offered advice and technical assistance on more effective means of agricultural production and instruction in home economics. Later, community development and citizenship training efforts were added.

Evening colleges were established in urban communities to provide opportunities for adults many of whom were fully employed yet eager to earn graduate, undergraduate, or professional degrees. Although the evening school of the Depression days is still recognizable, its activities have spilled over into weekend courses, retreats, and summer camps. Its content has shifted from degree requirements to occupational and life enrichment programs: management training, recreation, film or play series, and therapeutic activities.

The open university, or university without walls, is a contemporary effort to regularize these innovations and to make extension education available to populations that may not be able to come to an extension center to acquire knowledge or skill. The open university has been accompanied by the development of learning centers that use sophisticated educational technology including computerized instruction, simulations, video broadcasting, and video playback. Some centers develop their own instructional materials for the use of individuals and groups in a given geographic area.

These changes have moved the university beyond meritocracy, which excluded large sections of the population that could not compete on the basis of merit alone. Current efforts to institutionalize "open door" policies, ensuring entry for the "less than qualified," draw heavily on the experiences of university extension.

By the end of the 1960s the university was well established as a service center for society. Grants and contracts from both government and the private sector resulted in an enormous proliferation of research and research facilities. Today most universities have more than one research or service center that engages in partnership relations with industry, government, and human service organizations.

A number of universities have developed an "urban extension" focus. Urban extension is an attempt to enlist multiple university resources (research, instruction, facilities, expert staff) in solving urban or metropolitan area problems. These programs complement those of professional schools.

THE PROFESSIONAL SCHOOL AT THE UNIVERSITY

The two principal aims of professional education have always been to prepare qualified entrants for a particular profession and to ensure a sufficient number of those entrants. These aims are little different today from what they were twenty or thirty years ago. What has changed, however, is the emphasis on "entrants." It is no longer considered appropriate for professional schools to concern themselves solely with entry-level competence. The growth in new knowledge and new types of practice and the changing nature of a professional practice require that practitioners at least keep up if they can't stay ahead.

The requirements of new health care settings have made a twenty-year-old nursing degree virtually obsolete. The utility of a social work education has been estimated at no longer than five and a half years. Studies sponsored by the American Medical Association suggest that at least 5 percent of the nation's physicians are incompetent. Moreover, in many human service settings, the demands of practice have drawn in new categories of personnel, some trained at the associate arts level, others through short courses and seminars, and others not at all.

The aims of sufficient quality and quantity can no longer be achieved merely by persuading qualified students to apply for entrance into the professional school or establishing new schools as demand increases. This fact has propelled many professional schools to shift their focus from exclusive concern with on-campus instruction to concern with off-campus and continuing education.

This shift has several implications for the professional school. By extending its program to practitioners currently providing services, it emphasizes instruction that is directly relevant to practice. Through feedback from CE students, the professional school's faculty can modify on-campus instruction to include new material drawn from practice. CE activities enable the school to provide an ongoing and continuing service to its graduates. In several professions the alumni return the favor through substantial donations.

Continuing education also serves as a means of recruitment. By enrolling in a course or workshop, students can find out about the profession without making a long-term commitment. Both the school and the student assess the student's ability to do required academic work. CE activities also provide an opportunity for the professional school to train ancillary personnel—lay people and volunteers, paraprofessionals, or representatives of other occupations who perform tasks that complement those of the professions, thus freeing professional personnel to do other work. Finally, continuing education activities perform a public relations function. They give the professional school an image of being responsive, service-oriented, and relevant to the particular issues of the day.

This shift in focus has had a number of unanticipated consequences for the administration of the professional school. First, it has required the school to consider alternative faculty assignments. Second, it has forced some schools representing different professions into cooperative efforts. Although it may be true that mental health and other human service professions can remain somewhat isolated from each other on the campus, this is less true in the field. Representatives of different professions work with similar clients, frequently in the same agencies or in increasingly complex patterns of relationships. The multidisciplinary nature of practice has suggested the need for multidisciplinary CE efforts. In turn, such efforts have had an impact on the content and structure of the on-campus curriculum and on the nature of the research done by the faculty.

A third unanticipated consequence of the shift toward CE is seen in improved teaching and in the use of more varied instructional formats. Schools that have conducted short-term workshops and minicourses or that have used electronic and audio-visual media in continuing education find that the same approaches also work in on-campus educational programs. Their internal students may in fact demand this diversity.

Continuing education programs also provide research-oriented faculty with an opportunity to disseminate their findings and to test them in the field. Many instructors have discovered what one researcher calls "the joy of being able to share your findings directly with people who will make use of them," rather than publishing them in a journal. Furthermore, the proliferation of CEPs has stimulated the conduct of research. It has been instrumental in helping faculty identify new areas and new partners for their research. Because continuing educators tend to be closely attuned to the needs and interests of professionals in the field, they may be among the first to identify issues of concern to practitioners. They are in an ideal position to carry these concerns back to their colleagues.

THE CONTINUING EDUCATION PROGRAM
AND ITS HOST INSTITUTION

These plus factors notwithstanding, most mental health and human service continuing educators at the university would agree that their programs are often balanced precariously between acceptance and rejection, support and abandonment. The reasons for this ambivalence are not hard to fathom.

Most CEPs are located in a host institution upon which they are dependent. The host may be the university's extension center, an interdisciplinary institute, or a degree-granting professional school, entities that generally have a long tradition which antecedes the continuing education program. None of the changes in higher or professional education noted above have been complete; most institutions of higher learning still maintain vestiges of earlier periods. The function of a human service CEP is often not fully understood; it is perceived as an interloper and a competitor for scarce resources.

Until the mid-1960s few medical schools had clearly identified continuing education units. Prior to 1970 no more than a handful of schools of social work had full-time continuing educators. Even today many schools of nursing, and public health have no one assigned to a full-time role in continuing education. Although many extension services welcome the growth of CE activities within the professional schools, some feel that such growth creates competition for fiscal resources, clientele, and prestige.

The continuing educator is at once an outsider and an insider, sitting on the boundary of his or her institution. He or she tends to have one foot in the world of practice and one in the world of the academy. Like other "boundary" personnel, the continuing educator may perform tasks that are essential to the host institution's mission and its maintenance needs. But the tasks performed may not be fully understood or appreciated at first. Many of the educator's actions may be suspect. They have to be justified. And justification comes only from his or her own successful practice or the successful practices of others in similar positions. Because the practices of other continuing educators, even within the same professions, are extremely varied, few agreed-upon models of practice exist. Most human service CEPs are still in their developmental stages; standardized patterns are only now in the process of evolution.

Although our research was far from exhaustive, we were able to interview more than thirty directors of continuing education programs or deans of professional schools of nursing, social work, and medicine. We also spoke with a number of continuing educators located in institutes and extension programs. We found a number of patterns well established in certain institutions, with new patterns emerging in others.

THE CEP IN THE MEDICAL SCHOOL[1]

The dean of a medical school describes the establishment of his school's CEP as follows:

> Before Charlie joined our faculty, I don't think anyone ever seriously considered the implications of postgraduate or continuing education. We knew we had to do something in this area, but not what. I had no idea

---

[1]A number of the CE patterns described in this section are also becoming more common in other professions and professional schools. Names and settings have been disguised to preserve confidentiality.

it would lead to this when I told Charlie to start off with a lower teaching load and to get to know the state. Well, he did. He traveled up and down for four months, getting to know everybody in and around the mental health field. And I don't mean just psychiatrists. I mean social workers and public health nurses, probation officers, schoolteachers, and anybody who seemed to identify with mental health practice. He has a natural way of relating to people, because he listens to what they say and he hears what concerns them.

What seems to concern him is helping people to do their work better and to get support from each other in the process. The four months were up, and Charlie asked for an extension of his reduced teaching load. He didn't want to teach less, he wanted to teach more, only he wanted to teach in the communities he had visited. Well, we could afford it in those days, and my policy is to encourage faculty to develop in those areas they seem committed to. I sensed that Charlie's commitments were important to a lot of people.

Within a few months Charlie was doing even less formal teaching and more facilitating. His natural respect for people in the field was translated into efforts to help them teach each other. He began building CE programs around the capacities of those people he ran into, using the facilities and the materials available.

I can't tell you how important this use of available resources is to our program. It costs us very little to operate, because it's really operated by the clients out there. That's how Charlie works. He builds on other people's capacities to help themselves. And that's the character our continuing education program has taken on. It's no longer a one-man operation. It's a statewide operation.

This may indeed have become a statewide program, but its "personality" is very much an extension of Charlie's own. Although there are other Charlies at other medical schools, his effort cannot be said to fit the modal pattern.

More typical is the "post graduate medical education program," a separate and identifiable unit within the medical school that may have its own staff of physicians to do the teaching, while adult and continuing educators do the program development, coordination, and management. These postgraduate medical education programs were developed in the 1960s in reponse to the need to upgrade the skill and knowledge of medical practitioners. This need was recognized simultaneously by medical school faculty, by professional medical societies, and by medical practitioners themselves. For the most part the offerings were voluntary and included weekend courses and seminars or a series of lectures on specific topics. Although many of these activities are well attended, the continuing educators we spoke to complained that fewer than 10 to 15 percent of the physicians in their areas ever attended the educational activities available to them.

In many cases the medical school may have been inaccessible because of distance. In other cases physicians found that they could not spare the time to attend. In perhaps a larger number of cases the psychic costs of attendence were too high. It is difficult for some physicians to admit to the obsolescence of their knowledge. For these reasons a number of medical schools cooperate with local and state medical societies in the establishment of credentialing or recertification programs. (These will be discussed in the next chapter.) Other medical schools have developed a variety of outreach programs. Some, like Charlie's program, reach out to providers within a certain service sector at the local level, regardless of their previous professional training. Their efforts are community-oriented and developmental. They focus on building up people's capacity to learn from each other and to make effective use of university resources.

One medical school aims its efforts directly at hospitals. It selects particular services or wards within hospitals that require change and provides consultation on how that change might occur. Consultation is followed by training activities aimed at all the personnel on that particular ward or service. The strategy employed is described by a physician who readily admits that his efforts are manipulative but "highly effective in terms of benefits to the patient":

When I'm called in to consult on a training program, I first find out who are the key people in the hospital who can determine whether or not a change is to occur. There's no sense in training people for something that the powerful people in the hospital are going to block.

I then ask these people to serve as my consultants. I tell them right from the start that I'm going to be designing the curriculum but that I need their help. I tell them that they know the hospital better than I do and that I don't want to make any decisions that will be off the mark. I also tell them that I'm going to ask them to do more than what is usually expected of an advisory committee.

I ask them each to read a number of articles that I've clipped out of newspapers or professional journals. Based on these articles, I ask them to outline a teaching curriculum they think makes sense. This shows them I respect their opinion, and it also shows that I'm not there as a threat to them. The fact that I've selected some articles also indicates that I'm no "dodo." I know the literature, so I'm not just turning to them to design the program.

You can bet I've selected those articles pretty carefully. They represent the best thinking of leaders in the field. If there are differences of opinion, I include them. I know that anyone who reads these articles will come to certain conclusions. They may vary a little bit here or there, but they'll pretty much stay in the ball park.

I then take each of their curriculum outlines and weave them together into a single curriculum with a few suggestions of my own. By the time I'm through, I've got a product that looks pretty much like their work. It includes their content, but it includes objectives that I cleared with the hospital administration. Now you can bet again that my task force people will be politically active in supporting many of the changes that will emerge from the training program.

Most schools of medicine do not have sufficient staff to provide on-site consultation on demand. In order to reduce the costs in manpower and yet maintain a posture of responsiveness, the Medical Information System Terminal (MIST) in a Southern medical school provides telephone terminals in hospitals throughout the state. Medical practitioners with a particular problem can pick up a telephone at any time and call the medical school or teaching hospital, where faculty and senior medical personnel are on call just as they might be in an emergency room. Several other medical schools have created their own variations of the MIST model. They generally limit calls to certain hours during which the experts are available.

Another approach to extending CE to the learner is exemplified by the "circuit rider," who travels to outlying areas providing consultation and clinical instruction and who acts as a reference person for practitioners in the field. Local physicians and other mental health professionals anticipate the circuit rider's visits by preparing descriptions of problems with which they need help. The circuit rider, perhaps a psychiatrist, then consults with each individual at an open session attended by other professionals. Each local person may present a problem of his or her own.

In other settings clinics may involve a team rather than an individual circuit rider. The following vignette illustrates an arrangement that involved a medical school and a state department of mental hygiene:

We felt for a long time that we could not deal adequately with local problems by bringing people to the university. So we set up a partnership arrangement with the state agency. At first we dealt with only a single issue—interagency collaboration around reentry problems for ex-mental patients. We selected a small group of experts to be potential team members. Three were from the state agency and were knowledgeable about state regulations. Two people were chosen from local agencies, and four university people who were familiar with some of the psychodynamics and social aspects of reentry were selected. Everyone on the team knew the relevant agencies outside of the mental health system well and had good rapport with those agencies.

The composition of our team is well thought through. But the content of a particular consultation is purely ad hoc. The team goes into action either when somebody at the state level identifies a community in which there is a problem or when somebody in the community contacts us. Once a referral is made, we select one of our people to be the team captain. The team captain travels to the community to better assess the problems involved. He or she will talk to anybody who seems relevant, starting with the person who originated the contact. These may include mental hospital officials in the area or from where patients are being discharged, local agency people, volunteers and civic groups like the Kiwanis, the chamber of commerce, the Junior League, civic council people, and media representatives.

Based on what he or she discovers, the captain selects two or three other team members for the clinic. We don't like to take more people than we need. The team members set up a design that seems to fit the local situation, and the captain conveys it to the original contact person and the small local coordinating committee that may have been organized during the initial field visit.

Finally, the team goes into the locality and may run a whole series of activities within a one- or two-day period. These may include individual and group consultation sessions; an actual therapy or counseling session with an ex-mental patient or his family, conducted in the presence of appropriate social and mental health agency representatives; one or more interagency exchange sessions; or problem-solving seminars. The team members are experts and share their knowledge by applying it to the problems presented by the local people. In a sense, the locals get "treatment for their ills."

Additional activities found in medical school CEPs include the publication of training materials for use in hospitals and in clinical practice, the conduct of policy conferences and forums, medical information workshops for policymakers and legislators, and in-service training of interns and other hospital staff. Many of these activities are service-oriented; others are oriented toward change. Sometimes the same activity reflects both orientations simultaneously or in sequence. Some CE activities are aimed at the individual who is the recipient of service or the target of change or are aimed directly at the service system. These possibilities are illustrated in Chart 2. The same range of possibilities exists for CEPs located in schools of nursing and social work.

Chart 2 Medical School CE Activities Categorized

Target or consumer	Orientation	
	Service	Change
Individual	1 Consumer choice • on-campus courses and workshops • MIST model or telephone consultation • circuit rider and clinic • CE publications activities	2 Training • on-campus courses and workshops with certification component • in-service training in hospitals and clinics • teaching-hospital activities
Service system	3 Consultation • MIST or telephone consultation • circuit rider or clinic • consultation on staff development activity • community resource workshops (Charlie's work)	4 Systems change • staff development • community resource workshops • CE activities aimed at legislators and policymakers

THE CEP IN THE SCHOOL OF SOCIAL WORK

Although most schools of social work have conducted conferences and short workshops throughout their histories, no more than a handful had recognizable continuing education programs prior to the 1970s. By 1975 more than half the graduate schools had at least one faculty person designated as coordinator of continuing education, and one out of four schools had at least one full-time person responsible for CE. Two schools employed more than ten full-time continuing educators, some with faculty appointments and others with professional and administrative appointments. These schools had annual continuing education budgets that ranged from $5,000 to more than $1 million per year, depending on the volume of training or contracts.

The schools we visited evidenced an enormous diversity in administrative structures and locations of their CEPs as well as in their programmatic activities. In the most common arrangement a faculty person was designated coordinator or director of continuing education, responsible directly to the dean's office. In a number of instances the same person also served as an assistant or associate dean. Most CE programs have advisory or faculty policy committees; some may have a variety of committees utilizing input from representatives of social agencies or service systems. As social work CEPs become more established, they develop administrative structures of their own, generally becoming semiautonomous. They may develop their own internal budgeting procedures.

CE activities tend to include one or more of the following: extension courses for academic credit, short-term courses, workshops, and clinics with or without credit, thematic conferences, consultation and staff development, training for specific populations, and certification.

Extension Courses

Although a few schools of social work permit part-time students to enroll on campus, many others offer courses for academic credit in the evenings on campus or in communities throughout the state or region. Although many of these courses can be applied toward an advanced degree, the bulk of those enrolled participate for purposes of skill and knowledge development and individual career growth and, in some cases, in pursuit of credentialing requirements imposed by civil service commissions. In most instances half or more of the students enrolled are human service workers outside the profession of social work (e.g., schoolteachers, clinical psychologists, and rehabilitation counselors).

The public response to social work extension courses has led some schools to experiment with both format and purpose. Several schools regularly send faculty to outlying sections of the state to conduct courses on weekends. One school uses closed-circuit TV to reach populations in social agencies. Several schools have established task forces for the purpose of conducting feasibility studies that may lead to the creation of off-campus degree programs and/or advanced certificates in certain areas of specialization, such as management, child welfare, and community mental health. Although degree-granting programs are not strictly continuing education, the fact that most extension offerings include non-degree seekers as well as degree seekers makes it difficult to draw the line between one and the other.

Short-Term Instructional Activities

Once relegated primarily to the summer months, workshops, seminars, and short-term courses are now offered periodically throughout the year at many schools. Four or five courses may be offered simultaneously on as many topics. One schools offers a choice of forty-five to fifty workshops, attracting more than 1,500 practitioners each June. Workshop or course content may be organized into two- or three-day programs. Individual consumers select the one they are interested in; some choose to stay on campus for a week or more, putting together two, three, or more discrete programs. Academic credit is not generally available, although CEUs may be offered.

Some summer courses, workshops, seminars, and institutes are scheduled so that consumers can participate in several simultaneously. A seminar in supervision might run from ten o'clock to twelve noon, a course on behavior modification from one to three, and a workshop on the application of behavioral techniques from three to five. Many professional schools prefer to scatter their noncredit offerings throughout the year or to locate them off-campus in agency or community settings. Consumer demand and faculty interests are major determinants of what is to be offered, its location, and its format.

The Conference and the Forum

The conference, which a major CE activity of the professional association, has also frequently been used by schools of social work to attract social workers concerned with specific issues. Conferences are generally intended to accomplish any of the following four objectives: information dissemination, problem solving and decision making, information exchange, and fact finding. At the information-giving conference, it is up to the participant to decide whether or not to use that knowledge for action or problem solving subsequent to the conference.

The problem-solving or decision-making conference is designed to obtain group agreement or action on some problem, issue, or policy. The convener expects that decisions will be made or problems will be solved at the meeting. The hoped-for outcome could be a plan of action or a strategy to be used by the participants. Schools of social work sometimes cosponsor conferences with community mental health centers and boards or other human service agencies. Several CEPs report using problem-solving conferences for proposal writing and CE project development. CE directors report that when the objectives of the conference are modest, success tends to be higher than when they are more complex or ambitious.

The information exchange conference provides participants with an opportunity to gain and share information with each other rather than get it exclusively from a convener or an outside source. The convener's objective is to provide a setting or an atmosphere conducive to a comparison of notes between participants. The focus of an information exchange conference is generally on the work participants do, the problems they share, or the approaches they have found useful in solving these problems.

The primary function of the fact-finding conference is to elicit information and opinions from participants to be used as a basis for future planning. It is similar to the information exchange conference in that the participants are chosen as resource persons because of their knowledge in a particular field. It differs in that the information is not necessarily secured for use by its participants. Information generated may be directed at policy groups and others who may need it to make more effective decisions or to allocate resources.

The educational experience may begin prior to the actual start of the conference or the convening of its participants. This is especially true when there has been a planning committee representative of those for whom the conference is intended. If a committee is not used, inputs from expected conference participants may be elicited in advance of their attendance through questionnaires that obtain facts, attitudes, interests, and definitions of problems. Interviews and pre-conference meetings are also used.

One school of social work has developed an interesting variation of the conference, which it calls a "public policy forum." We found the following excerpt from our interviews instructive:

> We run our public policy forum whenever an issue is hot and we think public attention and perhaps some public action are warranted. Over the years, for example, we've run forums on "narco-politics" (while a bill on services to drug abusers was before the state legislature), mental health insurance, the impact of integration of the state's departments of health and mental health on local service integration, and so on. The way it works is simple—sort of a cross between a TV talk show and a university teach-in.
>
> The policy issues are broken down into their component parts and assigned time slots in a two- or three-day period. Twelve or more "experts" on the issues, each with a different perspective, are invited as the principal resource people. Depending on the issues, we may pick people from different professions, from national, state, or local agencies, from different occupational levels, ethnic minorities,. and work settings. We pick them because they are known or have something to say. We like to mix people with national as well as local reputations or orientations.

Then we team them up in threes and fours for issue sessions. We rotate members on these teams so that at each session the experts have at least one new person to relate to. Maybe the word "team" is inappropriate. We group people who are not likely to agree. A moderator, usually one of our staff who is well versed on the issue, then opens up the session with introductions and a few well-placed questions. Panelists respond in five-minute presentations.

The moderator then probes, pushing panelists to express disagreement as well as consensus. A dialogue among the panelists then proceeds for about forty-five minutes, much like a David Susskind TV show. An audience of forty to a hundred listens in. Then we open it up to the audience, and they engage in an extended dialogue with the panelists and each other for an hour or so. The moderator sums up, and people go to the next session. Several sessions go on simultaneously. Side rooms are available for audience participants to meet with the panelists during the breaks between large sessions or when speakers are not on a panel.

Several times the issues were so hot that extension of the policy dialogue to local communities made sense. Once we cosponsored a forum with the National Association of Social Workers and published a guide to setting up similar forums at the chapter level. Another forum resulted in such an outpouring of political concern that subsequent action led to major revisions of a bill before the state legislature.

Consultation and Staff Development

Although some social work CE programs shy away from staff development activities because of their demanding nature and the CE program's lack of resources, others do it as one of their primary functions:

Staff development is the most important thing we do. It's not that I think academics know more about what needs to be done in an agency than the people who work there. On the contrary. But we do have certain knowledge and expertise that we must share with the field. The best way we know to do it is by engaging in collaborative staff development activities with social agencies.

We got into it in a sort of roundabout way. Several years ago we ran a series of small-group institutes for our field instructors on how to supervise students and how to train staff. We soon discovered that a number of field instructors were utilizing their newly gained skills to conduct other training activities for staffs in their agencies. This was a revelation. First we had the notion of using these people as junior partners or adjuncts of our own staff. But as we consulted with our supervisor-trainees, we found a new kind of relationship developing—one based on more equal partnership relationships.

Based on this experience, we conducted a series of summer workshops for all human service personnel interested in learning how to conduct staff development and in-service training activities. We used some of our former trainees as faculty and resource persons. Following the workshop we provided on-the-spot consultation in person or by telephone. Some of our workshops included a requirement to design a staff development plan and to bring it back to the campus for group consultation one to six weeks after the initial session.

Now we're into something that excites us even more. A federal grant has made it possible to establish a team made up of university and department of social services people. The team has designed several models of staff development that mesh with new management approaches the department is establishing. The new management system builds heavily on MBO [management by objectives] concepts and on team service delivery structures. The project's task is to develop models whereby staff development and training activity can support management and programmatic objectives.

We're building several models. One puts the primary responsibility for training on the unit supervisor, another on the district office manager and his staff, a third on the central office staff. We'll test these out in the field and evaluate them.

Because our project staff includes university personnel, we can stand back and take an objective look. Because it is also composed of agency personnel, we have a direct line to people who control policy and some assurance that whatever we come up with that works will be institutionalized within the system.

Community Development

Social work CE programs also engage in community development activities. In one instance the community mental health center administrator from a rural area approached a school's CE coordinator at a campus-based workshop. "Isn't there some way in which similar programs could be run in the northern part of the state?" he asked. "We have mental health workers in six communities, all isolated from each other, all in need of professional upgrading. It's too expensive to bring them to the campus, and we don't have the skill to conduct our own programs."

The CE coordinator agreed to visit the northern part of the state in order to develop an educational program if the administrator would agree to convene a "planning committee" of representatives from each of the communities involved and if the committee would agree to survey interest, select alternative study topics, promote any resultant educational program, evaluate it, and suggest subsequent activities. In return the school would agree to send an educational planner at its own expense to meet with the committee, to provide, for a set fee, one educational program to be determined jointly by the school and the committee, and to return any surplus to the committee for its use in planning or sponsoring future programs. The expense of any future field visit by a representative of the school would then be borne by the committee. The CE coordinator's reasoning went as follows:

> If we had simply agreed to bring a faculty member up there for a two- or three-day workshop, everyone would have been pleased, but little would have been accomplished. The establishment of a working committee, however, accomplishes a lot more. Some of their sense of isolation has been dispelled. They have a working, contractual relationship to the university. They have their own budget and sense of autonomy, and they get to choose and evaluate programs in relation to the practice problems they perceive as critical to their practice.

Grant-Supported Projects

Most schools of social work do not depend exclusively on general fund support or on fees for service from individual clients or contracts from agencies requesting specific service. Instead they seek grants from federal and state agencies, foundations, and civic associations. In some instances the school may have sought grants only in specialized areas (e.g., management training, substance abuse, child welfare). More often the school and its CEP tend to be much more opportunistic, addressing their proposals to the interests of the grantor and looking for sources of support wherever available. When questioned, however, many social work continuing educators reveal a set of guidelines that inform their choices about what kinds of grant support to seek and which proposals to write. The following quote is illustrative:

> When you look at the grants we've had over the years—alcoholism, skills training in community mental health, board training, training of adoptions and foster-care training, human relations for public-housing managers, a conference for juvenile court judges—it looks as if we were just terribly opportunistic, with no rhyme or reason to the things that we do. But if you look deeper, it all hangs together. We impose the following criteria on every opportunity:
>
> 1 The project has to have some impact on service delivery. We don't take on a project that relates only to the career interests of individual trainees. In our substance-abuse project, for example, we trained other trainers in community colleges and agencies, thereby making it possible for the state agency to establish a certification

Chart 3   School of Social Work CE Activities Categorized

Target or consumer	Orientation	
	Service	Change
Individual	1 Consumer choice • extension courses • workshops, seminars, etc. • conference	2 Training • conferences and some forums • in-service training
Service system	3 Consultation • consultation and staff development • community development • projects	4 Systems change • forums • community development • projects

program for 4,000 to 5,000 drug counselors in the state. When we developed a proposal for the mental health skills project, it was with the understanding that all the agencies in the metropolitan area would have input into the project's policies and be able to draw on the project for their own purposes.

2   The project has to result in a product or products that have lives of their own. The product might be training materials like those we developed in our child welfare and substance-abuse projects. These materials have successfully been used in graduate and undergraduate programs, in in-service activities, and in other government-supported training projects. The product might be a process or a set of relationships that have been established in some locality or within the managerial hierarchy of an agency.

3   Someone else has to care about this project as much as or more than we do. When someone else has as much of a stake in its success as the project staff, there is a greater likelihood of having impact on either persons or programs.

4   The project either has to reflect some current interest or expertise on the part of our faculty or has to contribute to its development. First of all, we don't like to take something on unless there is at least one person on the faculty who has a career commitment to the area and some expertise in it. On the other hand, we do sometimes buy the expertise from the outside, particularly when we feel the project provides an opportunity for faculty at the school to grow and develop. The mental health skills project provided an entry point for both faculty and

master's degree students to make connections with mental health agencies in the state's largest metropolitan area. The project dealing with planning in the field of aging gave us an opportunity to develop a collaborative relationship and some joint appointments with the university's gerontology institute. The net result was an increase in faculty interest and in curriculum content on aging within the master's and Ph.D. programs.

5 The project somehow has to meet the CEP and the school's maintenance needs. These may include bringing in new sources of funds and support for faculty and students, increasing our prestige, opening up avenues for other projects, and developing collaborative relationships outside the university.

Like those of the medical school, the social work CE program's activities can be categorized in a chart that accounts for the target or consumer of intervention and the program's orientation (see Chart 3).

THE CEP IN THE SCHOOL OF NURSING

Continuing education programs in schools of nursing conduct many of the same activities as those described for medicine and social work. Like doctors, nurses are health practitioners. The same kinds of changes in the health field that affect physicians affect nurses as well. Like social workers, most nurses are employed in organizations. The delivery of CE activities, therefore, is often facilitated through collaborative relationships by schools of nursing and employing organizations—hospitals, clinics, public health agencies, and others.

Because the American Nurses' Association has taken active leadership in promoting both standards and guidelines for continuing education, schools of nursing tend to be more extensively involved with their state professional associations than schools of social work. They also tend to have close-knit relationships with hospitals. This is understandable in light of the accreditation policies of the American Hospital Association, which requires its member agencies to provide in-service training to nurse employees.

We find that nursing CE offered through the university is in the same state of flux as medical and social work CE. This dynamic quality is illustrated by the example of a Southwestern school of nursing that regularly conducts summer institutes. Enrollment is always above capacity, yet the faculty members on the continuing education committee were nagged by doubts about the utility of the content being presented. A survey revealed that practice did not change significantly following participation in the workshops.

Accordingly, seminars for the following summer were designed to focus primarily on skill development. Publicity indicated that follow-up assignments would be required. In the staff development seminar, for example, participants designed training plans to be implemented on return to their places of employment. Faculty time was made available for consultation during the next three months. The participants then returned to campus to share their experiences. A number of nurses reported being frustrated in trying to apply what they had learned. Their home agencies were not particularly supportive of their efforts or of the implied changes in management and technology that might result from staff development activities. The school's director of post graduate training explained:

The director of nursing in one state hospital even called us to complain, threatening never to send us any more of her staff if we didn't respect the agency's right to do what it considered correct. At first this response threw us.

The school's committee now had to grapple with the question of whether the agency or the individual nurse who attended our training programs was the consumer. We decided that in some cases it was one, in some cases the other, and at other times both. But we hadn't ever thought of the hospital or agency as the consumer before. This new awareness created a major change in our approach to planning our summer workshops. Since that time we have gone beyond conducting occasional surveys of our former students to find out what they were interested in. We have also met regularly with the administrators of major hospitals in the area and with officials of the state health and mental health agencies.

It has had terrific payoffs. First of all, they understand us better now. We no longer worry about offending people. Secondly, involving administrators assures us of full registration—administrators who have been involved in the planning process usually are willing to commit a certain number of dollars or a certain number of heads for attendance so that we can preregister even before we officially announce the program. And we can build in an implementation process right from the start.

Before conducting our last seminar on the "Application of Behavior Principles for Nurses," we invited the nursing supervisors of several major hospitals to attend a two-day workshop at our expense. We then told them what their staffs would be getting at the seminar later in the month and examined with them the implications for nursing services. We pointed out that those nurses from their staffs who attended would leave the university with some new concepts and real motivation for putting them into practice. If the learning was to be effective, they would have to be supported and given an opportunity to try things out. We examined what this meant in terms of shifting or changing assignments in relationships on the ward. The response was really positive. The supervisors were much less threatened. Several even decided to attend the seminar. Later we brought back groups of nurses and their supervisors for a one-day institute on campus to examine what worked, what didn't work, and why.

Unfortunately, time did not permit us to visit a sufficient number of schools of nursing to design a chart like those developed for medicine and social work. In general, however, it was our impression that the range of activities sponsored by nursing CEPs would include most of those listed in Charts 2 and 3.

OTHER HOST INSTITUTIONS FOR THE HUMAN SERVICE CEP

There are additional administrative and programmatic hosts for the human services CEPs in higher education. These include other professional schools and academic departments, universitywide extension "services," and specialized research service and teaching institutes. Other professional training programs include schools of public health, education, and library science and departments of psychology. Because of our decision to examine only those professions most closely linked to mental health, we did not systematically gather information on CE in any of these professional schools.

Psychology

We did, however, seek evidence of CE activities in graduate departments of psychology. There was almost none to be found. The profession of psychology, as contrasted to the discipline, is considerably behind other mental health and human service professions in the development of continuing education for its practitioners.

Perhaps because of lack of opportunities to engage in the delivery of continuing education through their own profession, psychologists are heavily involved in the CE activities of other professions. They are engaged in the conduct of courses and workshops under the auspices of schools of nursing, social work, medicine, public health, and education. This bodes well for the future. A former national officer of the American Psychological Association states optimistically:

We're behind now, but when we take off, we'll be moving like a Fourth of July firecracker. There's an enormous hunger for knowledge in the profession. We know it by reading the ads in *Psychology Today* and in other journals. We know it by watching psychologists flock to almost any kind of educational opportunity, no matter who conducts it and what the quality.

And you can see some real changes even here at the university. Our clinical psychology programs haven't moved as rapidly as they should. But our new community and industrial psychology programs are already committed to training people on the job. By 1980 the gap between us and the other mental health professions will have been narrowed considerably, if not erased entirely.

Extension Services

At many universities the extension service or department plays a major role in planning continuing education and providing it to human service practitioners. As with professional schools, the patterns and the activities vary considerably. These patterns are affected by the nature of the relationship between extension and the professional school. These relationships can be charted along the following continuum: (1) no involvement whatsoever, (2) provision of administrative services to the professional school, (3) equal partnership with the professional school, (4) major partnership, (5) total responsibility for continuing education.

Although schools of medicine rarely make use of the extension service, partnerships with schools of social work, public health, education, and nursing and with departments of psychology are common. The extension service may assume responsibility for administrative tasks such as record keeping, taking in fees, and paying out salaries. The professional school, however, may plan and schedule the offerings, assign the faculty, and maintain major control over curriculum. The professional school or department generally sets policy on instruction, whereas the extension service sets policies on fees, format, location, and so forth.

Some extension departments include a subunit called a conference department responsible for forums, short-term workshops, institutes, and other noncredit offerings. An instructional activity may be planned by the professional school but managed by the staff of the conference department. Tensions often exist in these relationships. Allocation of responsibility and of authority is not always clear. The partners to the relationship may have differing perceptions of their prerogatives. Their relationships tend to change as new personalities are introduced, funding sources shift, or external demands change. Far from being unhealthy, these tensions tend to produce a dynamic interchange within which considerable experimentation and innovation occur.

Sometimes the extension service competes with a professional school or department. It may conduct its own conferences, workshops, and courses, hiring faculty from within that school or department or outside the university. In many instances the lead taken by the extension service has jolted a professional school into action. On those campuses where no professional schools exist or where the professional schools are relatively weak or inward-looking, the extension service may conduct the great bulk of human service continuing education.

The Special-Focus Institute

Many universities also sponsor special-focus institutes. Examples include institutes on developmental disabilities, early childhood, gerontology, and research in mental health. These institutes are generally multidisciplinary or interprofessional in nature. Some are degree- or certificate-granting, whereas others conduct research or provide service to agencies and communities in their environment. Many of them conduct continuing education activities. For some, CE is their major reason for existence.

Typical institute-sponsored CE activities include (1) a summer program, which may be anywhere from a week to several weeks long and which may result in the awarding of CEUs, academic credit, or a specialized certificate, (2) a variety of conferences and workshops, (3) a combination of research and service leading to more effective manpower utilization and/or staff development within a particular service sector, and (4) specialized publications or information retrieval services.

OTHER VARIATIONS

Additional variations exist. Foremost among them are the colleges of lifelong learning, summer or camp retreats, and CE schools.

Colleges of Lifelong Learning

Extension programs at some universities have either spawned or been transformed into colleges of lifelong learning. These are non-degree-granting institutes that offer a wide variety of courses and workshops, some of them aimed at professional personnel and others at lay consumers. The distinctions between them are not always clear. A ten-week evening course on "group leadership skills" may be perceived by some students as an opportunity to increase their ability to work on boards and committees in the community. Others may take the course with a view toward increasing their competence in classroom management, in the conduct of staff meetings, in agency-group supervision, and so on. Thus the individual may choose a course or workshop because of a variety of needs and interests. The CE planners offer the course recognizing that it is the consumer who will decide to what purpose he or she will apply the new knowledge or skill gained. This is a pure consumer choice model.

The Camp or Retreat

Some universities also sponsor periodic camp or retreat programs. In some instances these camps operate throughout the summer months and are open to university alumni and their families. In other instances they are open to the general public. In some cases special weeks are open only to people from certain professions or occupational groupings. Even when the program is not aimed directly at human service professionals, the content often has relevance for them.

In addition to recreation, arts, and cultural activities, both daytime workshops and evening sessions are often devoted to topics dealing with the human potential for growth and development, to social policy issues, and to other matters of professional concern to human service practitioners. It is not uncommon for university extension services or professional schools to conduct regularly scheduled retreats on topics for which their faculty is well known, such as behavioral treatment, the management of hypertension, or family counseling.

The CE School

Despite the prevailing image of human service CE as ad hoc in its response to particular needs or consumer demands, many continuing education and staff development programs are administratively and programmatically similar to the degree-granting professional school. Patterned after the external degree programs conducted by business schools at Columbia and Carnegie Tech, they hold classes, award certificates, have permanent or semipermanent instructional staff, and attract students who commit themselves to completing curricular requirements. Requirements may include several courses and extend over a prolonged period of time.

Some course offerings parallel those of basic graduate or professional education. Instructional content may be geared explicitly to the students' career aspirations and future occupational roles rather than to increasing their competence in the performance of current task assignments.

Some CE schools require as much as twelve months of full-time participation. Harvard University's Laboratory of Community Psychiatry provided a good illustration. Most have more limited offerings and are more modest in their expectations and demands. For example, a school of social work in New England established a ten-week certificate program meeting four afternoons a week for B.A. graduates who were employed in social work settings but had no former social work education.

Several university-based CEPs have reported a move toward regularizing previously ad hoc offerings and restructuring them into a semblance of curriculum. As one continuing educator explains:

> We found ourselves offering certain courses and workshops over and over again every year. We always ran at least one workshop in grantsmanship, another in staff development, and a third in supervision. Periodically we ran workshops in fiscal management, program design, and interagency relationship. On examining our registration, we discovered that a number of agency middle-management people were attending pretty regularly and that some had already taken four or five of our management workshops.
>
> It seemed like a natural idea to package these into a single program. We now offer a certificate in management to anyone who completes six of our courses or workshops, of which three are required and the other three can be selected from seven or eight electives that we pledge to give at least every other year for the next four years.

Varied as these patterns may appear, we saw no evidence that the range of possibilities has been exhausted. New patterns evolve continuously.

SUGGESTIONS FOR FURTHER READING

Alford, H. F.: *Continuing Education in Action*, Wiley, New York, 1968.
American Council on Education: *Higher Education and the Adult Student: An ACE Special Report*, Washington, D.C., 1972.
Barzun, Jacques: *The American University*, Harper & Row, New York, 1968.
Bebout, J. E.: "University Services for the Urban Community," *American Behavioral Scientist*, vol. 6, no. 6, February 1963.
Becker, Marshall L.: "Factors Affecting Diffusion of Innovations among Health Professionals," *American Journal of Public Health*, vol. 16, no. 2, 1970.
Bennis, Warren G., and Philip E. Slater: *The Temporary Society*, Harper & Row, New York, 1969.
Blakely, Robert J., and Juan M. Lappin: *New Institutional Arrangements and Organizational Patterns for Continuing Education*, Syracuse University Press, Syracuse, N.Y., 1969.
Carnegie Commission on Higher Education: *New Students and New Places: Policies*

for the Future Growth and Development in Higher Education, McGraw-Hill, New York, 1971.

Gross, B.: *Beyond the Open Door*, Jossey-Bass, San Francisco, 1972.

Dill, William R.: "Obsolescence as a Problem with Personal Initiative," in S. S. Dubin (ed.), *Professional Obsolescence*.

Drucker, Peter F.: *The Age of Discontinuity*, Harper & Row, New York, 1969.

Dubin, S. S. (ed.): *Professional Obsolescence*, D. C. Heath, Lexington Books, Lexington, Mass., 1972.

Eurich, Alvin C. (ed.): *Campus, 1980*, Delta, New York, 1968.

Friedman, C. H., et al.: *Inventory of Federally Supported Continuing Education Programs: A Report to the President's Council on Continuing Education*, parts I & II, Greenleigh Associates, New York, 1972.

Gould, Samuel B.: *Today's Academic Condition*, McGraw-Hill, New York, 1970.

Halpert, Harold P.: "Communications as a Basic Tool in Promoting Utilization of Research Finding," *Community Mental Health Journal*, vol. 2, no. 3, 1966.

Havelock, Ronald G.: *Planning for Innovation through Dissemination and Utilization of Knowledge*, Center for Research on Utilization of Scientific Knowledge, Institute for Social Research, University of Michigan, Ann Arbor, 1969.

Hespberg, Theodore P., Paul A. Miller, and Clifton R. Wharton: *Patterns for Life-long Learning*, Jossey-Bass, San Francisco, 1973.

Hodgkinson, H. L.: *Institutions in Transition: The Study of Changes in Higher Education*, McGraw-Hill, New York, 1971.

Houle, Cyril O.: "The Comparative Study of Continuing Professional Education," *Convergence*, vol. 3, no. 4, 1970.

————: *The External Degree*, Jossey-Bass, San Francisco, 1973.

Ingham, Robert J. (ed.): *Institutional Backgrounds of Adult Education: Dynamics of Change in the Modern University*, Center for the Study of Liberal Education for Adults, Boston University, 1966.

Knowles, Malcolm: *Higher Adult Education in the United States: The Current Picture, Trends and Issues*, American Council on Education, Washington, D.C., 1969.

Liverwright, A. A., and David L. Masconi: *Continuing Education in the United States: A New Survey*, Academy for Educational Development of the National Institute of Health, New York, 1971.

McGlothlin, M. C.: *The Professional School*, Center for Applied Research in Education, New York, 1964.

Moses, Stanley: *The Learning Force: An Approach to Politics of Education,* Syracuse University Educational Policy Research Center, Syracuse, N.Y., 1969.

Roberts, A. O. H., and J. K. Larsen: *Effective Use of Mental Health Research Information*, American Institute for Research, Palo Alto, Calif., January 1971.

Roger, Everett M.: *Diffusion of Innovation*, Pergamon, New York, 1962.

Second Round Table on Permanent Education: *Towards an Education System,* Council of Europe, Strasbourg, Paris, June 8–9, 1971.

Shaunton, Theodore J., and C. Schoenfeld: *University Extension*, New York Center for Applied Research in Education, New York, 1965.

Smith, Robert M., George F. Akar, and J. R. Kulik (eds.): *The Handbook of Adult Education*, Macmillan, New York, 1970.

Striner, H. E.: *Continuing Education as a National Capital Investment*, W. E. Upjohn Institute for Employment Research, Kalamazoo, 1972.

Valley, J. R.: *Increasing the Options (A Look at the External Degree)*, Educational Testing Service, Princeton, N.J., 1972.

Wolff, Robert C.: *The Ideal of the University*, Beacon Press, Boston, 1969.

Chapter 4

Continuing Education in the Professional Association

Professional associations have been under pressure from two sources to expand their CE functions. Pressures from within are exerted by members seeking new knowledge and skills that are applicable to their practice. External pressures are exerted by the general public and by third-party payers (government agencies, insurance companies) who increasingly demand assurance from the mental health and human service professions that their members are up to date and are utilizing accepted professional practices. Professions are compelled to establish mechanisms ensuring the quality and availability of their services.

Internal demand has been somewhat less commanding than external pressure. If anything, it has tended to result in some shifts in emphasis and priorities rather than in basic structure or form. Until the mid-1950s professional associations could point to almost no CE activities other than their publications and professional conferences. The content of each tended to be less practice-focused than scientific in nature. From the mid- to the late 1960s one could perceive a slight shift in emphasis as policy issues became the central theme of most plenary sessions at conferences and lead articles in journals. By 1970 pressure from members created a second shift in emphasis from science and policy to practice and method. Although this emphasis is still far from predominant, it will clearly deepen during the next decade.

Simultaneously, the public demand for accountability has challenged professional associations to pay increasing attention to improving the quality of professional practice. In both nursing and medicine, for example, continuing education may be a condition for continued membership in the professional association or one of its societies and academies. In a number of states it may be a requirement for license renewal or certification. In social work there has been a strong move to vest membership in the Academy of Certified Social Workers with requirements for ongoing and regular continuing education. Although mandatory continuing education is far from universal, it has become one of the major issues in virtually every professional association in the human services.

Proponents argue that mandatory requirements for continuing education will provide a broad exposure to new knowledge and skills and thereby have an advantage over reexamination programs to maintain licenses or certification. Others argue that many CE activities have no measurable impact on practice and that requiring CE may result in a proliferation of low-quality continuing education. This argument is countered in turn by those who propose "certifying certification programs"—a proposal which presumes that although a professional association may not be able to conduct all the necessary CE activities for its members, it can certify those programs that meet certain minimal requirements.

MEDICINE AND PSYCHIATRY

Relicensure and the Physician's Recognition Award

In 1967 the American Medical Association's National Advisory Committee on Health Manpower concluded that a "physician's education must continue as long as he practices" and suggested that "professional societies and state governments should explore the possibility of relicensing of physicians and other health professionals." In 1969 the AMA established the Physician's Recognition Award (PRA).

Physicians who wish to receive a PRA must participate in 150 hours of the following activities every three years: courses and workshops under accredited sponsorship, generally under the auspices of a medical-society teaching hospital or medical school; activities with nonaccredited sponsorship; teaching of medicine; contributing to papers, books, and exhibits; independent study; and other meritorious learning experiences.

Relicensure is not popular among individual physicians, nor is mandated continuing education. Nevertheless, in 1970 the AMA House of Delegates convened a number of specialty boards to consider the desirability of establishing periodic recertification programs based on continuing education, self-assessment programs, and other appropriate actions. The boards were also encouraged to consider adoption of a policy requiring participation in continuing education programs as a condition for continued membership. In at least a dozen states physicians are expected to meet PRA requirements in order to remain members in good standing of their medical practice's specialty society. In a smaller number of states, the PRA pattern is currently a requirement for relicensure.

AMA Criteria

The AMA's Council on Medical Education evaluates and sets guidelines for training and certification of training programs. A document entitled "Essentials of Improved Programs in Continuing Medical Education" identifies six categories of institutions that could be accredited for continuing medical education: (1) medical schools and affiliated hospitals with departments of continuing education, (2) specialty medical societies at national and regional levels (e.g., the Academy of Family Physicians or the American Psychiatric Association), (3) voluntary health organizations, if national or regional in influence, (4) state medical associations or societies, (5) hospitals that have annual CE activities, and (6) other organizations or institutions of national and regional significance that attract physicians in appreciable numbers and that offer recurring continuing medical education activities.

Individual Self-Assessment

The medical profession seems to be alone among the professions directly related to mental health in having made extensive use of self-assessment instruments. Virtually every medical society has its own self-assessment examination. The American Medical Association distributes a *Directory of Self-Assessment Programs for Physicians,* which summarizes programs already operational and others currently being developed. The procedures described vary in the time required for completion. Some are "graded" confidentially by a central source such as a medical school, a state association, or a national academy, whereas others are designed to be scored by the physician taking the exam. There are no penalties for poor performance.

In 1972 a "Psychiatric Knowledge and Skills Self-Assessment Program" sponsored by the American Psychiatric Association became available. It complements and expands the association's Self-Assessment Program of 1969,[1] shifting emphasis to various aspects of patient management. It attempts to confront the everyday realities of the psychiatrist's practice, including recent developments in diagnosis and treatment. Questions are designed to have clinical relevance. Available to nonmembers, the program is composed of eight clinical cases on patient management and 240 multiple-choice questions, divided equally between diagnosis, treatment, and special-interest areas.

Psychiatry

Despite the extensiveness of psychiatrically oriented CE, psychiatry may not have kept up as much—or put as much emphasis on keeping up—as other medical specializations. Much of what is labeled continuing education in "psychiatry" is in fact conducted by or with the aid of psychiatrists for nonpsychiatric physicians and allied personnel—not for the psychiatrists themselves. These "physicians' education projects" are generally aimed at the family physician or general practitioner in private practice. Many were and continue to be extremely effective. They are often conducted at low cost and build heavily upon local initiative. The following description of "vest pocket" continuing education is illustrative:

> Part of my job as a half-time coordinator for the state's Academy of Family Physicians is to coordinate what I call the vest pocket continuing education project in mental health. I've got about twelve course outlines and study guides that we have developed over the last two or three years. Some come from the national association and others from the medical school at State U. Every year we add one or two new outlines as family practitioners express interest, or we modify some of our old outlines based on new knowledge or discovery. Every month or so I send out a mimeographed letter to all of our members telling them about some new practice or highlighting an article in some journal they should be reading. And I announce the availability of our vest pocket courses.

[1]See the Carmichael entry in the reading list at the end of this chapter.

Then, if some local physician wants to sponsor the course, all he has to do is call me and tell me which course he is interested in. The courses are structured to run eight weeks. In addition to the initiator who acts as convener, the local people need ten to fifteen participants and a psychiatrist who acts as a consultant. I have a string of consultants all over the state. So if I get a call from Maryville, I put the local convener in touch with a psychiatrist who may be living in the next county. The convener calls ten to fifteen of his buddies together and gets each to pay a $50 fee, which is sent to my office. These fees go into a budget account that helps to cover my mailings and to pay the psychiatrist his honorarium. The whole operation is really pretty simple to run, and the overhead is very low. No files to keep, no administrative apparatus. I can run it out of my "vest pocket."

More recently, however, the APA has turned its guns on its own membership. The American Board of Psychiatry and Neurology is examining the relationship of continuing education to recertification, following the pattern already established by the American Board of Family Practice. In response to recommendations by the Committee on Continuing Education for Psychiatrists, the executive committee of the American Psychiatric Association has concluded that 150 hours of CE credit over a period of three years should be required for continued membership in the association.

Built-in Resistors

Despite what at first seems like an impressive array of available CE activities, many of them of high quality and some quite innovative in their format and approach, there is some evidence that psychiatry and medicine as a whole may have some built-in resistors to continuing education. Foremost among these are the habits inculcated during formal education in the medical school. Although professional medical educators recently have emphasized problem-focused learning, this is far from standard practice. Old knowledge continues to accumulate in disparate and discrete disciplines or divisions within medicine. Students continue to be taught bodies of knowledge rather than where to look for knowledge and how to use it. Some continuing educators suggest that medical school education may be an effective demotivator of CE.

Built-in resistors are also located in the structure of medical service delivery and in the organizational structure of the American Medical Association. The majority of American physicians are in private practice. Although they may have hospital or clinical affiliations, these are often peripheral or part-time. For this reason agency-based staff development and in-service training programs are not apt to reach large numbers of physicians. A staff member in the national office of the AMA comments on the structure of organized medicine:

> Organized medicine is its own worst enemy. It is a loosely knit conglomerate of fragmented disciplines and programs, so that many physicians hardly speak to each other. The reasons are ideological, philosophical, scientific, political, and historical. Each specialty and subspecialty is broken up into its own committees and boards. Continuing education activities follow this same cleavage, so that far from being interdisciplinary across professions, they are not even interdisciplinary within our profession. The outcome of all this is that patients are looked upon as fragmented organs and seldom as whole individuals.

NURSING

American Nurses' Association

More perhaps than any other professional association in the human services, the American Nurses' Association has been concerned with helping its members to keep abreast of new knowledge. Each specialty division offers continuing education workshops for its membership, often in cooperation with other health organizations having the same specialty interests.

In 1971 the board of directors of ANA took the position that there was to be a CE membership group within the association. Under the aegis of the Commission on Nursing Education, the Council on Continuing Education in Nursing was formally established in 1972. It now has a membership of more than 300 nurses who have primary interest and responsibility for planning, implementing, and evaluating continuing education in nursing. These are nurses involved in staff development/in-service education programs as well as voluntary health agencies and governmental agencies (the Air Force, Navy, U.S. Public Health Service, Army, missions, and Veterans Administration).

In 1974 this council published standards for continuing education in nursing. These were accompanied by a pamphlet, *Continuing Education Guidelines for State Nurses' Associations* (no longer in print). It differentiated the ANA's responsibilities for continuing education from those allocated to state nurses' associations and included guidelines for the development of CE recognition programs at the state level. This pamphlet has been replaced by *Guidelines for*

State Voluntary and Mandatory Systems, which documents the 1974 House of Delegates decision that:

> ANA express its strong support for establishing participation in continuing education approved by state nurses' associations as one prerequisite for continuing registration of the license to practice nursing, and that the American Nurses' Association assist state nurses' associations in developing systems for implementing this requirement which will ensure maximum interstate mobility of licensed practitioners of nursing.[2]

The ANA Commission on Nursing Education has interpreted the motion as follows:

> The intent of the motion was in support of states' rights and is not a mandate for all states to move ahead to establish continuing education requirement for relicensure.
> [The] motion directs ANA to provide support to those states which choose to establish continuing education as one prerequisite for relicensure as well as those states who choose to encourage continuing education through a voluntary program. In either case the quality of the continuing education must be assured by the professional association.

Every state nurses' association in the United States is involved in the development of a Continuing Education Approval and Recognition Program (CEARP). Some CEARPs are in full operation, serving to acknowledge those nurses who meet voluntary requirements for maintaining competence through continuing education. Evidence of involvement in CE activities is the basic requirement of all certification ANA programs. Records are kept by state nursing associations and made available to the ANA certification board. This consistency between state and national association standards increases the ability of nurses moving from one facility to another or one section of the country to another to transfer their credentials.

However, there is considerable difference between ANA certification of excellence in clinical nursing practice and ANA recognition of participation in continuing education. The former is based on an evaluation of the nurse's work performance, the latter on participation in learning activities. Under CEARP guidelines a minimum of

---

[2]American Nurses' Association, *Guidelines for State Voluntary and Mandatory Systems,* Kansas City, Mo., 1975, p. 1.

thirty contact hours per year of instruction is suggested, but state associations may elect to require more or less of their own members. CEUs are often used to record contact hours and as a means of maintaining a transcript of individual educational efforts. Files are maintained by the state nurses' associations. These provide evidence that the nurse has met the requirements. Efforts are under way to establish a National Data Bank for Continuing Education under ANA auspices in which these instructional records will be stored.

Licensure and Relicensure

All professional nurses must be licensed according to the laws of the states in which they work. Two states have recently revised these laws to require continuing education as a provision of license renewal. Two other states have enabling legislation that permits state boards of nursing to require CE. Two other states require refresher courses for nurses who have not been in active practice for three or five years. Other similar developments can be expected to snowball within the decade.

Problems and Promise

In comparison with other human service professions, nurses, in the American Nurses' Association, give truly impressive prominence to continuing education. Placing responsibility on state nurses' associations spreads the responsibilities throughout the system from the national to the local level. It increases the likelihood of collaborative relationships between the professional association, local training institutions, and employers. Ultimately, however, the responsibility devolves on the individual nurse to keep his or her practice current.

A number of problems remain. First, the ANA has not yet fully addressed the question of occupational mobility. Because the levels of formal education in nursing vary, continuing education may become the means of moving up the career and occupational ladder. In a number of locales CE programs have provided individuals with an opportunity to move from practical to M.A.-level education outside a formal or campus degree program. As such programs prove worthwhile, they can be expected to be highlighted in ANA literature and replicated elsewhere.

Second, the emphasis placed on an individual nurse's continuing education somewhat limits the association to either a consumer choice or training model of CE. This might be appropriate in a profession most of whose members are in private practice. But such is not the case with the nursing profession, in which the majority are employed by agencies and hospitals. Theoretically the possibilities of participation in in-service training or staff development activities are much greater for the nurse. This is true in many hospitals in which accreditation by the American Hospital Association is contingent upon provision of in-service training to the nursing staff. In other situations, however, nurses are often the last to receive training. Although their services may be essential to the organization that employs them, that organization is rarely managed by nurses. Nurses often occupy positions with relatively low status and influence at their places of employment. The result is neglect of their needs and, by implication, neglect of their patients' needs as well.

Finally, nursing CE would benefit through collaborative efforts with other professions. Although CE activities under state or national ANA auspices may include faculty from many disciplines and professions, the learning population tends to be unidisciplinary. The director of continuing education in a nursing school who has been active in the professional association explains:

> We don't like to expose our ignorance to other professional groups. In many ways, it's an expression of self-consciousness because of our traditional second-class role. We have to move out to others and learn together with them if we're ever to convince ourselves that we need not be second anymore.

This, too, can be expected to pass. Nurses now more frequently work in multidisciplinary settings in which they interact from strength and with clearly recognized competence. The CEARP can only be expected to add to that competence.

SOCIAL WORK

National Association of Social Workers

The profession of social work has three national associations concerned with continuing education. The National Association of Social Workers (NASW) is open to all social workers with a degree in the field—B.A., M.S.W., or Ph.D.—and to a small number of allied professionals. In a 1972 survey of its 60,000 members, the association found that more than half identified CE as a service they wanted from the national office—the highest percentage by far of any service requested. NASW has been active in promoting continuing education by grants to individual chapters, by conducting an annual national symposium, and through its publication services.

In 1972 grants up to $2,000 were made to those chapters that designed and submitted proposals for innovative training programs to be run at the local, state, or regional levels. This was an effort to respond to membership interest and to revitalize and give meaning to local chapter activities. The content of training was generally focused on broadening knowledge and expanding members' skills. In some cases it complemented the association's priorities for expanding services and opportunities to minorities and for political action. Consultants were available to local chapters. The NASW consultants report that CE activities conducted at chapter meetings were least well received, whereas retreats and collaborative ventures with universities or agencies were much more successful.

The NASW annual symposium is a national meeting organized primarily to provide social workers with an opportunity to share the latest knowledge about practice. It was conceived as a reaction against other conferences that did not adequately address practice issues. Its sessions include descriptions and analyses of practice programs as well as sessions oriented toward skill development and expansion. Several state associations have conducted similar symposia in their own areas.

The publications section of the national office is one of the association's major operations. In addition to a journal and newsletter, it publishes numerous volumes and guidebooks related to social work practice which fill large gaps in information. In addition to serving individual members, these materials are used extensively in graduate and undergraduate social work education programs, in organized CE activities, and in staff development programs.

Like the AMA and ANA, NASW has expressed concern over licensure and certification. But it has been slower to lobby for licensure laws. By 1975 only nineteen states had licensure laws. However, under pressure by third-party paying agencies, licensure bills have been introduced in almost all of the other thirty-one states. In some cases states with existing statutes are considering provisions that require continuing education for relicensure. Relicensure requirements are currently being reconsidered in thirteen states. NASW has a model licensure statute that includes a continuing education provision. It serves as a guide for most state bills. A bill being considered in one state would require fourteen hours of continuing education per year.

Academy of Certified Social Workers

Within the association the Academy of Certified Social Workers certifies all social workers with at least a master's degree and two or more years of practice in approved settings for the performance of specified tasks. The academy has debated for some years whether or not to require continuing education to maintain certification but has not as yet come to a decision. The academy is also examining the possibility of creating certification programs related to practice at certain levels or in certain settings: management and agency administration, supervision, family treatment, community organization, and so on.

Council on Social Work Education

The Council on Social Work Education (CSWE) is a service and coordinating body for schools of social work in the United States and Canada. Like the other associations mentioned, it also has a publications program. The council's publications, however, are designed primarily for use in basic professional education.

CSWE has sought and received external funds for expanding continuing education through its network of schools. It publishes an occasional newsletter that summarizes CE offerings throughout the country, provides information on innovative approaches to CE, and mentions literature and other references useful to the continuing educator.

The council has also coordinated several national and regional meetings of social work continuing educators in an effort to upgrade their skills and to provide them with opportunities to learn from each other and to find mutual support. A CSWE *Guide to Continuing Education* spells out the responsibilities of professional schools for CE and discusses approaches to program planning and administration. Virtually every graduate school and a large number of undergraduate programs conduct some CE activities, many in collaboration with local or state NASW chapters.

National Conference on Social Welfare

The National Conference on Social Welfare (NCSW) is really an umbrella organization for many professional groups, national agencies, and volunteer associations. Although it is not a professional association per se, it has close ties to social work and views its annual forum as a vehicle for dissemination of knowledge and the conduct of continuing education on a national scale. In addition to the usual array of research reports, professional papers, and policy guidelines found at most national conferences, the annual forum has included an increasing number of practitioner-oriented sessions that are instructional in nature. Membership and participant response suggest that the annual forum may increasingly become a major CE activity in social welfare.

Inhibitors of Effective CE for Social Workers

The very factors that compel large numbers of social workers to engage in continued learning militate against the success of that learning. First, the knowledge base undergirding professional social work education undergoes continuous revision. This flux stems from an ongoing challenge to "what is," coupled with dissention over "what ought to be." Second, the rapidly changing nature of social work practice makes almost any skill or knowledge base obsolete within a few years. More than any other occupation in the human services, social work is affected by changes in national priorities and public perceptions of social problems. Social work is indeed social.

The impact of individual social work CE activities has a way of being canceled out by non-CE activities. There are sometimes too many messages coming from too many sources. These messages are often contradictory or left unreinforced in the work setting. The vast majority of social workers are employed in relatively large, public bureaucracies. Organizational requirements are frequently at variance with professional prescriptions. What is learned in a CE activity may create tensions in the work environment. These tensions are healthy if they produce creative and innovative solutions to practice problems. They are unhealthy if they produce apathy or cynicism.

Perhaps the biggest inhibitor is the chronic sense of marginality with which many social workers seem to be afflicted. They are often caught between identifying with the profession and identifying with the agency in which they are employed, the service areas in which they work (e.g., community mental health, health, poverty), and the populations they are committed to serve. Many social workers tend to relegate the professional association and their professional identity to a level of secondary importance. These social workers may seek continuing education activities in other settings and from other sources: multidisciplinary training institutions, university-based CE programs, or staff development activities within their own agencies. Fortunately, such CE activities under these auspices are increasingly available to them.

PSYCHOLOGY

Of the four professions examined, psychology appears to have the least investment in continuing education. As of 1974 the American

Psychological Association had no special section on continuing education, nor did it offer any formal guidelines for the conduct of CE activities. At the time of our interviews, however, the issue of its responsibilities to continuing education was being examined by a national task force within the association. One of the group's findings was that psychologists, individually and collectively, attend a wide variety of CE activities. Why this discrepancy between the official actions of organized psychology and the activities of its members?

Factors that Inhibit and Support CE for Psychologists

Psychology is both a discipline and a profession. Unlike other professions, its basic educational program is conducted through academic departments rather than professional schools. Departments do not have the same administrative structures or fiscal autonomy as schools. For this reason one would not expect university-based CE programs to develop in psychology as they have in medicine, nursing, and social work.

As members of a segmented profession with many divisions, psychologists tend to think of themselves either as members of a discipline or as professional practitioners. Disciplinary psychologists tend to build CE directly into their work and consider it integral to their research and teaching. They can report on their work and learn of the work of others through such channels as conferences and professional meetings, professional journals, and books. They devote more time to mental health research than the combined efforts of psychiatrists, social workers, and nurses. The results of this research make up much of what goes into the CE programs of the other professions. Professional psychologists are also the recipients of these contributions.

According to the American Psychological Association, basic education in psychology has a "half-life" of seven years.[3] Although journal proliferation and conference attendance were the first responses to the growing demands by these psychologists for increasing their knowledge base, psychologists now are examining alternative sources. This is especially true of practicing psychologists, who make up a significant number of the consumers of CE activities developed by other professions. They also benefit from in-service and staff development activities conducted in their places of employment— schools, guidance clinics, courts, mental hospitals, community mental health centers, and so on.

---

[3] "Half-life" is the time after completion of training when, because of new developments, a professional finds himself or herself only half as competent as a recent graduate.

Licensing and Recertification

Like NASW, the American Psychological Association has proposed a model bill for state licensure of clinical psychologists that would require continuing education for the renewal of a practicing psychologist's license. Several states are currently considering introduction of bills based on this model. They would include the use of the CEU as a basis for accreditation of programs and certification of completion for the individual participant. In a parallel effort the association's Committee on State Legislation has recently revised the official association policy to include CE as a precondition for license renewal.

Search and Retrieval

More than any other association, the American Psychological Association has undertaken to mount an intensive effort to retrieve knowledge and disseminate it broadly within its own profession and to all others who might find it useful. The association maintains a search and retrieval system called PASAR (Psychological Abstracts Search and Retrieval).

OTHER ASSOCIATIONS

Developments in each of the professional associations are supported by parallel developments in other organizations, including national voluntary associations such as the Family Service Society of America, the National Association of Mental Health, the Group for the Advancement of Psychiatry, the Child Welfare League of America, the American Public Welfare Association, and the National Council on Alcoholism. Like the American Psychological Association, each of the professional associations provides at least some information-and-search services to its members.

TARGETS AND CONSUMERS

When a professional association sponsors and conducts continuing education activities on its own, the target or consumer is invariably the individual—the member of the association who is the professional worker and whose education would qualify him or her for membership. When CE offerings are voluntary, consumer choice is the model. When CE activities are related to credentialing certification or relicensure, the emphasis frequently shifts from consumer choice to a training model. The content may be preselected according to criteria established by the association or a licensing review board. A learner may have some choice of content within categories but relatively little choice about whether or not to participate.

Professional associations also employ the consultation model. Associations that function as societies of individual professionals (e.g., the AMA, ANA, and NASW), however, are not likely to be as consultation-oriented as those that are composed of organizational affiliates. These include the Council on Social Work Education, the American Public Welfare Association, and the Family Service Society of America. Although these associations may also include individual members, their services tend to be oriented toward institutions. But because they are membership organizations, they sometimes find it difficult to go much beyond where their affiliates are in terms of readiness.

We have found that they tend to be service- rather than change-oriented. It is somewhat difficult for membership organizations to identify a target for change and to systematically go about trying to change members through training and related activities. At best they may press for the development of standards and performance criteria. These may then be used as the basis for leadership seminars, which, broadly speaking, are integral to the association's continuing education responsibilities.

A wider range of possibilities opens up, however, when professional associations team up with agency or university collaborators. A particular project or program can be change-oriented and might be directed at either individuals or a component-service system. The project, even if time-limited, develops a life and identity of its own. Although it may draw legitimacy from its cosponsoring institutions, it generally has the freedom to engage in strategic activities not otherwise feasible. Examples of such activities will be given throughout the chapters that follow.

SUGGESTIONS FOR FURTHER READING

American Association of State Psychology Boards: "Continuing Education for Psychologists" and "Uniform Professional Continuing Education Act," mimeographed, September 1973.

American Medical Association: "Continuing Education for Physicians," Supplement to *Journal of the American Medical Association,* 1974.

————: *Essentials of Improved Programs of Continuing Education,* Council on Medical Education of the AMA, Chicago, 1974.

————: *A Guide Regarding Objectives and Basic Principles of Continuing Medical Education Programs,* Council on Medical Education of the AMA, Chicago, 1974.

————: *The Physician's Recognition Award,* Chicago, 1974.

American Nurses' Association: *Continuing Education Guidelines for State Nurses' Associations,* Kansas City, Mo., 1974.

————: *Guidelines for State Voluntary and Mandatory Systems.* Kansas City, Mo., 1975.

————: "Recognition for Continuing Education," *American Journal of Nursing,* Vol. 74, no. 5, May 1974.

————: *Standards for Continuing Education in Nursing,* Kansas City, Mo., 1974.

Arnhoff, F. N., E. A. Rubenstein, and J. C. Speisman (eds.): *Manpower for Mental Health,* Aldine, Chicago, 1969.

Brenner, M. N., and W. H. Koch: "Continuing Education among Social Workers: Patterns and Profiles," in *Approaches to Innovation in Social Work Education,* Council on Social Work Education, New York, 1974.

Brown, C. R., and H. S. Uhl: "Mandatory Continuing Education: Sense or Nonsense," *Journal of the American Medical Association,* vol. 213, no. 10, September 1970.

Carmichael, H. T.: "A Psychiatric Knowledge and Skills Self-Assessment Program," *Journal of the American Medical Association,* vol. 213, no. 10, September 1970.

Carmichael, H., S. M. Small, and P. F. Regan: *Prospects and Proposals: Lifetime Learning for Psychiatrists,* American Psychiatric Association, Washington, D.C., 1972.

Clark, Kenneth E., and George A. Milled (eds.): *Psychology,* Prentice-Hall, Englewood Cliffs, N.J., 1970.

Council on Social Work Education: *Guide to Continuing Education for Schools of Social Work,* New York, 1974.

Curtis, Frieda, et al.: *Continuing Education in Nursing,* Western Interstate Commission on Higher Education, Boulder, Colo., 1969.

Educom: "A Study of the Common Elements in Continuing Professional Education," *Bulletin,* Interuniversity Communications Council, January 1968.

Grosser, Charles, et al.: *Nonprofessionals and the Human Services,* Jossey-Bass, San Francisco, 1969.

Horns, Howard L.: "Relicensure and Recertification," *Journal of the American Medical Association,* vol. 229, no. 4, July 1974, pp. 61–62.

Katahn, Martin: "A Survey of the Interest in Continuing Education among Mental Health Professionals in the Southeastern States," *American Psychologist,* vol. 23, no. 3, 1968.

Lauffer, Armand: "Continuing Education in Problem-Focussed Extension," *Journal of Education for Social Work,* vol. 8, no. 3, Fall 1972.

Lawler, Edward: "Postdoctoral Training for an Industrial Psychologist," *Industrial Psychologist's Newsletter,* Spring 1967.

London, Perry: "The Psychotherapy Boom: From the Long Couch for the Sick to the Pushbutton for the Bored," *Psychology Today,* vol. 8, no. 1, June 1974.

McPheeters, Harold L., and Robert M. Ryan: *A Core of Competence for Baccalaureate Social Workers and Curricular Implications,* Southern Regional Education Board, Atlanta, 1971.

Miller, George E.: "Continuing Education for What?" *Journal of Medical Education,* issue 42, 1967.

Naftulan, D. H., J. D. Ware, and B. H. Meyers: "Psychiatric Interest in Continuing Education," *Archives of General Psychology,* vol. 24, 1971.

National Association of Social Workers: "Legal Regulation of Social Work Practice, Policies for a Continuing Effort," mimeographed, Washington, D.C., 1975.

National League for Nursing: "Position Statement on Nursing Licensure," statement by board of directors, New York, February 1975.

New Careers in Mental Health: Status Report, University Research Corporation, Washington, D.C., 1970.

Ross, Alan O.: "Continuing Professional Development in Psychology," *Professional Psychology,* vol. 5, no. 2, 1974.

Rushing, William A.: *The Psychiatric Professions,* University of North Carolina Press, Chapel Hill, 1965.

Schiff, Samuel B.: "Continuing Education for Professional Personnel," in Henry Grunebaum (ed.), *The Practice of Community Mental Health,* Little, Brown, Boston, 1970.

Shore, Milton F., and Fortune V. Mannino: *Mental Health and Community: Problems, Programs, and Strategies,* Behavioral Publications, New York, 1969.

Simon, Ralph, Sam Silverstein, and Beatrice M. Shriver: *Explorations in Mental Health Training: Project Summaries,* U.S. Department of Health, Education and Welfare, NIMH, Rockville, Md., 1975.

Webster, Thomas G., Margaret E. Hoffman, and Warren C. Lamson: "Continuing Education: Agent of Change," *Proceedings of a National Conference on Continuing Education in Mental Health,* Publication 2167, HEW, NIMH, Washington, D.C., 1971.

Williams, Richard Hayes: "The Mental Health Professions: Who, What, and Whither," in M. Levitt and B. Rubenstein (eds.), *The Mental Health Field,* Wayne State University, 1971.

————: *Perspective in the Field of Mental Health: A View of the National Program,* HEW, NIMH, Washington, D.C., 1972.

————, and L. D. Ozarin (eds.): *Community Mental Health: An International Perspective,* Jossey-Bass, San Francisco, 1969.

Chapter 5

Continuing Education in the Service Agency: The Staff Development Process

A Community Mental Health Center Requests Help with Staff Development

When the director of the Community Mental Health Center [CMHC] called to request that we conduct a series of training sessions to "get the staff moving," I agreed right away. I explained that for our educational approach to be successful we had to involve the CMHC staff in identifying needs and setting their own objectives. We would then collaboratively develop an educational format and a system of evaluation. Once this plan for staff development was complete, I would select faculty members with the requisite skills.

The center's director convened a committee the next week. At our first session, I found that half the people there didn't fully understand the purpose of the meeting. I've been in situations like this before, and I do have a way of building rapport.

Once they felt comfortable with me, things began coming out that had never been expressed publicly before. Unfortunately, there were so many problems expressed that it was difficult to decide which ones ought to have priority over others. To get over the impasse, I suggested that the staff development activities we engage in might focus on problem identification and problem solving instead of narrowly defined training. We would develop study and action groups within the agency that would work together prior to training. Our faculty members would serve as consultants and resource people at weekly or biweekly meetings. The first consultation session would focus on problem identification and group formation. The second would be focused on identifying change strategies and the third on selecting a strategy; at the next session training in those strategies would begin.

We ended that meeting on a kind of high. I felt pretty good about salvaging a situation I felt the CMHC director had set up poorly. I got my staff together and started planning the first session. It never came off!

The agency sent me a formal letter explaining that its staff did not feel I really understood what was needed. It was all very straight, but accusatory. When one of my staff checked informally with a friend on the center staff, she got a barrage of hostility. I was accused of looking for problems where they didn't exist, of trying to foment dissatisfaction just so I could have some problems to work on. The director already knew what problems existed. Apparently these had to do with staff skills. He had wanted us to train staff to work with community people. I was thunderstruck. No one had ever even mentioned this issue before.

For many continuing educators this will have a familiar ring, the more so because the vignette is a composite drawn from three similar incidents in different sections of the country. None of the three staff development efforts ever got off the ground. The educators had not fully thought through the interests of the three principal groups involved: the agency administration, the staff to be developed or trained, and the CEP itself. The educators seemed to be pursuing one particular model of practice, unaware that other models might have been more appropriate to the consumer of service or the target of change.

THE SERVICE AGENCY ARENA:
FOUR MODELS OF PRACTICE

The very question of who is the consumer and who the target was not adequately addressed. In Chapter 2 we discussed CE orientations toward service and toward change. We also spoke of individuals or service systems as being the recipients of service or targets of change. Represented on a "two-by-two" table, these differences generate four models of practice: consumer choice, consultation, training, and systems change. Each of these becomes a model of staff development practice when applied to the agency arena.

The "continuing educator" quoted made the error of assuming

that a consultation approach in which all staff would be treated as both consumers and targets of change was appropriate. The agency administration, on the other hand, viewed itself as the consumer and its staff as targets of change. The continuing educator attempted to utilize a combined consultation–consumer choice model with agency staff prior to completing his consultation with the agency administration. He viewed his efforts as service oriented toward both the individuals and the agency. The administration viewed his activities as agency-change-oriented and did not approve.

STAFF DEVELOPMENT ACTIVITIES AIMED AT THE INDIVIDUAL

Instructional activities aimed at individuals fall within either the consumer choice or the training model. Learning activities may take place within the agency or outside.

In-Service Training within the Agency

In-service training is a management device used to ensure that staff perform required tasks at an acceptable level. Training can be designed for professional and technical personnel, for subprofessional, clerical, and maintenance personnel, or for volunteers. Some in-service training programs begin with an orientation for new employees and continue throughout the duration of employment. They may include refresher training for current responsibilities as well as retraining for new tasks or new responsibilities. Although training activities are not oriented toward preparing people to leave the agency, some do include preretirement orientation.

Effective in-service training requires that the tasks for each level of work be specific in relation to the organization's service missions and maintenance needs. The objectives and content of training are determined by the administration. Training is aimed at fitting the individual to the organization through enhancing the effectiveness or efficiency of her or his performance.

Training Outside the Agency

This aim can also be achieved by sending the individual to training activities outside the agency. Thus it is not unusual for a university-based CEP to conduct campus-based workshops in grantsmanship or management techniques on behalf of an agency or complex of agencies that send their staff for such training. What distinguishes such activities from the consumer choice model is that the employer determines who is to go where for what kind of training. The service agency is the consumer, and the individual learner the trainee is the target of change.

Individual Development and Consumer Choice

In a number of agencies, however, we found that the choice is left entirely to the individual, who may be given the opportunity to engage in continuing education for his or her own purposes. Typical arrangements include conference attendance, educational leave for several hours per week or several days per year, and sabbatical with partial pay along the academic model. Some agencies provide staff with leave without pay; others give them time off but no reimbursement for out-of-pocket expenses; still others give total reimbursement. The alternatives sometimes depend on the level of the staff person within the organization. What they have in common is that the individual learner is perceived as the consumer who makes the choices about what to learn and where to learn it.

Nevertheless, such activities are generally viewed as beneficial to the agency. The learner might be expected to bring back and share what has been learned. But consumer choice activities are also oriented to job enrichment and may be perceived as fringe benefits or rewards for dedication or longevity.

One executive director of a large agency suggests that these activities are

> important not only to the individual's self-renewal, but to agency renewal too. You can't measure the payoff in terms of specific job performance. But you do see it in heightened staff morale, the exchange of creative ideas, and a sense of openness about the place.

Many educators agree that the atmosphere of the agency must be supportive of creativity and openness; otherwise, no amount of consumer choice activities will do much good. Sometimes, in fact, they may be disruptive to the agency. One of our respondents, a state-agency staff development specialist, made the following complaint:

> When my staff go outside the agency for training, they come back unsatisfied and want to put something totally unrealistic into practice. Take Transactional Analysis, for example. TA just doesn't fit into this agency. One of my staff went off to a three-week intensive TA workshop last year. Now she's off on her own, doing her own thing. We lost a pretty productive staff member.

STAFF DEVELOPMENT ACTIVITIES
AIMED AT THE AGENCY ITSELF

Education for Agency Development: Consultation Model

The objectives of agency development are complementary to and yet quite different from individually oriented training and learning opportunities. Rather than attempting to change the individual to fit the organization or providing multiple choices to the individual, agency development focuses more directly on changing the organization to fit its members. It utilizes instructional and other means to effect changes in the way the organization is managed and the manner in which staff relate to each other.

The underlying assumption is that greater job satisfaction and better internal relations will ultimately increase effectiveness and efficiency. In management terms, education for agency development draws on the "human relations school" for its orientation, whereas in-service training draws on the "scientific management school." Agency development draws heavily on consultation approaches in which units within the agency (and sometimes the whole agency) are engaged in a collaborative process. The emphasis is on process, communication, and better management.

This may be the most difficult form of staff development to conduct. It requires participation in decision making from various staff levels in the organization. The most common activities do not look like traditional training but include group problem solving, team building, and the development of new communication channels.

Systems Change Model: Education for Program Development

When the objective is program or service development, the educator uses instructional and related activities to expand the staff's capability to undertake new or modified responsibilities. The systems change model differs from in-service training in that emphasis is placed on the solution of practice problems or the expansion and extension of agency programs and services rather than strictly on training for effective performance. Staff are involved in identifying the problems to be addressed and determining their educational objectives. Although internal management issues may be addressed, the focus is always on improvements that better agency programs and services. In general, this orientation complements a "management-by-objectives" approach to administration. It differs from the consultation model in that administration is often central to the determination of what problems are to be examined and who should be assigned to dealing with them.

Institutional versus Individual Change

Agency and program development are oriented toward institutional change, whereas individual development (consumer choice) and training are oriented toward more effective or efficient performance of individuals within their assigned tasks. Under the consumer choice model the individual determines his or her individual development objectives, although the options are circumscribed within certain limits imposed by the agency. The nature of in-service training is determined by administration. The objectives, content, and format of agency and program development reflect the concerns of a wide range of people. They may require input from staff at every level, from different units within the organization, from members of the board, and from representatives of the populations served by the agency.

For these reasons some continuing educators feel that in-service training is conservative, whereas other forms of staff development are change-oriented. This is an oversimplification. It does not recognize that management is frequently more change-oriented that lower-level staff. A change effort, whatever its origins, can produce tensions. Tensions can arise when one person or group in the agency either resists or promotes changes that are not acceptable to others. Tensions also arise when one person or group in the organization perceives a staff development activity according to one of the four models discussed, while others perceive the activity as serving other functions.

In the example cited earlier, the administrator of a mental health center perceived staff development in in-service terms, whereas the trainers were oriented toward an agency development strategy. Similar results are likely when the trainees perceive staff development activities as opportunities to engage in efforts to change their relationships to each other but the administration perceives the same activity as a means of shaping the learner's behavior.

Conflicts often arise when the administration, motivated by a desire to help staff improve or modify their relationships, hires an outside firm to conduct an agency development activity. The staff may be resistant because of the threats implied in giving up existing patterns of relationship, in self-exposure, and in trading the tried and understood for the new and uncertain. When there is no mutual understanding among management, the staff to be trained, and the trainers of staff developers, tensions leading to failure or partial blockage of goal attainment are not uncommon.

Both in-service training and program development require distinct activities for different subgroups within an organization. No two subgroups are the same. In-service training activities are generally oriented toward subgroups composed of people at the same level within the organization or those performing similar tasks (i.e., secretaries, maintenance workers, ward attendants, intake workers, psychiatric nurses). In program development, staff may be grouped around service areas. Thus psychiatrists, caseworkers, nurses, volunteers, and others engaged in efforts to transfer patients from the hospital to the community may be involved in collaborative learning experiences.

While agency development activities may also involve a group of individuals performing similar functions, they frequently aim at increasing communication between persons in different types of positions. Thus, although an agency development program may begin with opportunities for maintenance workers, nurses, attendants, and occupational therapists to ventilate within their own occupational groups, the staff developer may have something else in mind as the final outcome. Once peer group ventilation has occurred, he or she may arrange for representatives of each group to express publicly how they feel about the others. By inducing people to express themselves, the staff developer hopes to increase work-related insights, improve communication, and ultimately move the staff toward collective problem solving.

These are not exclusive models. One leads to and complements the other. It may be appropriate to begin the staff development process without prior committment to a specific approach and move from one approach to another as the agency and its staff are ready for such movement. Movement from one model to another, however, is not automatic, nor is it always possible.

INITIATING STAFF DEVELOPMENT

Responding to Pain or Anticipated Pleasure

Popular wisdom has it that organizations begin the process of staff development when someone internal to it either recognizes that things are not going as well as they should or perceives the possibility of doing things better. The first is a response to pain, the second to anticipated pleasure. Both perceptions may be correct, but the reality is somewhat more complex. The following illustrations of initiating incidents, drawn from interviews with staff developers, demonstrate that complexity:

1   Nurses feel that their work is not fully appreciated or understood by physicians and that they do not have sufficient authority. They ask for an opportunity to exchange information with other staff so that they might instruct them about nursing functions.

2   Social workers feel ignored and resentful when only physicians and psychiatric interns participate in seminars within the hospital and receive funds to attend conferences and workshops outside. They demand similar consideration.

3   Increasing relationships between staff of several agencies around the needs of shared clientele result in new roles for "boundary" personnel. Interest emerges in learning about each other's services and sharing knowledge and skill.

4   New types of staff are added to the agency (paraprofessionals, ex-patients or clients, volunteers). The old staff must be prepared to work with them, while the new staff must be prepared for effective job performance.

5   A shift from individual supervision with a semitherapeutic orientation to management by objectives with a program orientation changes the relationships between staff. New lines of communication are opened up and new access to information is made available. But the new MBO system works well only in some units and is blocked elsewhere.

6   Participation of agency staff in workshops or courses outside the agency stimulates interest in a particular subject and a desire to bring outside experts to the agency.

7   The breakup of a formerly large hospital system into detached or decentralized units requires that staff perform a broader range of tasks.

8   Accreditation of an agency is dependent upon periodic or regular in-service training activities (e.g., a state agency will license the substance-abuse counseling center only after full staff has undergone forty hours of training). Money available for training.

These illustrations suggest that staff development activities may be initiated by forces or interest groups either internal or external to the agency. Someone internal to the organization, of course, has to want a staff development program or be willing to accept it. But the reason for wanting it may stem from external events and promises of rewards or from internal pressures. Staff development activities may be conducted by the agency itself, or the agency may contract for services from an otuside agent. Sometimes the outside vendor initiates the contact leading to staff development.

In four of the illustrations cited (3, 6, 7, and 8), we later discovered that a CEP outside the agency had taken advantage of a perceived need and initiated contact with the agency or agencies involved. This outside vendor may have been a university-based CEP, a state training unit, or a private entrepreneur. In one instance

(4), an allocating or planning body identified the need and initiated contacts between the agency and a university-based CEP. In each of the other illustrations, staff development efforts were initiated internally, but external resources may have been used to conduct CE activities.

Initiation by an Outside Vendor

When a continuing education program external to the agency attempts to initiate a relationship that might lead to staff development activities, it will generally employ one or more of the following strategies: (1) providing information about its own resources, (2) increasing the agency's awareness of its need for and the potential benefits of staff development activities, and (3) increasing pressure on the agency to move toward needed change, while pointing out that staff development activities can serve as instruments toward achievement of that change. Outside vendors frequently employ a number of promotional devices to make their services known. These include brochures, press releases, use of third-party "common carriers," and direct contacts.

Our observations suggest that effective brochures tend to be brief, attractively laid out, and quite explicit. They not only specify what the CEP is prepared to offer but also give details on the nature of the relationship that is to be established between the CEP and the contracting agency. Brochure copy may also specify the obligations of each. In some cases brochures warn the potential contractor of possible unanticipated consequences once the staff development process is initiated.

Press releases and occasional feature articles in newspapers or interviews on radio and TV may serve as advertisements. Satisfied customers often act as referral agents, either informing the CEP of an agency's need for staff development or informing the agency of the CEP's services. Typically, satisfied customers may be members of the agency staff who have recently participated in workshops they feel will be useful to their colleagues or administrators of a second agency who convey their enthusiasm to the agency in question.

Third parties are frequently responsible for bringing the consumer and the provider together. They serve as common carriers, bringing messages back and forth between the relevant parties. Sometimes the third party is itself a CEP that cannot undertake a particular staff development activity:

> The job may be too big or too small for us, we may be too busy, or we just don't have the capacity to take it on. But we do know a lot of people who

can. Because I've got a good line into what the agencies need, and good contacts with educators around the state, I'm in a good position to broker a lot of relationships. To be honest with you, I consider this one of my major functions. We obviously can't do everything that people want us to do, or be everything to everybody. Yet the training and staff development needs out there are enormous. What better service could we provide than that of matchmaker or broker?

More typically the continuing educator initiates the contacts with an agency himself. One educator reports that he regularly calls agency administrators in his community, ostensibly for social purposes or to ask about the usefulness of a workshop that someone on the staff may have attended. Another periodically drops in on agencies in different cities throughout the state. Still another regularly calls agency representatives together for coffee meetings or luncheons to discuss innovations in mental health services and uses the opportunity to establish contacts that may lead to staff development contracts. Several CEPs send out newsletters or bulletins to former or potential consumers informing them that new or extended services are now available. Written materials may be followed up with a telephone call.

The style employed by one continuing educator in the Southeast may be illuminating:

For me, working toward a contract in staff development has always been a continuing process. Both parties sort of mutually woo each other.

At first I don't like to come on too strong. Over a cup of coffee, I might make an innocuous-sounding remark to the agency person, like: "I understand these new regulations are going to create some problems for you." He has two options. He can say, "No, it won't be too serious," in which case he cuts me off. Or he can tell me about some of the problems to see how I respond. At this point he doesn't know whether I want his business or he wants my services. I don't either.

We might both go on this way for fifteen minutes or so, moving from innocuous openers to more specific examination of the possibilities. I might tell him, for example, that we have already had some experience training people around similar practice issues elsewhere, or I might entice him with some ideas about how he might get his staff moving to either do their work better or grab a bigger piece of the action. Of course, by now I'm sketching out how our training could be helpful in doing these things.

The person I'm talking to knows what I'm doing. And I know that he knows. It's a sort of mutual seduction process. Either of us can cut it off at any time if we think we're getting in too deep or if our explorations suggest our relationship might not be satisfactory.

However, there may be times when a mutuality of perspective is not likely. A more direct approach may be necessary:

If we had waited for the directors of community mental health centers to discover they weren't doing a good job of community consultation, or if we had tried to convince them that there were better ways of doing it, we'd be waiting until doomsday or until CMHC goes out of business. But when the state issued directives about new forms to be filled out if centers were to be reimbursed for consultations, then we let people know that we were available for consultation and training in the new procedures. We didn't have to convince anybody that our services were necessary. We just made doubly sure they knew we were available.

An external authority is sometimes used to induce people to attend the course or the training program. In the illustration given, the state agency's requirement provided a threat of economic or administrative sanctions. Although such sanctions may induce an agency to provide training as staff development, they do not necessarily motivate staff to learn or to change in the desired directions. A state-agency staff developer explains:

You can induce change through instituting new regulations or procedures. You don't necessarily need training or education. But when you do use instructional means, you've got to move people from feeling that they're being forced into something to feeling that they really want to learn and apply what they're learning. I've seen more "good" in-service training programs go sour because the learners weren't convinced that what they were supposed to learn was in their interest. Training techniques, methods, and sophisticated gear mean nothing unless the learner is motivated. The agency atmosphere has to be such that it supports learning and change.

Perhaps a melding of the training and consumer choice models is necessary. The agency must also be prepared to accept the possible consequences of change and must be prepared to deal with them as they emerge. The illustration at the beginning of this chapter is a case in point. The CMHC was not prepared to deal with problem identification as suggested by the university continuing educator. Despite protestations that "I thought I had adequately prepared the agency," the educator had not been aware that informing the agency about a process might not be the same as informing it about possible outcomes.

THE STAFF DEVELOPMENT UNIT WITHIN AN AGENCY

Although many service agencies must go outside for some or all of their staff development activities, large agencies tend to maintain their own continuing education units to which designated personnel may be assigned full or part time. The location or auspice of the CEP may vary considerably. For example, in a state department of mental health, the staff development unit may be located within the man-power and planning division, it may be totally independent, or it may be located in a programmatic or administrative division such as community mental health or hospital services. It may be made up of expert trainers or may be no more than a committee of representative staff. It may be responsible for one or all of the following: approving all consumer choice requests, conducting in-service training activi-ties for personnel at all levels, consultation or problem solving with local agency affiliates around issues pertaining to management and communication, and developing new service plans while preparing staff to carry them out.

In most cases the staff development unit may not be able to carry out each of these functions without access to other personnel:

> We've got several in-service training programs down pat. But we're not experts on everything. Sometimes we're dependent on outside experts. Usually we can find them within the state agency system. I find it works best to use program personnel to train other program personnel. We may know something about training, but they know what needs to be known about services. If we can't find the right people inside the organization, we find an expert from outside.

The emphasis on using program personnel was carried even further by another state social service agency that perceives most CE or staff development activities as being conveyed through the normal supervisory channels. One of the agency's workers reported:

> From our perspective, training and staff development activities are an integral part of management and programming. Oh, we may run an occasional special event. But most of the time we're trying to help the system operate without us.

First of all, most training is conducted on site by the unit supervisor. After all, she has to see to it that the work gets done. We back the supervisor up by designing training packages and how-to-do-it guides.

We also train administrative staff up and down the line in the use of a number of problem-solving methods. That way, when an operational problem presents itself, they don't have to bump it up the line right away or call us in. They can use our step-by-step procedure on their own. We come into the process when the procedure doesn't work. Sometimes we do no more than refer them to an expert in the particular area when added expertise is needed.

Although patterns vary considerably, we have observed that state training or staff development units tend to do their work at the central level, training other trainers, approving leaves, and designing packages to be used at the local agency level. At the local level, staff development activities sometimes must be farmed out or outside consultants and CE specialists brought in.

THE INSIDER VERSUS THE OUTSIDER IN STAFF DEVELOPMENT

The internal staff developer may be a program specialist, department head, middle manager, planner, or supervisor whose principal tasks lie outside training and development or sometimes may be responsible exclusively for staff development activities. The outside vendor may be an individual entrepreneur with experience in staff development, an expert in a subject matter, a university-based CEP, or a staff development person in another agency. Outside vendors may also include the field staff of a professional association or a consulting firm. There are both advantages and disadvantages to using either an inside or an outside source.

Knowing and Being Known

The insider has the potential advantage of knowing the system. He or she knows where the power lies and where the strategic lever points are—the gatekeepers, opinion leaders, and innovators. Under the best of circumstances the insider speaks the same language as other members of the staff, knowing who talks to whom and about what. Insiders understand the norms and the commonly held beliefs and attitudes of the staff and generally share them. They identify with the system's needs and aspirations because they are members of it. Its successes are their successes.

Insiders are generally familiar figures and known quantities. They may be in a good position to make suggestions that relate to changes in job descriptions and work plans. They may be able to go directly to an administrator after reading a new directive in order to point out that a policy needs clarification because it confuses people. Insiders are familiar with the issues that need correcting, with staff learning needs, and with the practices of the agency.

Outsiders may have no such knowledge. If an agency's problems are deeply hidden and if staff are reluctant to be open with an outsider, they may never acquire the requisite knowledge. On the other hand, staff may feel much freer to speak openly and more willing to expose lack of knowledge or competence to an outsider who is neither a peer nor a representative of the administration.

However, a stranger, being both an unknown and an unpredictable quantity, may present a potential threat. The outsider's very demeanor sometimes causes initial discomfort, reinforcing the fears people may have about training. Sometimes the outsider is not aware of this anxiety until it is too late. Since she or he does not have the knowledge of the insider, it might take too long to find out what is going on.

Yet the outsider has the advantage of starting out fresh, unburdened by negative stereotypes, conflicts, or deep obligations. The outsider's perspective may be unencumbered by the tunnel vision often characteristic of personnel within the organization. The outsider can function independently of the organization's power structure and, in the long run, is generally unaffected by its view of him or her.

The outsider's advantages may be the insider's disadvantages. The insider may lack perspective, being unable to perceive the agency in its totality because he or she views it from a particular vantage point. He or she may not have the specialized knowledge or skill relevant to the situation at hand. Frequently, the internal staff developer is without an adequate power base to effect changes. The insider's familiarity to others within the agency may breed contempt or indifference. The "halo" that sometimes makes it possible for an outsider to achieve quantum leaps in one bound is rarely present. The insider may have to live down past failures. He or she may be further limited because of obligations to other members of the staff that have been built up over time.

Although tightened agency budgets may leave few dollars for training, other resources may be available to internal staff developers, such as staff time and energy, agency facilities, and available training materials. When no outside experts can be paid, there is often an internal staff person who can do training. When materials can't be purchased, they can often be modified and/or duplicated internally. Internal staff developers have almost no marketing costs; their trainees are available through face-to-face contact, memos, or telephone calls. The agenda for the training session can be posted in the coffee room.

Sources of Authority

There are also differences in the sources from which insiders and outsiders draw authority. The insider draws authority from his or her formal position within the agency and informal relationship and reputation with the agency staff. This can be both advantageous and disadvantageous. When management's authority is clear and legitimate in the eyes of the staff, there may be clear advantages to being an insider.

The authority of the outsider may stem from his or her presumed or known expertise either in a content area or in training and staff development. It tends to be based more on exposure than on position. To the extent that authority is based on position (i.e., a representative of administration or a consultant to a multistaff development committee), the authority is time-limited. No one expects the outsider to remain in that position beyond the life of the project, contract, or activity.

Team Approach

Staff developers frequently use a team approach that includes insiders and outsiders, because of the disadvantages of using only one or another. The staff development person who is an insider may employ an outsider for a specific task (consultation, leadership of a workshop, lecture). An outside developer may convene a planning or training team composed of agency staff representing various interests. Often the team will be composed of representatives of the administration, middle management, supervisors, area specialists, on-line professionals, paraprofessionals, and, in some cases, clients and lay leaders (such as board or advisory committee members). Sometimes a number of teams are convened. These may represent a single discipline or profession, a work unit or staff from one geographic location, or staff representing many disciplines and from several locations.

Team members may be engaged in both training and other staff development activities. Typically a planning team will set goals, decide content and format; select faculty, workshop leaders, and resource persons; and assess and evaluate. The planning team is the group in which general anxieties and more specific concerns can be expressed freely and severe problems can be headed off. Planning teams provide information on staff interests and concerns to the educator and provide a buffer against inappropriate criticism.

RELATIONSHIP BETWEEN THE AGENCY AND THE STAFF DEVELOPER

Whether the staff developer is an insider or an outsider, the quality of his or her relationship to team members and other relevant actors may be a critical variable in the activity's success. The relationship begins with the very first contact. Once the decision to establish a staff development relationship has been made, it is strengthened to the extent that each partner in the relationship clarifies the expectations he or she has of the others and of himself or herself. What is to be done? How is it to be done? Who is to do it? What are the alternatives? The assessment process is often ongoing, but frequently it will terminate at a given point. The staff developer continuing educator may determine that the agency no longer needs help or that the purposes of that help are misunderstood.

Mutuality of Awareness

The process of building the relationship and a mutuality of perspective is extremely important. It leads directly into both problem definition and the beginning of staff development activities. One continuing educator describes how she typically initiates staff development in a mental hospital setting by meeting with all the different work groups separately: attendants, rehabilitation workers, occupational therapists, nursing staff, psychiatrists, and social workers. She begins by asking what disturbs them the most about their work in the hospital or their relationships to others. Then she asks them whether they think people in other occupational groups feel the same or understand their feelings. Finally she asks them what they would like to see changed and how they would like to see the changes put into effect.

She uses this information to assess organizational readiness for change and to let people know how much she is prepared to do with them and what they must be prepared to do on their own. Many educators report similar approaches. They variously label them as problem-solving sessions, force field analysis,[1] or sensitivity or consciousness-raising activities.

Others approach things quite differently. Rather than meet in groups, they may begin the process by interviewing key people within

the agency who represent different points of view or different occupations. They may focus on problems of management, communication,
or service delivery within the organization. Sometimes they focus
exclusively on the nature of the tasks to be performed. This process
can be highly formalized and quite technical. It may include a
"functional job analysis" (FJA),[1] which requires delineation of every
task performed by every worker in an organization. The very act of
using a technical instrument like FJA in contrast to sensitivity
sessions or group problem solving defines the relationship between
the staff developer and the agency. In this case, as in others, the
medium is very much the message.

Costs and Benefits

Defining a relationship also requires estimating costs and benefits.
How much will a staff development program cost in dollars, in time,
in energy, in opportunities lost? Whom will it benefit? The director of
manpower and training in a state agency directly addresses the issue:

> Before I engage in a staff development process, I ask myself if the time
> spent is the best way of creating the changes desired, or if it wouldn't be
> better just to initiate some administrative changes or give people more
> time on their own. If I'm going to take people away from clients, it had
> better result in more efficient operations or better service to those
> clients.

One might also investigate how much of the initial problem might
be solved. What is the probability of goal accomplishments at a 75
percent level of satisfaction? At an 80 percent level? At a 100 percent
level? How will costs differ for different levels of satisfaction?

**Supporting Agency Staff during
the Process of Change**

There are almost always vested interests in maintaining the status
quo. These interests may be so strongly entrenched that they prohibit
the accomplishment of the staff developer's or administrator's objectives. A staff developer's assessment of feasibility is unrealistic if it
does not take into account the fear and anxiety that may be generated
by facing an unknown.

A staff development specialist in a large public mental hospital
talked about the "grieving" behavior she noticed among some hospi-

---

[1]See Chapter 12, "Assessment in Continuing Education."

tal staff. She found that after a new set of procedures was introduced, they behaved like people mourning a lost friend. This behavior was in direct response to developing skills in a new method that, although objectively more effective than older methods, was not yet as familiar or as comfortable.

In some cases learning or change is retarded simply because of a reluctance on the part of the learners to admit ignorance or lack of skill. Staff may fear exposing their ignorance or looking awkward while using a new approach to treatment or referral. Lack of successes in earlier attempts in staff development or change may create a sense of fatalism about current efforts.

For these reasons staff developers must help learners develop a sense of confidence in their own abilities to learn and to apply their new knowledge and skill. This requires an atmosphere that is conducive to change: one that permits innovation, error, and even failure. As one of our informants puts it: "The environment within which learning and problem solving take place may be of greater import than the activity itself."

SUGGESTIONS FOR FURTHER READING

Barker, Robert L., and Thomas L. Griggs: *Using Teams to Deliver Social Services*, University of Syracuse School of Social Work, Syracuse, N.Y., 1969.
Bertcher, Harvey, and Charles Garvin: *Staff Development in Social Welfare Agencies*, Campus Publisher, Ann Arbor, Mich., 1969.
Craig, Robert L., and Lester R. Bittel (eds.): *Training and Development Handbook*, sponsored by the American Society for Training and Development, McGraw-Hill, New York, 1967.
Frey, Louise: "Organizational and Social Change," *Psychiatric Annals*, vol. 3, no. 31, March 1973.
Gane, Christopher: *Managing the Training Function: Using Instructional Technology and Systems Concepts*, Darvin Publications, Beverly Hills, Calif., 1972.
Glasser, Robert (ed.): *Training, Research, and Education*, Wiley, New York, 1965.
Guttentag, Marcia, Thomas Kiresuk, Marjorie Oglisby, and Jerry Cahn: *The Evaluation of Training in Mental Health*, Behavioral Publications, New York, 1975.
Katz, Daniel, and Robert L. Kahn: *The Social Psychology of Organizations*, chapter 13, "Organizational Change," Wiley, New York, 1965.
Kirkpatrick, Donald: *A Practical Guide for Supervisory Training and Development*, Addison-Wesley, Reading, Mass., 1971.
Kuriloff, Arthur H.: *Organizational Development for Survival*, American Management Association, New York, 1972.
Lippitt, Ronald, Jeanne Watson, and Bruce Westley: *The Dynamics of Change: A Comparative Study of Principles and Techniques*, Harcourt, Brace & World, New York, 1958.
Lynton, Rolf P., and Udai Pareek: *Training for Development*, Richard D. Irwin and Dorsey Press, Homewood, Ill., 1967.

Mager, Robert F., and Peter Pipe: *Analyzing Performance Problems, or "You Really Oughta Wanna,"* Lear Siegler/Fearon Publishers, Belmont, Calif., 1970.

Meyer, Carol H.: *Staff Development in Social Welfare Agencies*, Columbia University Press, New York, 1966.

Morgan, John S.: *Managing Change: The Strategies of Making Change Work for You*, McGraw-Hill, New York, 1972.

Odiorne, George S.: *Training by Objectives: An Economic Approach to Management*, Macmillan, New York, 1970.

Otto, Calvin P., and Rollin O. Glasser: *The Management of Training: A Handbook for Training and Development Personnel*, Addison-Wesley, Reading, Mass., 1970.

Shay, Phillip W.: *How to Get the Best Results from Management Consultants*, Association of Consulting Management Engineers, New York, 1965.

Signell, Karen A., and Patricia A. Scott: "Training in Consultation: A Crisis of Role Transition," *Community Mental Health Journal*, vol. 8, no. 2, May 1972.

Spielberger, Charles D.: "Case Seminars of Group Mental Health Consultation," *Professional Psychology*, vol. 5, no. 3, 1974.

Stearns, Norman S., Marjorie E. Gitchell, and Robert Gold: *Continuing Medical Education in Community Hospitals*, Boston, Massachusetts, Medical Society, 1971.

Studt, Elliott: *Administration and Staff Training in Institutions for Delinquency,* The Children's Bureau, HEW, Washington, D.C., 1959.

Weiss, Carol H.: "Evaluation of Staff Training Programs," *Welfare in Review*, vol. 3, no. 3., March 1965.

Whitesaill, William E., and Joseph E. Pietrus: "Training and the Learning Process," *Personnel*, July 1965.

Part Two

The Growth of the CEP and Its Institutional Relationships

Chapter 6

The Continuing Education Program in Its Task Environment

Several months ago an ex-drug addict I know invited me to observe some pushers, former buddies of his, working the street. He knew I was in the midst of preparing a project proposal to train drug-abuse counselors and thought I should have a firsthand view of the client population those counselors would be working with.

I was fascinated. For two days I was submerged in a world I'd had almost no contact with. The small-time pushers were living a precarious existence, their activities circumscribed by those of the police, on the one hand, and the norms of the street, on the other.

The pushers were addicts, dependent on other addicts to buy their products and on their suppliers to provide them with the necessary hard goods—heroin and cocaine. I remarked to my friend that the pushers seemed a sorry lot. "Yeah," he answered, "the pushers are being pushed. Consumer demand is up, but supply is down and there are too many pushers around. Competition is fierce, not just for the customer's money but for the supplier's goods."

"Dammit," I said to myself, "I am that pusher." It wasn't a moment of existential truth or an act of transference. It was nothing but a simple realization that as the director of a continuing education program, I was just as dependent as the pusher on my suppliers, on my program's consumers, on my competitors, and on those rulemakers and rule enforcers that circumscribe the limits of my program's operations.

These four elements—suppliers, consumers, competitors, and regulatory groups—make up the CEP's "task environment." They impinge directly on the program's ability to accomplish its objectives and to maintain itself.

THE ELEMENTS OF THE TASK ENVIRONMENT

Consumers

A continuing education program's consumers include both individuals and organizations. Individuals may be organized or unorganized. An individual who registers for a course or workshop independently—that is, not as a member of an organized entity—can exert only minimal influence on the nature or direction of the CEP's offerings. But an individual consumer who belongs to an organization to which the CEP is responsible or which can exert pressure on it is in a more powerful position.

The alumni association of a medical school, for example, may be in a powerful position vis-à-vis the school's postgraduate medical education program. Its members command money, teaching facilities, and prestige—all commodities of considerable importance to the school. Members of a professional association can demand CE services from their association. These may be direct services (i.e., consumer choice) or change-oriented activities. As an example of change-oriented activities, the association may demand staff development services from employing agencies or engage in political action to ensure passage of a relicensure bill that requires CE activities. In staff development programs, the learners may belong to administrative or work units.

In many instances the consumer is an organization rather than an individual learner or an association of individuals. If a federal agency contracts with a university-based CEP for the design of a training manual, the federal agency is the consumer. The user of the manual is referred to as the target of change. Similarly, if a mental hospital contracts with a state-agency staff development unit to conduct its in-service training seminars, the hospital administration is the consumer, while the individual learner is the target of change.

In other situations, the relationship between target and consumer is blurred. For example, a mental hospital may contract with a CEP to improve communications between staff at different levels and recommend new approaches to service delivery and, in addition, to train the staff to use new and more appropriate skills. In this case the hospital is simultaneously the consumer and the target of change.

Consumers are usually thought of as "output constituencies"—those individuals and organizations to which the CEP has an obligation and which act as recipients of its outputs or services. Output constituencies are rarely as powerful as input constituencies—those suppliers and regulatory groups that have access to resources the CEP needs in order to conduct its program or accomplish its missions. For this reason most continuing educators have not sought to organize their consumers.

Some, however, have found it advantageous to convert consumer populations from output to input constituents. Although they may be relinquishing some autonomy to the consumer population, they may be increasing their access to needed resources from other suppliers:

> The first thing I did when I got here was organize the program's potential clientele. I organized advisory groups in communities throughout the state. By getting their input into the planning process I gave up some of my autonomy vis-à-vis individual learners, but I increased my range of program options vis-à-vis the school.
>
> First, by involving potential consumers I was able to increase both demand and commitment to course offerings. Second, the consumers' ideas and the energy they invested made it possible to broaden our offerings. Third, I was able to draw on them for personnel to coordinate or teach in the programs. Finally, having a constituency out there increased my power within the school.
>
> The school is very dependent on agency personnel for the supervision of students. Their goodwill is essential to the success of our M.S.W. program. When they demand new CE services—a demand I am not loath to encourage—the school sits up and listens. The dean may like and respect me as an individual, but my clout, if I have any, comes from my advisory committees of agency people.

Suppliers

A CEP's suppliers are those individuals and organizations that provide it with the resources necessary to produce its product, give its service, or maintain itself. Resources can be defined as any of the commodities or means that permit an organization to accomplish its objectives. In addition to money and such tangible items as facilities and personnel, these resources also include intangibles such as knowledge and expertise, goodwill, prestige, and community influence.

Prestige makes it possible to attract both consumers and other resources. It can be conferred on an organization by those who participate in it or by those with whom it associates. Thus a CEP's stature can be enhanced by recruiting prestigious learners or prestigious instructional personnel.

A new CEP might depend upon the prestige of the host institution—an agency, a university, or a professional association. It also may be important for the continuing education program and other institutions to develop collaborative relationships around specific projects. An agency or department within a hospital with a rather weak reputation might seek to conduct a series of training activities with the university's medical school, a rather prestigious body. Such collaboration may do more than attract individual consumers. It may also make it possible to attract top-notch instructional personnel, grants and contracts, or other resources from other suppliers.

Typically these suppliers include host institutions, academic schools and departments, human service agencies that are repositories of knowledge and expertise, funding agencies, and community institutions that can provide the CEP with materials and facilities. Libraries and media or materials centers may provide the CEP with needed instructional equipment and materials.

Competitors

Most continuing education programs must respond to a variety of competitors. "It's funny, but I can get all the consumers I need and more money through grants and gifts than I can spend. I just can't get sufficient faculty to teach. I've reached the limit with my director," complains the training coordinator in a state mental health agency. "He claims I'll be killing the service program if I use any more program staff for training." This situation is further complicated when there is also competition for other resources, such as money and facilities. CEPs also compete with each other to the advantage and disadvantage of both:

> When there are just so many dollars available for the whole federal region and there are seven states in the region, you know that the training bucks are going to have to be divided with some equity. No state is going to be left out unless the proposal is so bad no one would consider

it. Even then, the feds are likely to intervene and help people design a better project.

So you begin by cutting the dollar pie into seven pieces and figure out approximately what might be available to your own state, give or take 50 percent on either side. Then you figure out who has the capacity of designing a project proposal in your own state and who might be likely to do so. A few well-placed phone calls might help you find out. Then you figure out whether you stand a chance of designing a better proposal or being more on target with federal and state priorities than the other people you are competing with. If the answer is yes and you've got all the manpower you need to run the project, you go it alone. If the answer is no, then you had better figure out how to accommodate to some of your competitors and collaborate with them on a program design. Although this takes up time and energy that might be better spent on other things, you find that the competition is helpful; it keeps you on your toes.

Other continuing educators have spoken of both formal and informal arrangements with competing institutions:

We can't cover the whole state, so we've agreed to split the territory with several other universities. Periodically we collaborate on a particular activity in the northern or western part of the state, but we've more or less made a gentleman's agreement to stay out of those places.

Some continuing educators may not be aware of the competition or might not consider it legitimate. One of our interviewees claimed that his was "the only continuing education program for the mental health professions" in his area. When quizzed about the other educational activities that the mental health professions participated in— agency staff development projects, sensitivity weekends, ad hoc seminars conducted by psychiatrists and other private practitioners—he replied that these activities weren't "really professional" and that he did not consider them continuing education.

Many participants in CE activities apparently do not have the same qualms about auspices as the educator quoted. By not recognizing these competing activities, the continuing educator was ignoring a large potential market for his own CEP's services.

Legitimizing and Regulatory Groups

Legitimizing and regulatory groups are those boards of directors, legislative bodies, credentialing institutions, or governmental agencies that establish the boundaries of an organization's operation and determine some of the basic procedures that it may employ. Most organizations are subject to regulations from more than one external source. For example, a community mental health center's board of directors might provide it with both auspices and legitimacy at the local level.

But the board's policymaking options are limited, because they are regulated by local, state, and national governmental agencies that are subject to legislative guidelines. A school of medicine may be subject to regulations imposed by the state in which it is located, the American Medical Association, the state medical association and the many academies within it, the university board of trustees, and the American Association of University Professors.

The same holds true for a continuing education program, whether it be a staff development program in a local mental health center or a postgraduate program in a medical school. Regulations are imposed directly and indirectly. For example, fees established by the extension service of a university for a nursing school's CEP are directly imposed. A university's regulations limiting work for extra pay, which result in a decrease in the school of public health's faculty available for teaching in CEP, are indirectly imposed regulations.

Although the CEP may not have much leverage over its regulating groups, it need not assume a passive role toward them. Regulations and guidelines, after all, are subject to interpretation and modification. Because a CEP may be subject to multiple regulations, it may be possible to modify some while responding to others:

> The terms of our NIMH grant specifically call for training paraprofessionals from minority populations, whereas the terms of our Justice Department grant exclude paraprofessionals. At one point last year we were able to get Washington's OK to use part of our NIMH grant to train professional workers because of a tie-in between the two grants.

SPECIAL RELATIONSHIPS
TO THE HOST INSTITUTION

The extent to which the continuing education program is free to engage in exchanges with its task environment depends on its practice arena and the relationship it maintains to its host institution. Few CEPs are independent entities. Most are part of an organizational complex.

Perhaps no aspect of the task environment is as influential as the host institution. It regulates the range of activities in which a CE program legitimately may engage. It may specify the objectives, consumers and targets of intervention, and methods and procedures of the program. It often supplies the CEP with most of its resources, such as money and credit, staff, facilities, knowledge and expertise, legitimacy, and legality. A CEP's autonomy is directly linked to its degree of dependence on the host institution for these resources.

The host institution may also act as the principal consumer of the CE program's services. A mental health department or local agency is the consumer of the services provided by its staff development or training unit. A medical school may use training materials in its basic degree program developed by its postgraduate medical education program.

Conflict and Tension

Conflicts are inevitable. They arise out of contradictory perspectives and as consequences of growth and development. Whenever a new segment or subsystem within an organization grows and develops an identity and an image of its own, it can be expected to compete for resources with other units in that organization, to press for its own definition of mission, and frequently to upset existing patterns and relationships. The developing CEP is no exception.

From the perspective of a school of social work, for instance, the CEP may perform a needed function by taking the pressure off the school to provide other services to social agencies in its environment. It may be used to compensate those agencies for providing student field placements. The continuing educator, however, may perceive the function of the CEP much more broadly. He or she may be concerned with improving the delivery of services to populations at risk, and this may require inducing those very same agencies to change. These efforts may generate productive controversy from the continuing educator's perspective but counterproductive controversy from the perspective of other faculty at the school.

If conflicts get out of hand, the CEP may attempt to develop total autonomy. Or its autonomy may be stripped as it is absorbed by another unit. In one university a library extension program split off from the university's extension service to become absorbed in a new unit within the school of library science. In other cases accommodation is achieved by granting the CEP almost total autonomy in areas such as programming but not in other areas, such as fiscal accountability. In such cases the host institution may disassociate itself from sponsorship of certain projects or activities, which then become identified solely with the CEP.

Because human service CEPs are relatively new, continuing educators are forced to deal with the ambiguities of their situations and solve problems as they arise. The lack of precedent makes it difficult to anticipate conflicts or resolve them once they happen. This is not always a comfortable position, as the director of a university-based CEP points out:

> It's the hardest thing to live through. We've been great at program planning, but we're lousy in planning our relationships to the school. Tensions arise periodically. The associate dean calls me in and puts me on the carpet whenever she thinks that I'm overstepping my bounds. But it's all part of the growth pains of establishing ourselves and proving that we are academically respectable and professionally responsible.
>
> Sometimes it means I have to go slow; at other times it means I have to redefine what I am doing in a language that is acceptable to my colleagues. When I ran a survey a couple of years ago, some of the faculty thought I was asking questions that were too sensitive. When I redefined what I was doing in research or diagnostic assessment terms, however, the survey made perfect sense to them, and they could accept what I was doing.

AUTONOMY AND INTEGRATION: FINDING THE RIGHT MIX

In the *Guide to Continuing Education Programs in Schools of Social Work* recently published by the Council on Social Work Education, an attempt is made to deal with some of the ambiguities in relationships and to provide guidelines to schools establishing new CEPs. The task force that drew up the *Guide* concludes that a continuing education program tends to be strengthened to the extent that it:

1 has departmental status on par with other departments or divisions within the sponsoring institution (not subordinate, committee or ad hoc status);

2 has a separate and distinct entity within the auspice-giving body with some degree of responsibility for budgeting, staffing, and the planning of specific activities and projects;

3 has basic financial support for planning, overall, administration, and program development from secure sources such as from the university's general budget;

4 is integrally related to the sponsoring unit's educational service and research missions, complements or extends those missions and contributes to their development;

5 establishes clear lines of communication and collaboration with other academic research or extension programs within the school and the university, in order to maximize opportunities for school multidisciplinary efforts where appropriate.

These observations parallel our own. We find them to be equally true of continuing education programs in professional schools, local mental health agencies, state human service departments, professional associations, and coordinating bodies. Although the specific mix of autonomy and independence may vary, the CSWE's inventory might very well provide general principles for most continuing education programs. Each continuing educator must find the formula that works in his or her own situation, although this may change over time.

This chapter concludes with a vignette that illustrates how one university-based continuing educator deals with the twin issues of independence and effective relationships to his host institution. We present it in its entirety because it indicates a range of connections that benefit both the CEP and the host institution:

> Without a base in the school, we could have no legitimacy of our own. It would be tougher than nails to get the resources we need to operate. Still, we can't afford to be too thoroughly identified with the school without losing our freedom of action.
>
> For me, the answer is to get as wide a variety of CE activities going as possible and to draw from multiple sources of funding: core support from the university, a fairly regular, predictable flow of funds from individual consumers who pay for courses and workshops, and a more unpredictable income from grants and contracts with state, federal, and local agencies. The grants and contracts really give us our autonomy. We can pitch projects in a variety of different directions, moving into areas that might otherwise be considered too innovative by the university because of the risks involved. The greater the variety of projects we conduct, the greater the autonomy we have.
>
> The neat thing about projects is that they permit you to do things that you might not otherwise because of lack of funds. But you can't just go off in any direction. Somehow our projects have to relate to other faculty and departmental interests. Otherwise our colleagues would begin to wonder who we are and what we're doing here. Whenever possible, I try to build projects around the expressed interests of the faculty. The result is access to manpower and expertise. At other times I design projects in such a way as to stimulate new interests.
>
> When we ran our crisis intervention project, for example, we drew heavily on our own faculty's research and interest. If it wasn't for their reputation, we never could have gotten the grant we applied for. But

when we got into the drug counseling workshop, we did it with the knowledge that we had no faculty experts in this area. I discussed the projects in advance with both our dean and the department heads. They wanted the project because they saw it as an opportunity to expose the faculty to an arena of practice while giving them experience in developing teaching materials in collaboration with agency personnel. The materials, incidentally, are now fully integrated into our teaching program at the master's level.

It wasn't an easy project to do. The grant wasn't really big enough to cover all our expenses, but our dean was convinced that releasing three faculty people quarter-time to the project wasn't an absolute expense to the school; it was an investment in something that would have real payoff. And I don't mean just for the continuing education program or its consumer populations, but payoff to the school in terms of more competent teachers, better teaching materials, and better instruction in the M.S.W. program. What's more, it directly linked us up with the medical school, the department of pharmacology, and the department of psychology—connections the dean was anxious to strengthen.

SUGGESTIONS FOR FURTHER READING

Carey, James T.: *Forms and Forces in University Adult Education*, Center for the Study of Liberal Education for Adults, Chicago, 1961.

Council on Social Work Education: *A Guide to Continuing Education Programs in Schools of Social Work*, New York, 1973.

Emery, F. E., and E. Trist: "The Casual Texture of Organizational Environments," *Human Relations*, vol. 18, no. 1, February 1965.

Evan, William: "The Organization Set: Toward a Theory of Inter-organizational Relations," in James D. Thompson (ed.), *Approaches to Organizational Design*, University of Pittsburgh, 1966.

Lawrence, P. R., and J. W. Lorsch: *Organization and Environment: Managing Differentiation and Integration*, Harvard Business School, Boston, 1967.

Thompson, James D., and William J. McEwen: "Organizational Goals and Environments: Goal Setting as an Interactional Process," *American Sociological Review*, February 1958. Reprinted in Mayer N. Zald, *Social Welfare Institutions*, J. Wiley, New York, 1965.

Chapter 7

The Management of Exchange

EXCHANGES WITH ELEMENTS IN THE TASK ENVIRONMENT

Continuing education programs interact with many elements in their task environments, elements with which they are interdependent. The continuing educator's freedom to maneuver depends on her or his ability to manipulate exchanges with these elements so as not to be totally dependent on a single supplier of resources, a single consumer population, or a single source of legitimacy.

Such exchanges have significant consequences for the realization of the CEP's goals or objectives. Exchanges may be unilateral, as when a hospital without a staff development unit sends its staff to the university-based continuing education program. The relationship is somewhat more reciprocal when the hospital pays a fee for the service, helps the university secure a grant, or locates faculty resources for the university-based instructional program. The determinants of exchange include the accessibility of the partners to each other, the extent to which each expects to gain from the exchange, and each partner's perception or his or her own and the other's domain.

When a continuing education program lays claim to a domain, it specifies (1) the populations it serves (by profession or level of training, geographic location, occupational or work setting, etc.), (2) the issues covered by its educational offerings (substance abuse, child mental health, gerontology, delinquency, or any combination of these), and (3) the services it renders (extension courses for academic credit, instructional materials development, staff consultation, the conduct of conferences, problem-solving clinics, etc.).

Domain Consensus

The claim made for a particular domain, however, does not result in automatic consensus over the legitimacy of that claim. Physicians may not accept the claim of the school of nursing or the school of social work over a certain training area and may refuse to attend programs sponsored by that school. A university may not agree with its school of social work that the mental health CEP should be under its auspices. The university administration might prefer to see it located in a campuswide extension service. A state agency might be reluctant to relinquish its training prerogatives to a training committee representing the staff of a local hospital. The same committee, on the other hand, may refuse to acknowledge either the authority or the legitimacy of the training division of the state mental health agency.

At least some consensus over domain is necessary if organizations are to agree to an exchange. This agreement on who can service whom, how, and for what purpose is a requisite for engaging in exchange relationships.

Mutual Gain from Exchange

A successful exchange also requires that some benefit accrues to each of the parties involved. It is not necessary for both partners to gain equally; it is only necessary that the exchange process have value for each. Thus, referring interested parties to a university's continuing education program may serve to take the pressure off one organization, a minimal gain, while increasing the consumer and resource base of the second organization, which may have great need for them. Cosponsoring a series of workshops with a graduate department of psychology may have only minimal value to a school of social work. It may be of great value to the psychology department, which could not have conducted the workshops without the knowledge, expertise, and administrative structure of the school's well-established CEP. Unfortunately, expectations sometimes exceed benefits:

> We expected that contracting out all the administrative work, such as registration and bookkeeping, to the university's conference department would free us to do more in the area of programming. But the conference department had different ideas. They wanted a voice in program design. They had all kinds of standards and regulations they wanted to impose on us. It was three years before we finally understood each other. For a while it looked as if our relationship might generate more minuses than pluses.

Accessibility

Whatever its potential benefits, an exchange may never take place if the appropriate parties are unknown or inaccessible to each other. This experience of the training director of a community mental health services board is illustrative:

> It took a long time before I began to appreciate the wealth of resources on the university campus—the teaching and learning center, the TV and radio studios, the conference facilities. It took even longer for others to get to know us. How could they, when we were just one of many local agencies? But we had something the university wanted: training placements for students, problems to research, and access to funds for program evaluation. So we made our resources available in a trade for what the university has. The swaps have had terrific payoff. We get into new exchanges all the time.

The range of exchange possibilities is enormous. For the purpose of reporting, we have grouped them into three categories: (1) programmatic exchanges, (2) administrative and facilitating exchanges, and (3) fiscal collaboration. Exchanges in each category may occur between a CEP and other educational enterprises including actual or potential competitors, the CEP's consumers, and those elements in their environment that serve as suppliers of resources. Chart 4 briefly describes the range of exchanges common to CE programs in different parts of the country. Although no CEP conducts the full range of exchanges discussed, most are capable of substantially increasing their range and number.

PROGRAMMATIC EXCHANGES

No mental health or human service CEPs are self-sufficient enough to respond to all requests for service without establishing programmatic exchanges with other CEPs, their consumers, and their suppliers. Although the range of these exchanges almost defies categorization, the following tend to be the most common: swapping of instructional packages, joint projects between two or more institutions, the establishment of multiprogram centers that conduct more than a single type of educational activity or that are oriented to many consumer populations, lending staff from one institution to another, and the training of trainers.

Swapping Packages

Continuing education programs engage in a number of "swapping" arrangements in which one institution exchanges a program package in return for a package from another institution. In a Midwestern community, three mental health agencies that had conducted successful staff training programs on three separate topics agreed to swap their programs. The exchange was so successful that they decided to plan future offerings jointly. Each continued to take major responsibility for a particular training topic, but the selection of topics and resource persons was determined jointly. Several professional schools in different parts of the country have engaged in similar enterprises. A successful three-day institute on sociobehavioral techniques conducted by one school was swapped with several other continuing education programs in return for two- or three-day workshops on topics for which the other cooperating institutions were well known.

CE programs also conduct programmatic swaps with elements in their host institutions. The staff of a university extension service developed publicity materials for the mental health CEP in a professional school in return for a workshop on the use of games and simulations conducted by a staff member of the CEP. Trades of this type are similar to purchases of service and replace the exchange of funds for service. Unlike most purchase-of-service arrangements, however, these trades do not always require the exchanges to be of equal monetary value. Exchanges of unequal monetary value often arise out of the desire by both partners to build more positive relationships, to reach new constituent or consumer populations, to enhance their prestige, or to broaden their repertories.

Chart 4 Types of Exchanges with Elements of the Task Environment, Grouped by Category of Exchange

Category of exchange	Type of exchange	Elements in the task environment		
		Competitors*	Consumers	Suppliers†
A Programmatic linkages	1 Swapping packages	X		X
	2 Joint projects	X	X	X
	3 Multiprogram centers	X		X
	4 Staff			
	a Loaners	X	X	X
	b Outstationing		X	
	5 Training of trainers	X	X	X
B Administrative and facilitative services	6 Referral	X		X
	7 Intake/registration		X	X
	8 Publicity	X	X	X
	9 Bookkeeping/disbursements		X	X
	10 Record keeping		X	X
	11 Help with grants		X	X
	12 Use of facilities	X	X	X
	13 Consultation	X	X	X
	14 Program evaluation		X	X
C Fiscal collaboration	15 Purchase of services	X	X	
	16 Joint investments	X	X	X
	17 Joint budgeting	X	X	

*Potential competitors can be brought into a collaborative relationship with the CEP through one or more of the exchange mechanisms found on this chart and discussed in the chapter.

†Refers only to suppliers within the CEP's host institution. Outside suppliers (government or foundation funding agencies) are not referred to in this chart.

Joint Projects

More extensive programmatic exchanges are also possible. At one university the school of social work regularly conducts joint projects with the CE units in the medical school, the school of public health, and the school of nursing. These may be as simple as a course or workshop offered jointly to hospital staffs or as complex as a three-year federally funded project that produces training materials and conducts in-service training activities. Joint projects may also be conducted with consumers, as when a university collaborates with a mental health agency to design training materials for the agency's staff and the university's students.

In a more complex example a university CEP conducted a collaborative project with the staff development unit of the state department of social services. A federal grant to the university required 25 percent local matching funds. These were donated by the state agency through in-kind contributions composed of office space, secretarial time, and allocation of professional staff to the project. In another example in-kind matches were disallowed. The agency then paid for another service by the university. The payment was banked and then used as the 25 percent contribution. In a third example a state department of mental health collaborated with several universities and community colleges to create a statewide mental health careers program.

Multiprogram Centers

Joint projects sometimes result in the establishment of multiprogram centers. In a large metropolitan area a joint project between a community mental health board and a state university resulted in the establishment of a mental health skills laboratory. The laboratory, which was intended to serve all of the mental health agencies in the surrounding county, became more than a training institution. It also became a vehicle for the management of exchanges and the swapping of packages between service agencies, the design of new training materials, and the provision of consultation on programmatic and staffing issues. This project provides technical assistance on program development and design as well as on the grantsmanship process. Agencies assign staff to the laboratory or provide loaner staff to it.

Among the more common multiprograms are the lifelong-learning centers on university campuses that include programmatic inputs from CE programs located in a number of autonomous academic units.

Loaner Staff and Outstationing

Loaner staff are employed by one organization but tend to operate as if they were in fact staff members of another organization. A pharmacologist from a medical school who conducts a series of workshops under the auspices of the school of nursing or the school of social work may be on loan from his or her own institution. In another example the director of training in a state hospital was lent for six months to a second hospital that was undergoing total overhaul of its treatment programs. The second hospital had no training capacity. The director conducted training and set up a new staff development unit. Other examples include the assignment of a fiscal officer from central administration to a postgraduate medical education program to work on accounting problems and the participation of a university librarian in the management of reference materials at a conference conducted by a school of medicine. The latter is an example of outstationing.

Like the loaner arrangement, outstationing also includes situations in which one organization places its personnel in the facilities of another. Unlike the loaner arrangement in outstationing, the first organization maintains administrative and programmatic control over its own staff. The relationship between the outstationed staff and the host organization must be clearly defined it conflicts of interest and misperceptions are to be avoided.

Training of Trainers

Myriad examples exist in which a training staff of one institution is involved in the training of trainers in another. It is not uncommon for central-office staff development personnel or for university-based faculty to be engaged in the training of local-agency-based trainers. These persons then serve as extensions of the central training institution. A Midwestern school of social work views its field instructors as potential staff developers in their own agencies and trains them to conduct such activities.

ADMINISTRATIVE AND FACILITATING SERVICES

Many continuing education programs depend heavily on administrative and facilitative services from their host institutions. In a number of cases, particularly those involving joint projects or arrangements, they also receive such services from consumer populations and from other CE programs. The CEP may provide similar services in return.

The most common of these include referrals, intake and registration, publicity, bookkeeping and disbursements, record keeping, help with grants, sharing of facilities, consultation, and program evaluation.

Referrals

Referrals may be purely ad hoc, as when a psychology department receives a request for training in management of community mental health centers and refers it to the school of public health. Or they may be built into the operation of a particular institution, as when a social agency or a health and welfare council refers requests for training to the appropriate instructional institutions in the community. Some organizations are known for their referral functions and are regularly called upon for information on training resources.

Intake and Registration

The registration and counseling of participants in a continuing education program are frequently handled by an institution other than the CEP itself. At many universities the extension service may be responsible for registering all participants in CE activities conducted by the medical school or the school of social work. Arrangements between academic departments and a professional association like the AMA sometimes include a decision that the university-based CEP will conduct the educational and instructional program, while the agency will handle recruitment, advising, and registration of its own staff.

Publicity

Publicity is often handled by a unit in the CE program's host institution. Most large agencies, universities, or national associations maintain centralized publicity, printing, or public relations services. In some cases one CEP might publicize the services of another by cross-listing courses and workshops in brochures or by mailing other CEP brochures to its registrants.

Bookkeeping and Disbursements

Bookkeeping and disbursements are frequently handled by a central office, relieving the CEP of the need to employ special staff for these tasks. This central unit, which may be a service agency's business office or a university extension service, may handle all accounting matters.

Bookkeeping arrangements might also be worked out between the provider and consumer of CE services. Thus a university-based

CEP that is prohibited from making payments to its own faculty because of university policy may arrange for a consumer agency to pay instructional personnel directly. Similar arrangements are sometimes made to bypass overhead payments to the CEP's host institution when such payments might price a contractual agreement beyond what a consumer could afford.

Record Keeping

Although most CEPs maintain their own records, certain information, such as attendance statistics or fiscal information, may be maintained by a central source within the host institution. In some cases all registration information is maintained centrally. This is invariably true in university settings, because registration and participation information may also include academic credit, continuing education units, and information on certification.

Help with Grants

Many CEPs have their own procedures for grants management. Others need help with the technical aspects of proposal writing and submission. Universities and large agencies generally have research and development centers that provide information on the potential availability of funds from various federal and state programs, through local revenue sharing, or from private and voluntary sources. Similar help may be available to local mental health agencies through their state agencies or through local government sources. National associations generally provide such services to their local affiliates.

Facilities

The sharing and exchange of facilities are extremely common and probably require little elaboration here. They may include the use of one agency's conference room by another or the use of a medical school's closed-circuit TV facilities by a school of social work in return for the latter's gaming facility.

Consultation

Consultation activities complement many of the others discussed. Examples include consultation on management by the director of one CE program to the director of another, consultation by a university educator to a local-agency staff development person or by the psychiatric head of a gerontology ward to a university CE project, or consultation by experts on instructional techniques to faculty in a professional school's CEP.

Program Evaluation and Needs Assessment

Assessment and program evaluation are more fully discussed in Chapters 12 and 13. Assessment refers to procedures for determining needs or interests, and evaluation refers to an examination of the efforts that went into a CE activity or project, its effectiveness, and its efficiency. Because many CEPs do not have staff trained in evaluation and assessment, they may contract these functions to an outside source or exchange other services for them.

FISCAL COLLABORATION AND EXCHANGE

Three forms of fiscal exchange are relatively common between CE programs and elements of their task environments. These include purchase of service, joint investments, and joint budgeting.

Purchase of Service

Many of the examples given above include some purchase of services. Purchase-of-service agreements usually require contractual arrangements between two equally autonomous agencies. One has funds and needs the services of the other, either for itself or its consumers. A CEP can be a contractee or a contractor. When a community mental health center contracts with a university for the provision of consultation on staff development, the university CEP becomes a contractee. Such arrangements permit the purchaser to provide its members with services not otherwise available. The contractee finds these arrangements helpful in increasing its operating budget while simultaneously extending its own services.

A CEP may purchase the services of a printer, a bookkeeper, or secretaries instead of employing such workers directly if such services are required only at peak periods. Purchasing these services when needed may be much less expensive than hiring permanent staff. As the CEP grows, however, it may find these purchases less economical than employing its own specialized personnel.

Joint Investments

Joint investment refers to arrangements made by two or more institutions to finance the development of a training project or materials related to it. Thus a nursing school's CEP and a teaching hospital might agree to joint investment of funds in the development of self-instructional materials that will later be distributed by the university's extension service as home study courses. The course will be offered "by" the school "through" the extension service "based on" materials developed in the hospital. In addition to money, joint investments might also require such resources as time, energy, and facilities.

Joint Budgeting

When several providers agree to share decisions regarding the financing of existing or new services, they are involved in a joint budgeting process. The most powerful incentive for joint budgeting is often the availability of additional money. Joint budgeting does not require joint investment. The fiscal resources of two or more institutions need not be pooled into a common fund or a common bank account. When the schools of social work, nursing, and medicine in a university agree on the joint sponsorship of a series of summer workshops, it is not necessary for any money to change hands or change accounts. It may be necessary to view the collaborative effort as a single project with a single budget for publicity, administration, instructional personnel, travel, materials, and so on. Each of the collaborating institutions is allocated a share of responsibility for one or more of these areas. The funds are disbursed by each collaborating institution individually. Only the decision on how such disbursements will be made is part of the joint budgeting process.

NURTURING THE EXCHANGE PROCESS

These exchange mechanisms do not operate effectively without considerable nurturing by the collaborating parties. Satisfactory exchanges require time, goodwill, and imagination. Exchange mechanisms may not be quick to prove themselves. Stresses and strains resulting from unequal benefits may suggest that it is better to have less than more exchange. Comfortable working relationships are not easy to achieve. Even well-tested exchanges need continued attention and support so that the gains made are protected and further progress becomes possible.

SUGGESTIONS FOR FURTHER READING

Aiken, Michael, and Jerald Hoge: "Organizational Interdependence and Interorganizational Structure," *American Sociological Review*, vol. 33, no. 6, 1968.

Beisser, Arnold: "Continuing Education and Community Mental Health: A Social Systems Perspective," *Exchange*, vol. 1, no. 2, 1972.

Lauffer, Armand: "Inter-agency Linkages: Coordination at the Operational Level," in A. Lauffer, *Area Planning for the Aging*, HEW, Administration on Aging, Washington, D.C., 1975.

Levine, Sol, and Paul White: "Exchange as a Conceptual Framework for the Study of Inter-organizational Relationships," *Administrative Science Quarterly*, vol., 5, no. 4, March 1961.

Litwak, Eugene, and Lydia F. Hylton: "Inter-organizational Analysis: A Hypothesis on Coordinating Agencies," *Administrative Science Quarterly*, vol. 6, no. 4, 1962.

————, and Jack Rothman: "Towards the Theory and Practice of Coordination between Formal Organizations," in William R. Rosengrin and Mark Lifton (eds.), *Organizations and Clients: Essays in the Sociology of Service*, Bobbs-Merrill, Columbus, Ohio, 1970.

Chapter 8

Financing Continuing Education

Perhaps no aspect of resource exchange commands as much attention as financing. Few of the continuing educators we interviewed reported stable and secure sources of funding. Many CE program directors spend an inordinate amount of time searching for funds. One educator describes his feelings about this in the following way:

> The hustle isn't so bad if in searching out funds you are also involved in program design and relationship building. In fact, it is almost an exhilarating feeling . . . like being on a hunt where the target is a grant to do a significant piece of work. But it can be awfully depressing if you have to scramble for a few bucks just to maintain your staff or your office.

Another CE director complains that despite grants and contracts totaling nearly ½ million dollars, her program receives so little from university general funds that there is almost nothing available to support administrative and coordinating staff. She finds herself "nickel and diming" just to have a half-time secretary who is not responsible to any of the projects.

SOURCES OF FUNDING: PRIMARY, SECONDARY, AND TERTIARY

Continuing education programs draw on at least nine sources of funding: (1) general fund allocations from their host institutions, (2) project awards and grants, (3) contracts for service, (4) fees paid by individuals for courses, workshops, conferences, and so on, (5) sales, copyrights, and royalties, (6) gifts, (7) investments, (8) reserve funds, and (9) in-kind services or contributions. One or more of these may be the primary source of funding for a CEP, whereas the others will constitute secondary or tertiary sources.

By primary source we mean the funding that underwrites the CEP's central staff—that source which would provide a basic floor under the CEP if all other sources dried up. Primary sources may be relatively stable, as when they come from general funds, or precarious, as when they come from short-term grants. Secondary sources refer to those that underwrite one or more of the CEP's regular activities but that do not underwrite the CEP itself. Without these funds a particular activity (e.g., an annual conference or series of summer workshops) might disappear, but the program itself would survive. Tertiary sources support ad hoc, one-shot, or short-term activities. At a given time any one of these sources may overshadow the others in the amount of cash flow.

Some continuing education programs draw exclusively on only one source, although most draw on multiple sources. The access to certain sources by a CEP depends in part on the program's auspices and arena of practice. State departments of mental health, for example, may be prohibited by law from soliciting income from sources such as fees from their own staff for in-service training, whereas fees might be a primary source for a university. Although situations in any particular institution may differ, Chart 5 reflects our observations of the typical range of sources accessible to mental health CEPs operating in each of the three major arenas of practice.

SOURCES DESCRIBED

The range of sources is quite broad. Successful continuing educators make effective and imaginative use of the multiple sources available.

Chart 5 Sources of Funding for CE Programs Operating within Different Arenas

Arena of practice	Source of funding								
	General funds	Grants and awards	Con- tracts	Fees	Sales, etc.	Gifts	Invest- ments	Reserve funds	In-kind contri- butions
College or university department or school	P	P or S	S	P	S	T	T	P or S	S
Service agency									
a State-level training division	P	T	T	–	S	–	–	–	P or S
b Local-agency staff develop- ment unit	P	P or S	T	T	–	T	–	–	T
Professional association (CE office)	P	P or S	T	P	P or S	T	T	–	P

Note: P = primary; S = secondary; T = tertiary.

General-Fund Allocations

Budgeted allocations from the host institution are the primary sources of funding for CEPs in the business of conducting internal staff development and training activities (state mental health training divisions, local agencies, etc.) and for an increasing number of college- or university-based programs. These allocations may take the form of basic support for core staff, office space, equipment, and supplies.

In state agencies the allocation may include the salaries of all training staff including those contracted for outside the agency. In a university-based CEP, general-fund allocations may constitute a primary source but cover only part of the cost of maintaining the program's core staff. A typical arrangement might include the payment of 75 percent of the director's salary and 100 percent of one secretary's salary by the university's general fund. In other cases general-fund support may constitute a secondary source:

> We pay instructional fees for some of our teaching faculty, but the school also allocates faculty time to teaching in the continuing education program. This doesn't show up in terms of dollar donations, but it does result in savings of some $30,000 or $40,000 per year. Much of it is recouped through the fees we charge for attending workshops, and these dollars can be reallocated to other activities for which university funds are not available.

Sometimes general-fund allocations constitute a tertiary source:

> One year we got $15,000 to run a conference on alcoholism from the university. The university figured it was a good investment, because it would generate grants and contracts to do research and training.

General funds can serve as multiple sources of dollars:

> Last year all of my salary was paid from the school's budget, and half of my associate's salary was paid by the extension service [primary]. All of the faculty who teach in our on-campus postgrad workshops get paid by the school [primary]. All the extension faculty get paid by the extension service [secondary]. This year we got $80,000 from the university's instructional-resources fund to design a videotaped instructional program which we may use in some of our CE courses but which will be used mainly by the school in its degree program [tertiary].

Grants and Awards

Project awards and grants are perhaps the largest single source of funds for continuing education activities that are aimed at systems change. A substantial number of mental health CE programs originated with grants from NIMH and other federal or state agencies. Although foundation grants have not been available extensively, in some cases they have been quite generous. They have provided for the underpinning of core staff, the construction and reconstruction of facilities, and the purchase of instructional equipment.

Both government and foundation grants are generally focused on particular social problems, populations, and areas of human service practice. They often circumscribe the range of activities permitted under terms of the grant. Awards are almost invariably time-limited. They sometimes require matching funds or in-kind contributions by the CEP and its host institution. In addition to providing primary support for some CEPs, the principal advantage of grants and awards is that they permit expansion into programming areas that might not otherwise be considered:

> Nothing has been as important to our development as the availability of federal grants. First of all, they influence us to consider new areas of service. Secondly, they permit us to do things we could never support through fees or through general-fund allocations. Projects limit the risk. If we screw up a project, we can take our lumps in a limited area. It's not the entire program that gets criticized, just the project. That makes it possible for us to take risks, to stretch ourselves in ways that we might not be willing to if we had to pay for the activity out of fees or general-fund support, or if the reputation of the entire program were at stake.

Because grants are based primarily on the capacity of the grantee to carry out the proposed activity, evidence that the activity is within the proved capacity of the CEP may be very important. Activities funded by other sources are sometimes used by continuing education programs to establish and prove their capacities:

> We use our conferences and workshops to establish our credibility. Once we have run several workshops on behavior modification, we can substantiate pretty well our claim of expertise in this area. I always send my brochures to potential funders, just to keep them informed, and

frequently attach them as appendixes to my project submissions. Sometimes the fees we charge for workshops result in a surplus that we can use as the matching fund requirement for grants and contracts.

Success often breeds opportunity. Thus successful completion of work under one grant may generate others.

Contracts

Contracts differ from grants and awards in that they generally require the performance of a specific service in a way determined by the funding agency or organization. Sometimes the terms of a contractual agreement are spelled out precisely in advance, as when a state agency tenders bids to train a certain number of paraprofessionals to perform designated tasks. The contract may be so explicit as to specify hours of training, content areas, and location of training. The CEP is held accountable for accomplishing the agreed-upon objectives. Taking on the contract signifies agreement.

At other times a CEP may initiate the relationship leading to a contract. The continuing educator may try to sell an idea or to build a product based upon the potential consumer's notion of what help he or she needs. Both parties may move gradually from their original disparate ideas of what should be done to a mutuality of perception. When mutuality is achieved, a contract spelling out each party's obligations is written up. Contracts awarded for purposes other than training are sometimes used for CE activities. Federal or state regulations may prohibit the use of certain funds for education but permit their use for consultation or action research. It is not unusual for a CEP to use instructional means as one approach to consultation or as a means of helping people do action research.

Fees

Fees charged to participants are another major source of funds. Most universities and professional associations have well-established mechanisms for collecting fees. Standard fee schedules by which the CEP must abide may be set by the host institution. Many CEPs establish stable fee schedules of their own for certain kinds of activities (e.g., so many dollars per hour or day of instruction, conference participation, etc.). These fees are sometimes increased or decreased depending on the cost of location or materials, the ability of a consumer population to pay, the number of registrants anticipated, and the popularity of the subject matter. One CEP regularly charges $24 per day for courses and workshops but may increase the fee if the facilities used are in a country retreat instead of university classrooms. Additional fees may be charged if participants are given expensive materials, such as books, tapes, exercises, and the like. In some cases excess income is transferred directly to the host institution's general fund. In other cases it can be banked or transferred to a reserve funds account.

Sales, Rentals, Royalties, and Copyrights

Although most human service CEPs do not engage in materials development or distribution, some are extensively involved in such activities. The Mental Health Materials Center and several other organizations described in Appendix 1 are primarily in the business of sales, rentals, and materials development. A growing number of other CEPs generate instructional materials in connection with such activities as staff development, courses, and conferences.

Sometimes these materials are duplicated by the CEP for sale or rental to the public. At other times materials developed by the CEP are published by a commercial firm, and royalties are paid directly to the CE program. When such work is a regular part of the program's operation, the program will establish procedures to eliminate any disagreements over copyrights and royalties. Generally they go to the CEP, not to the individuals employed to create them.

Gifts

In a relatively small number of cases, a continuing education program is the recipient of gifts from alumni or others who have some commitment to it or its host institution. If the gift goes directly to the CEP with no strings attached, it is usually treated like surplus income from fees. Gift giving is not a substantial source of funding for CE programs, although several CE directors speak about tapping this potential source.

Investments

The investment of funds to generate income is another idea that has come of age. Some educators report investing in the design of training materials for sale or lease as described above. Others, especially those in postgraduate medical education, have begun to invest in commercial and savings accounts, much as universities develop endowment funds. Earnings are then reinvested or used like reserve funds.

This pattern is common to most universities with a grant or research administration office. University rules may prohibit investments by individual units and departments. Although public agencies rarely permit such investments, CEPs can invest in their own products, publications, or future contracts.

Reserve Funds

As CEPs grow older, reserve funds tend to play an increasingly central role. A continuing educator in a professional school explains:

> Grants, contracts, and university allocations are made on a yearly basis, but effective programming requires some flexibility on our part as a way of carrying over funds. Without the ability to control a few thousand dollars here and there, we are really locked in. Most of our other money is earmarked, and we are held strictly accountable for it.
>
> It took two years, but we finally were able to get a special university account in which we could bank our surplus. We draw on it to cover deficits and to buy pieces of equipment that neither the university nor a grant will allow. It permits us to launch new activities for which other sources of funds are not available. For example, three years ago we started a newsletter, which is now totally self-supporting.
>
> We shortly hope to invest $10,000 in the design of two correspondence courses, which we will offer through the university extension service. The plan is to collect tuition fees from people who register and plow back some of this money into our bank account. We have an agreement with the university on how these funds will be used.
>
> Last month we heard about the possibility of getting 75 percent funding for training under Title XX of the Social Security Act. We're drawing on our reserve funds for the matching 25 percent. It's a very good investment, because we can use a substantial portion of the grant to support our core staff. This makes us much less dependent on the university or on the capriciousness of federal and state granting agencies.

In-Kind Contributions

Budgets generally do not reflect the broad range of in-kind contributions that CE programs receive from their host institutions, contractors, and others. The accounting, bookkeeping, mailing, and other technical facilities of a national association or state agency may be put at the disposal of a training unit. The cost of these services never appears in the training unit's budget line. Faculty may be assigned to a number of hours per year of teaching in the CEP as part of their regular work load. The contribution in time is not charged off to any

CE budget line. Sometimes a contractor or consumer organization absorbs a number of operational expenses by performing the administrative tasks (e.g., registration, publicity, evaluation).

PRACTICE MODELS AND FUNDING SOURCES

Securing the appropriate funding source is closely related to the pattern of CE activities sponsored by the CEP. Thus consumer choice offerings tend to generate fees, whereas training activities are paid for by the organization interested in training a particular population. Chart 6 summarizes some of the differences we observed among CEPs with different CE models.

Chart 6   Frequency of Funding Sources for Each CE Model

| | Model | | | |
Source of funding	Consumer choice	Training	Consultation	Systems change
General fund	rare	often	sometimes	sometimes
Project awards and grants	rare	often	often	often
Contracts	rare	often	sometimes	often
Fees	often	sometimes	never	never
Sales, royalties	often	rare	rare	rare
Gifts	rare	rare	rare	rare
Investments	sometimes	rare	rare	sometimes
Reserve funds	often	rare	often	rare
In-kind contributions	sometimes	often	often	often

CREATIVE USE OF FUNDING: THAT DELICATE BALANCE BETWEEN SKILL AND LUCK

The programming creativity demonstrated by continuing educators and staff developers in mental health is superseded only by the ingenuity used to finance CEP activities. Some show great resiliency and optimism, no matter how bleak the money scene might look. What chance has removed, skill has restored:

When money is loose, everything is great. We know we can expect agencies to fund staff attendance at our workshops and to give them released time to attend. But when money is tight, things can still be pretty good. We might cut back on a few workshops, but not too many. You might note that our summer workshops are all scheduled for June. In a tight money economy, agencies are very careful about their disbursements and tend to save so as not to run out at the end of the year. They usually wind up with a surplus in June which they have to spend before the start of the next fiscal year. And there we are, a ready-made program. They'd much rather send their staffs here than send the money back to the state capitol. Now that the fiscal year is shifting to October, we are adding a fall series of workshops.

Another continuing educator describes a shift in focus:

When money is tight, the first thing that goes is training. So we reach an agreement with the proper program and planning people at the state level to redefine our work as research, assessment, or consultation. It means a slight shift in our approach, but we're still "doing our thing" even if it's called something else.

Use of Volunteers and Personnel Exchanges

One CEP deals with financial problems by using retirees who may be skilled and experienced but who may be permitted only limited incomes under federal income tax laws. Other CEPs engage in swaps and exchanges. Still others shift from the offering of services to brokering activities:

If we can't pay for something in dollars, we do it in services. I'll do a workshop for somebody if they'll do one for me, or we make our mimeograph machine available in return for someone else's librarian.

Another educator explains:

When it became obvious that people couldn't pay their fees, and we couldn't run the courses without income, I started looking for people with knowledge and expertise who might be willing to share it with others without a fee. We've now got an enormous range of interagency exchanges going on. A guy from a mental health center in one part of the city who's got a reputation for effective consulting with the schools might go in and do a two-day workshop with the staff of CMHC in another neighborhood. The second agency might have somebody who's really knowledgeable about working with unions and who will consult with a third agency. Everybody benefits, although everybody may not benefit the same way or get an equal shake at any particular time. But over the long haul, I'm sure, it balances out. Frankly, I think it's a much better way to operate than the way we used to. It shifts the responsibility off our shoulders onto those of the consumer.

This approach does have its limitations and drawbacks, however. A number of continuing educators complain that the absence of planning grants makes it very difficult to shift from project to project without considerable disjunction:

> I've talked with SRS and other federal agencies about this, but I don't seem to be able to get anywhere. The average grant is enough to get something accomplished, but it doesn't leave you with anything to use for program development for the next year. We serve a fairly large region. It costs money to generate new projects.
>
> We've got to bring people together from a large number of places when we try to write a project proposal. Yet there is no guarantee that we'll even get funded. It costs a lot of money. When we ask the "feds" for a planning grant, they answer that we haven't shown enough evidence that the time invested would be really effective, so they can't fund it. My question is, why not?

Hiding the Fat, Budget Hopping, Tithing

Some CE planners have accepted these realities by creating reserve funds or seeking gifts to be used for investment purposes. Others do not accept this "reality" as unchanging or as a barrier that cannot be overcome. They build some "fat" into each existing grant that permits them to use staff time or to bring people together to examine the next steps. Some follow a rule of thumb that no project is complete without a thorough examination of whether other activities are warranted:

> When I was a group worker, I used to tell my teen clubs to begin the planning process for a new activity at least two weeks before finishing a current project. I don't know whether I taught *them* well, but *I* certainly learned the principle. I never finish a project witout having two or three more in the wings. In fact, the moment I get a grant, even before the project gets under way, I start thinking about the next project. This makes it possible to use activities conducted under one grant to initiate the development of a second grant.

"Budget hopping" is another device that CE directors use to increase their flexibility. It requires careful tracking. One project, for

[1]Social and Rehabilitation Service, Department of Health, Education and Welfare.

example, may be high on allowable expenditures for materials and supplies, whereas another is high on personnel. It is not uncommon for a CE director to absorb the cost of publicity on Project A by covering it out of Project B, while assigning a Project B staff person to perform a task of relatively equal monetary value on Project A.

A varient of this approach is the "hidden" overhead used increasingly by established CE programs:

> When you are financed almost exclusively out of projects, grants, and fees, you might find yourself with an enormous budget but no flexibility. This year, for example, we have six projects going on simultaneously. Each project is pretty well financed. The problem is, when you get this big an operation, you also have some coordination and management to do, and no one is going to pay you for that. So we designed a hidden overhead into each project.
>
> It works like this. When a person signs on to a project, he or she knows from the start that 10 percent of the responsibilities will be to the overall CE program. We may be asking the staff person to take responsibility for new project development, PR work, managing the CEP library, doing editorial work outside the project, teaching in our summer workshops for which we charge a fee, and so forth.
>
> If we don't call in the "tithe" on all the staff on a project, I might negotiate a special agreement with the project director in which the project picks up 25 or 50 percent of a staff person's salary. That person may be performing central CE functions rather than working on project tasks. It's a little shady, but I make it clear to every funder that this is how we operate. They appreciate the candor and tell us what they will allow and what they will not.

It is a little shady. Candor or not, budget hopping and hidden overheads require clear limits and agreed-upon guidelines if they are not to border on the unethical.

Joint Budgeting

Joint budgeting was referred to briefly in Chapter 7. "Tithing" and "budget hopping" are forms of joint budgeting within the CEP. It is also possible to joint-budget with other CE programs and other types of institutions:

> The medical school allowed us to use its conference facilities without any charge. In return we handled all the printing and distribution of the brochures without charging the medical school. It avoided the need to transfer funds or to make expenditures for which we may not have been authorized. Furthermore, it made it possible to charge some CE activities to the general fund.

FLEXIBILITY AND AUTONOMY

The wider the range of income sources, the greater the degree of flexibility and autonomy for the continuing educator. A single source of funding can be very constraining. If it dries up, the program disappears. Multiple sources, however, make it possible to shift costs from one to another. They also permit changing one category to another. Thus the CE program that has been using fees for services as a tertiary source may find its primary source from the general fund evaporating. The fees may be increased or costs reduced so that central CE functions are covered by fee income, which then becomes a primary source.

However, using multiple sources of funding makes it very difficult to examine the total budget of a CEP. Many programs do not have a single document on which their budgets appear. This has both advantages and disadvantages:

> I figure we must run through ¾ million dollars a year, but I couldn't show you in a single book how we do it. We just don't operate the way an academic department does. They have fixed allocations, and they know they put so much into faculty, so much into secretaries, so much into travel and equipment and materials, so much into attending conferences, and so much into student support and scholarships. It might be nice to operate that way, but we can't.
>
> We've got separate budgets for each of our projects and activities: extension, summer workshops, grants. This separation is both our strength and our weakness. The weakness is that almost all of our money is earmarked. Still, if the project money were to go, all we would have to do is retrench a bit for a year or two. I might not like that, but it would not hurt the program too much. That's where our strength lies.
>
> We may not have much dollar flexibility, but we have a lot of program flexibility. We could cut back to less than $100,000 from general funds and projects a year in expenditures, and all it would mean is that we would shake down to a small core staff. It's sort of like an accordion. You expand with volume when funds are available and contract when they're scarce. But you've still got the same instrument.

SUGGESTIONS FOR FURTHER READING

Kidd, J. Roby: *Financing Continuing Education*, Scarecrow Press, New York, 1962.

Shaw, N. C. (ed.): *Administration of Continuing Education*, National Association for Public and Continuing Education, Washington, D.C., 1969.

Smith, Norman R., et al.: *Getting the Most for Your Training Dollar*, Public Personnel Association, Chicago, 1966.

Steele, S. M.: *Cost-Benefits Analysis and the Adult Educator: A Literature Review*, American Education Association, Washington, D.C., 1971.

Striner, H. E.: *Continuing Education as a National Capital Investment*, Upjohn Institute for Employment Research, Kalamazoo, Mich., 1972.

Chapter 9

Growth and Institutionalization of the CEP

Although the variety in continuing education and staff development programs is prodigious, a number of similarities exist in their patterns of growth and development. This is particularly evident when one examines the initiation or establishment of the CEP and its processes of growth, institutionalization, and adaptation.

THE ESTABLISHMENT OF A CONTINUING EDUCATION PROGRAM

Continuing education and staff development programs are established in response to both predicament and opportunity. The availability of new funds may represent an opportunity. The need to respond in a new way to external demands for service may represent a predicament. The decision to conduct CE activities or to establish a CEP may be the result of a number of lesser decisions made at several points. The following scenario is illustrative of this process as it unfolded in a West Coast mental health agency:

We have a national reputation for innovation in our field. We've not only tried all kinds of new methods to deal with people in crisis, but we've been pretty effective in the prevention business as well. Our staff publishes broadly in many of the professional journals. The result is that when out-of-towners are here for a visit or a conference, many call us and ask if they can drop in to see what new things we are doing. This happens to be a pretty popular vacation area, and during the summers we had a full-blown "crisis" of our own with visiting firemen coming from all over. My staff were beginning to complain about the extra work demanded of them.

One summer I decided to schedule weekly consultations with groups of visitors instead of with individuals. One thing led to another. Setting up workshops and group consultation sessions on a scheduled basis seemed like the most natural way to bring some order out of chaos, to preserve our own sanity, and to share with others more effectively. By our second summer we were advertising workshops and conducting them on our own premises. By the third summer we were conducting them on site in other mental health agencies. Now we even run our own seminars and cosponsor credit courses with several universities.

Most of the CE programs we examined emerged out of organizational responses to (1) external demands on or expectations of the organization, (2) internal pressures for change or expansion, (3) increased availability of funds or other resources, and (4) loss of funds or other resources.

External Demands

External demands stem from potential consumers, as in the illustration above, from host institutions or sponsors, and from regulating bodies. The needs of researchers and requests from practitioners may lead to the establishment of information-disseminating centers and clearinghouses. Collective and individual requests from practitioners have convinced many professional schools to establish postgraduate or continuing education programs. The actions of state licensing boards put pressure on individuals to continue their education, thereby increasing pressure on the schools and associations to offer further training.

Internal Demands

Internal demands may stem from staff dissatisfactions with a particular situation or from staff ideas about what they need in order to do their work better. In one school of nursing, faculty members pressured the dean to extend the school's service function to hospitals and other settings on which faculty were dependent for student placements.

Sometimes the CE program reflects the interests of a particular staff person or organizational leader:

> When you have a superstar like Dr. Cameron[1] heading your agency, you get a lot of competent people wanting to work for you. Obviously we couldn't take everybody on and still maintain our level of quality. What we could do, however, was provide internships in psychotherapy and family counseling to a select few each year. The first internships lasted at least a full year and sometimes two. We conducted weekly seminars with the interns.
>
> There was something exciting about those seminars and the give-and-take between people from the agency and the outside. It was great for the agency staff. Our own people wanted more. Dr. Cameron was not one to miss an opportunity to do something novel and exciting, particularly when he had staff support. He decided to try some different formats, and before you knew it, we were in the continuing education business.

Availability of Funds and Other Resources

Although both external and internal pressures may be contributing factors, many organizations could not have established their continuing education programs without some financial underpinning. Examples include legislative appropriations for training state-agency staff, contracts, or grants. Many of the strongest CE programs we examined were funded in the late sixties by NIMH:

> We were one of the first schools to get money from NIMH's Continuing Education Branch. When we got NIMH's request for proposals, the dean convened a task force to write one up. It seemed like a good way to provide some service to the agencies that had been providing field placements for our students all these years. We wrote the proposal, got the grant, and were in business.

Essential as money may be, it is rarely sufficient when such other resources as facilities, staff, and expertise are unavailable. Nor are these resources sufficient if there are no demands upon the organization or interest from within the organization in the development of CE

[1]The name and situation have been disguised so as to respect the confidentiality under which the interview was conducted.

activities. Many CE programs have started with adequate resources but have lasted no longer than the period of the project grant because of their inability to mobilize consumer interest or demand.

Loss of Resources

Conversely, some CE programs grew out of an actual or potential loss of resources. CE can become a matter of self-defense. This was clearly the case in a Southern professional school:

> Money was tighter than a drum. We'd lost almost ½ million dollars in faculty grants and traineeships from the federal and state governments over the past two years. On the other hand, there seemed to be new money available for short-term training and continuing education. So we went for it to save some faculty positions. It meant changing some of our functions, a difficult thing to do. But it gets easier when it is a matter of survival.

A similar sentiment was expressed by the national director of special projects in a professional association:

> Our members wanted it. It's as simple as all that. You can't remain a broad-based-membership organization through political action and lobbying alone. You've got to give people something for their money. And what they wanted was to learn how to be better practitioners. We either had to get into the CE business or take a chance on losing members.

As the vignettes suggest, more than one factor generally is present if a CE program is to get off the ground. Whatever the external or internal pressures and supports, however, we do not want to minimize the importance of the role played by the first coordinator or director of a CEP. It is not unusual to find that the program style reflects the personal style of a program's leadership. This is particularly true in the early stages of development, when strong drive and charismatic leadership may be required to steer the organization through an uncharted sea.

CHARACTERISTIC INITIAL DEVELOPMENTS IN EACH PRACTICE ARENA

Higher Education

In professional schools and extension departments the CEP typically begins as a satellite of the host institution, a spin-off of some special activity within the degree program, or a dissemination component of a research project. The CEP operates outside the normal channels of faculty or administrative decision making. The term "trial balloon" may be more apt than the term "satellite." Once the first balloon has proved itself by not detracting from other functions or by enhancing the operation of the host institution, it may become a regularized, incorporated element within it.

This pattern has the dual advantage of permitting the CEP considerable latitude, while relieving the host institution of any ongoing responsibility for it. It has the disadvantage of forcing the continuing educator to devote considerable energy to recruitment of resources and justification of the program's existence. Although a satellite or trial balloon may be fun to watch, as long as it remains peripheral, it cannot achieve its potential.

The Professional Association

Like schools and universities, professional associations also send up trial balloons. These include special CE projects that have a limited life span and are aimed at specific populations. Initiated by an association, they may later become lodged in a professional school or human service agency. The extent to which a professional association exerts leadership in establishing continuing education programs seems to be directly related to the pressures on it to certify the competence of its members. Thus public demands for accountability may cause an association to encourage its members to engage in continuous education or to design model licensure and relicensure bills as self-protection. These bills, when passed, result in additional pressure on the association to provide CE services to its members.

Most professional associations are not structured adequately to offer a variety of CE activities. Instead, they tend to redefine in CE terms those services they have offered previously. Principal among these are the professional conference or meeting and the association's publication service. Both are modified so as to be less scientific in language and style and more practitioner-oriented. Thus CE, as defined by the association, quickly becomes integrated into the traditional structure.

The Service Agency

CE activities within a service agency are generally initiated in response to external demands or a legislative mandate to conduct training, internal pressure from staff, availability of new resources, or loss of existing resources. When the impetus is legislative mandate, the CEP generally becomes integrated fully into the administrative structure. When the CEP develops primarily because of the availability of outside funds, it may disappear when the funding period ends. Whether it is established in response to internal demand or external pressure, it may cease to function when the pressure is reduced. Under such circumstances, the difference between permanence and a short life may be the quality of agency leadership or the charisma of the CEP's director and staff. Charisma is ephemeral, however. It can be lost at any time. It tends to disappear when the individual who possesses it leaves. And unless the CEP's functions become integral to its host institution, they, too, may disappear with the leader.

GROWTH AND INSTITUTIONALIZATION

Institutionalization is the process by which a CEP becomes identified with a particular function or purpose, a complex of services, a characteristic form of planning and management, or a stable organizational structure. Initially a CE program may keep its administrative structure very loose and its purposes undefined. Program activities are inclined to be limited and somewhat amorphous. Initial choices about programmatic activities, however, may set the tone for the future. One choice or set of choices may preempt others:

> Our first offerings were a series of twelve workshops packaged together over a three-week period one summer. It seemed like a manageable thing, something I could put together with the help of a secretary and the services of the university's conference department. Well, it was such a success, we had to do it again the next year, and then the next. I found myself spending an increasing amount of time on the summer institute, getting support for it, promoting it, hiring and counseling staff, planning with groups of consumers, surveying others, and so on. It was becoming a Frankenstein's monster. It had a timetable and a schedule of its own: mailing lists, brochures, contacting speakers. As it grew from year to year, the procedures seemed to get more complex and more rigid at the same time. I got to wondering what else we should be doing.

The process of institutionalization can result in ossification if staff and others develop such an investment in "what is" that they can no longer envision "what might be." The director of a state-sponsored training division on the West Coast describes what happened when he took over a well-established organization and brought in a number of new people:

The staff that I inherited were not too sure what to make of me. They began looking at the new people I had brought in for clues to what I wanted. When they found that I wanted people to be open and expansive in their ideas and to be aggressive in seeking out training interests, they started moving. But the movement was generated by fear. They knew I could ask to have them transferred out of the department. Fear got them started, but it wasn't going to generate the open expressions of opinion I wanted. It took a while, but when they found that I did not punish them for honesty, we were able to establish some basic trust.

But trust isn't enough. Change is costly, and you've got to reduce the cost to people you are trying to change. After I got to know the division better, I realized that many of the old staff had a stake in the way things were, because over the years they had built strong personal attachments to leadership people in the agencies, people who had been their trainees. Now I was asking them to give up working with people who were their friends and peers and to start working with paraprofessionals, new workers, nurses' aides, and the like. The psychological costs were great. To reduce the cost, I organized planning committees chaired by former trainees who were now all administrative and middle-management personnel located throughout the state. It made a big difference.

Reducing psychological costs is not always possible, and the director of the CEP may have to veto the ideas of staff members who oppose new directions. In addition, he or she may attempt to counter the forces opposing change by allowing staff members to continue teaching the same courses to the same kind of learners as they have taught in the past, while increasing the size of the classes or the numbers of courses taught. Ultimately the resisting staff may come to see that shifting to other, more flexible formats is in their own best interest.

Several of the CEPs we observed attempted to maintain flexibility and retard institutionalization by developing diffuse ideologies and multiple services. One educator explains:

We have tried to stay away from defining the mission of the program. If you look at most of our literature, you'll find descriptions of our activities and the techniques we use. You will rarely find a mission statement, and if you do, it will be so diffuse as to be meaningless. We want it that way. You make a mission statement too explicit, and you're stuck with it forever.

There is some danger, however, in missions that are too diffuse. Some other entity with well-defined goals may become the provider by default. Those CEPs whose services are based entirely on consumer preferences have their goals set externally by the potential consumer. This leaves the continuing educator with little more than the technical task of responding to demand. It leaves the CE program inadequately prepared to work with new organizations with clearer missions or to protect itself from competition invading the CEP's field of work.

Many CE directors try to steer a course between rigidity and flexibility. Recognizing the many advantages to institutionalization, they may establish regularized procedures that increase operational efficiency, sufficiently clarify the program's mission, or reduce inappropriate demands for service. Institutionalization also permits the organization to establish a solid base from which to expand its functions or extend its mandate in a planned fashion.

Turning the Ad Hoc into the Routine

When CE services are repeated for a variety of consumer populations, they tend to become at least partially routinized. The CE planner may no longer be able to afford the luxury of ad hoc planning and program implementation, which is wasteful of time and resources. Rules and formal procedures are needed to deal with ongoing and recurring events so that tasks can be performed routinely. Advertising or registering participants for summer workshops are recurring events that utilize standardized procedures, requiring no more than minimum technical expertise of persons hired only for those activities, and should need little attention from the CEP director.

But not all activities can or should be routinized. Identifying the needs that individual clients or a client organization may have for specific services tends to be nonuniform. A number of skills in diagnosis, knowledge about existing programs and services, and interpersonal relations are needed. Yet some continuing educators, by developing a standard approach to consultation, have in fact routinized this procedure as well, turning it into a recurring event. Assessment efforts may be scheduled for certain times of the year. Requests for service may be put through a uniform screening process.

Most CE programs tend to develop specialized substructures to deal with routine events. Other may subcontract them out. It is not unusual for a professional school to contract with another campus unit for registration, mailings, and advertising. CE staff are thereby left with time that may be better applied to issues in their own areas of expertise.

Some events are unpredictable, not because their occurrence is random but because not enough is known about them to make accurate predictions. One can predict that a percentage of workshops and institutes will be overregistered and that another percentage will be poorly received, but one cannot always anticipate which ones they will be. One of the concerns of the continuing educator is how to make such events more predictable, or at least how to keep some resources available.

A state-agency staff development coordinator describes a situation in which ex-pushers, drug abusers, and other street people were invited to a training conference at which professionally trained social workers would constitute the bulk of the participants:

> We knew the street people could "blow" at any moment at the frustration of listening to professional jargon. On the other hand, you can't fully dispense with jargon when you have a bunch of social workers in a room together. So we decided to hire several blacks and Chicanos with street experience who were well known and acceptable to these folks. We trained them and involved them in the program design and asked them to be on the lookout for participants who might be having trouble. We asked them to be around when jargon or concept interpretation was necessary or to do a little "therapeutic bouncing" when that seemed warranted. It cost a few bucks to put them on our staff, but it was well worth it.

Preparing for the unpredictable may require some additional expenses. Not preparing may be even more costly.

Reliance on the continuing educator to make decisions is decreased as routine procedures increase in importance. The more rigid these routines, however, the more brittle the organization. On the other hand, the stronger and more responsive the procedures, the more capable is the CEP in responding or adapting to the pressures from its environment.

Adaptation, Expansion, and Innovation

Adaptation can be static or dynamic. Static adaptations entail only superficial responses, whereas dynamic adaptations may require changes in basic organizational purposes or structures. A shift from summer to year-round offerings and addition of staff to a series of oversubscribed workshops are examples of static adaptations. However, when the CEP shifts from campus-based summer offerings planned by its own staff to conducting staff development activities in collaboration with local-agency personnel on the agency site, it may be making a dynamic adaptation to environmental pressures.

Expansion is another form of adaptation. Like most organizations, CE programs have an inherent tendency to expand. Expansion may mean offering a wider range of services to an existing clientele or reaching out to new consumers. Normally expansion provides continuing educators with more independence and autonomy and forestalls the need to make some troublesome decisions about the core or central functions of the program. So long as sufficient resources are available to permit the CEP to grow at a relatively rapid rate, problems related to organizational structure, staff and personal relationships, and the clarity of purpose or mission can be brushed aside in deference to the more urgent matter of gearing up to new or expanded activities.

Concomitant with growth is an increased likelihood of innovation, which many continuing educators perceive as a value in itself:

> What makes us special is that we keep changing. We don't stay with one line of goods. We're always experimenting, growing, trying, learning. There is an excitement about what we do. And because we're excited, we generate excitement among the people who come to our programs.

Expansion and innovation complement each other. Just as expanding programs are likely to be innovative, successful innovations are likely to lead to program expansion. The likelihood of both is increased when staff include people with diverse experiences, capabilities, and points of view. This is not without danger, but it has its rewards:

> Although there are times when we can't seem to agree on anything, I wouldn't have it any other way. If everyone agreed with me, or if the staff were polarized into two competing camps, then we might either stagnate or be warring constantly. I purposely picked my staff for their independence. I like people to think as I do in some areas, but I require that they have opinions of their own too. That sometimes makes management frightfully complex, but it's also the reason why we've grown as rapidly as we have. All I have to do is turn some of my staff out on their own, and they really move.

Another requisite of innovation is diversity in sources of supply for income, consumer populations, and other resources. It is difficult to maintain a fresh perspective when a CEP is totally dependent on one or two sources of supply. Human service CEPs that wish to avoid limiting their programmatic options or avoid repetitive programmatic activities do better to expand their range of resource suppliers.

The likelihood of innovation and expansion is also increased when the CEP finds itself in a rapidly changing environment:

> At first we just did not realize that we couldn't have any influence on the mental health system by training social workers alone. But changes in funding patterns required us to consider other professions along with paraprofessionals and volunteers. I think this is the major reason we have become a truly dynamic program. As soon as we began responding to the needs of professionals with many backgrounds, and to para-professionals and volunteers, we had to learn to teach differently to different groups.

Some programs have been spurred on to innovate because of competition:

> We thought we had the entire state sewn up with our extension courses, and along came a rival school that began to run one-day institutes in cooperation with community mental health centers throughout the state. They brought in a few superstars, charged $10 a head, drew 200 people for a five-hour program, got a great deal of publicity, and made some money to boot. I may not think much of their program qualitatively, but it sure beats ours for visibility and image building. I know we've got a quality product, but I think our packaging is bad. I'm not sure how, but I know we have to make some changes.

In short, expansion and innovation complement each other. They are enhanced by increased autonomy over program directions and procedures, by building on staff with varied and diverse backgrounds, by immersing the CE program in a turbulent environment with a diversity of supply sources, and through competitive interactions. However, these activities may detract from the CEP's need to build and maintain routine relations with the host institution.

SUGGESTIONS FOR FURTHER READING

Bowers, David G., and Stanley F. Seashore: "Predicting Organization Effectiveness with a Four-Factor Theory of Leadership," *Administrative Science Quarterly*, vol. 2, no. 2, September 1966.

Downs, Anthony: *Inside Bureaucracy*, Little, Brown, Boston, 1966.

Golembiewski, Robert T.: *Renewing Organizations*, F. E. Peacock, Itasca, Ill., 1972.

Hersey, Paul, and Kenneth H. Blanchard: *Management of Organizational Behavior: Utilizing Human Resources*, Prentice-Hall, Englewood Cliffs, N.J., 1972.

Kahn, Robert L., et al.: *Organizational Stress: Studies in Role Conflict and Ambiguity*, Wiley, New York, 1964.

Mann, Floyd C.: "Toward an Understanding of the Leadership Role in Formal Organization," in R. Dubin et al., *Leadership and Productivity*, Chandler, San Francisco, 1965.

Simpson, Richard L., and William H. Gulley: "Goals, Environmental Pressures and Organizational Characteristics," *American Sociological Review*, vol. 27, no. 3, 1962.

Thompson, Victor A.: *Bureaucracy and Innovation*, University of Alabama Press, University, 1969.

Part Three

Programming and Program Development

Chapter 10

Program Development

Although continuing education and staff development in the human services have grown rapidly, they tend to be piecemeal responses to individual and organizational perceptions of need and to consumer demand. The ad hoc nature of their development has often led to brilliant innovations and responsive service. But it has also led to the creation of an aggregate of service programs and patterns that are variable in quality, uncoordinated, and difficult to evaluate and that leave large segments of the mental health and human service fields unserved or underserved.

Many continuing educators agree that a more systematic approach to program development is both possible and desirable. They apply rational means to problem identification, goal and means selection, and program implementation. Although continuing educators describe what they do in different ways, their program development activities can generally be grouped into the following phases:

1   Identifying the problem to be addressed and assessing the needs and interests of potential consumer populations

2   Building a structure or network of relationships through which the problem can be addressed and needs and interests responded to

3   Formulating operational objectives and selecting from among the alternative means of achieving them

4   Implementing programs

5   Monitoring, feedback, and evaluation

These activities are described on Chart 7. Each set of activities requires the performance of both analytic and interactional tasks. They are presented in logical order. In practice, however, the time sequence of these activities may vary. Often, building a network of relationships precedes problem definition. At other times both may occur during the process of program implementation.

TWO ILLUSTRATIONS FROM PRACTICE

In order to better understand the analytic and interactional tasks performed by continuing educators and to examine them within the context of the four practice models described in Chapter 2, it may be helpful to examine two vignettes drawn from practice:

Illustration 1: Interagency Cooperation

Interviews with mental health personnel in a medium-sized community resulted in the identification of a communitywide concern with the learning needs of black children in the school system. The courts were concerned about truancy, delinquency, and recidivism. School social workers were concerned about dropouts and classroom behavior problems resulting from emotional difficulties. The Urban League was concerned about the absence of meaningful curricula in the schools. And the Community Mental Health Center saw the problem as an opportunity to educate the other agencies and make its presence felt in the service area.

Because of historical and jurisdictional problems, three of the four agencies involved would not come together to discuss their mutual concerns. Only the CMHC, a relative newcomer to the scene, appeared untainted by earlier conflicts and personal animosities. All three agencies, therefore, responded positively to the center's initiative in offering a seminar to deal with the problems of black children.

So as to avoid any hint of bias, the center invited a well-respected and charismatic psychiatrist on the faculty of the medical school to act as the seminar leader. As the seminar progressed, papers were presented by staffs of all three agencies as well as the staff of the center.

Chart 7 Overview of Analytic and Interactional Tasks in the Program Development Process

Stage or phase	Analytic tasks	Interactional tasks
1 Identifying the problem and assessing needs and interests	Studying and describing a situation in preliminary terms, conceptualizing the problem. Assessing what opportunities and limits are set by the resources available to the CEP, the interests and needs of the consumer population, etc.	Receiving and/or eliciting information from those who might serve as sponsors or cosponsors, actual potential consumers, and other relevant parties.
2 Building the structure or network of relationships	Identifying the various actors who should be involved in the program development phases and choosing a means of communicating with them. Identifying people for roles as experts, communicators, influencers, etc.	Establishing formal and informal communication processes in task forces or planning committees, recruiting participants and helping them to select their roles, and establishing links with cooperating bodies or individuals.
3 Formulating objectives and intervention strategies	Analyzing past efforts to deal with the problem, thinking through those objectives that seem feasible or operational, examining the resources required to accomplish them, weighing the costs and benefits of one approach over another, and selecting from among them.	Promoting expression of opinions and exchange of ideas, testing out the feasibilities of various alternatives with relevant actors, assisting decision makers to weigh alternatives, and overcoming resistance to implementation.
4 Implementation	Working out the logistics of implementation in detail, specifying tasks to be performed and who will perform them, estimating costs.	Conducting the continuing education activity, e.g., assessment, consultation, training.
5 Monitoring, feedback, and evaluation	Designing a system for collecting feedback and analyzing information on operations and accomplishments. Analyzing consequences of actions and the possible need for change, specifications of necessary adjustments, and determining new problems that call for action or new program development.	Obtaining data from designated sources and receiving or eliciting information based on the experience of learners and other relevant actors. Communicating findings and recommendations to appropriate persons: consumers, auspices providers, and other interested parties.

Despite a history of separate efforts, it took little time before staffs were cooperating on issues of concern to their constituencies and mutual clientele.

Illustration 2: Hospital Social Services

The director of social services in a large mental hospital approached a nearby school of social work with a request for help in training his staff. "Social workers are used as psychiatric assistants at the hospital," he complained. "They can't make any decisions without the psychiatrists' approval. They often know four times as much as the psychiatric residents and, in fact, informally train the residents when they are fresh out of medical school. But they can't make any decisions without getting a resident's OK.

"I think the problem is that my staff doesn't know its own self-worth and can't argue its position with the medical staff. We'd be in a better position if we could, first of all, prove that we are really competent in what we are doing and, second, improve our competence through training. But I can't even get a training budget. Not a penny is allocated for training social workers in this hospital, whereas thousands upon thousands of dollars are spent in training physicians and psychiatrists. We're really low men on the totem pole."

The director of the CEP suggested that a first step might be to find out what social workers do on the job. After some discussion it was agreed that the school would conduct a "functional job analysis"[1] of the tasks performed by social work staff at the hospital.

With the help of the continuing educator, the social service director submitted a proposal based on the resulting data to the hospital administration for a training program that was to prepare social workers to better perform their functions and to interpret those functions to other hospital staff. The proposal was turned down, "not on the basis of its merit," the hospital administrator hastened to point out, "but because in today's budgets squeeze there just aren't enough dollars for frills."

"Some frill!" the social service supervisor complained later to the continuing educator. "We've got fifty social workers on the staff. Their salaries alone total up to nearly ¾ million dollars. All we asked for was a lousy 10,000 bucks, about 1⅓ percent of the salaries of the professional staff or 1 percent of all the salaries if you add the clerks and paraprofessionals. All we'd have to do is not fill one vacancy on the professional staff for half a year or so, and we'd have all the money we'd need. And our operations would be a damned sight more efficient, too. Can you imagine the staffs' morale when they hear this?"

[1]FJA is a technical process discussed in some detail in Chapter 12, "Assessment in Continuing Education."

In the first illustration a systems change model of CE was used to effect better cooperation between agencies. The "neutral nature" of an educational activity made it possible to attract participants for the activity on a consumer choice basis. Individual consumers were the participants, but the target of change was the interagency system. In the second example the CEP tried to respond to the interests of a small segment of a larger system by providing consultation services to that subunit, whereby the CE director hoped to influence the larger administrative unit. But he was not successful. Somewhere his analysis of the problem, his assessment of the possible, and his effort to influence the larger system on behalf of a subunit went wrong.

To better understand what goes into effective program development, it may be useful to examine the analytic and interactional activities that go on in each phase of the process.

ANALYTIC AND INTERACTIONAL TASKS
IN EACH PHASE OF PROGRAM DEVELOPMENT

Problem Identification and Needs Assessment

Logically, the program development process begins with problem identification and needs assessment. Problem identification may be initiated by a continuing educator, a consumer or consumer organization, or a third party such as a funding body, planning agency, or coordinating council. The problem may be defined in such terms as inadequacies in service delivery, inappropriate personnel assignments, low staff morale, or lack of necessary skill or competence among certain groups of human service workers.

Needs assessment is subsumed under problem identification. It refers to a technical process wherein an individual's or an organization's functional requirements are identified. A problem, for example, may be defined as poor communication between the social services staff or a mental hospital and providers of medical services. The assessment of needs might focus on functional requirements of the hospital's social services unit or individual medical caseworkers. To illustrate, the hospital may require more effective counseling and supportive services for bereaved families. Its social services unit may need more staff or better-trained staff. Individual caseworkers within that unit might need specific skills in counseling the bereaved or designing a treatment plan that can be understood and accepted by the medical staff.

Needs assessment is incomplete if it does not take into account the interests of those to be trained. When the hospital administration identifies a certain need but the trainees do not perceive the resultant training program to be in their interests, training may be subverted from the start. Conversely, if potential trainees express interest in a particular content area but the resultant training activity is perceived as counter to the agency's interests, the program will not be supported by administration. It is not necessary that all partners agree on the objectives of a CE activity; it is only necessary that they do not disagree on the legitimacy of those objectives or the need to allocate resources to accomplish them.

Problem identification and assessment of needs and interests require both analysis and interaction. Defining a problem in operational terms demands careful thought and critical analysis. To be useful, however, the analysis also requires involvement of the key or relevant actors. The reader is referred to the vignette in Chapter 3 (pp. 37–38) dealing with a community development project conducted by a school of social work. Representatives of mental health agencies in six rural communities were involved in developing an instructional program.

Sometimes the definition of a problem shifts as a program grows and matures or as greater attention is paid to the impact of educational activities. In Chapter 3 we reported on a shift in focus of a nursing school's summer institutes. The reader may recall that definition of the consumer population shifted from the individual learners who attended CE activities, to the agencies from which they came and to which they were to return, and then back again. When the consumer is the individual learner, the objective of instruction may be to help the learner make needed changes in occupational or professional performance. Thus the individual learner is both the consumer of education and the target of change.

It is also possible for individuals to be consumers while the target of change is an agency or the service system in wihch the learner works. This is also illustrated in the nursing school vignette, in which the CEP trained trainers to function as change agents in their places of employment. When the agency or service system is seen as the consumer, individual learners may be the target of change. The training effort is intended to modify their knowledge, attitudes, or skills.

Problem identification may begin with a consumer perception of need. The CE planner joins the consumer in defining the problem in operational terms to that it can be acted upon. In the hospital illustration in this chapter, the problem was identified less as a training issue than as a problem of staff morale. The continuing educator tried to expand the definition to include an analysis of functions that might lead to more appropriate task assignments. Unfortunately, the strategy suggested could not succeed without the involvement of others directly concerned with the hospital's functions. Had the continuing educator involved the hospital administration and medical resident staff, problem definition might have led to the design of a solution to the problem. The interaction and the relationships that would have emerged from this collaboration could have become part of that solution. Sufficient attention had not been directed at building a structure of appropriate relationships.

Building a Structure of Relationships

It may not be necessary for a formal structure of relationships to be built *after* a problem has been identified. Relationships may exist prior to problem identification or needs assessment. It is not unusual for planning and coordinating committees to be established on a permanent basis.[2] Many CEPs make regular use of planning and advisory committees, although such relationships need not be formally structured. They may be informal, as when a continuing educator maintains a colleague relationship to a potential contracting or funding source in a state of federal agency. Sometimes these relationships are initiated by the continuing educator; at other times he or she may be sought out by a funding source when potential consumer groups or an interested third party perceives someone else's needs and then links the CEP to a potential consumer. These relationships form the context within which decisions are made on objectives, generating needed information or support for the program and arranging for a rational distribution and management of resources.

Effective relationships are not easily substituted by other means. In the second vignette, efforts to use tools such as FJA on an ad hoc basis to identify worker or agency needs had little payoff, because the right persons—the psychiatric staff and hospital administrators— were not involved from the start in identifying the problems.

Although the development of structured relationships may be thought of as "phase 2" of the planning process, it is not a single act or necessarily a complex of acts that take place during a discrete period of time. These relationships may be formal or informal, planned or unplanned, permanent or ad hoc, or a combination of all of these. They should extend throughout the entire planning process.

[2]The use of committees, advisory groups, and planning bodies is discussed more fully in Chapter 11, "Marketing Continuing Education."

In some cases problem identification or needs assessment occur only because a formal structure of relationships already exists. This is the case in the vest pocket medical CE program described in Chapter 4. There a statewide network made it possible for people at the local level to initiate and conduct a learning activity. The very same structure might be used to move beyond vest pocket programming in formulating specific learning objectives, implementing programs, and monitoring and evaluating.

The formulation of operational or learning objectives and the selection of the structure or structures to be built first require clarity about the focus of the intervention. Is the focus to be on the individual, the organization, or a complex of organizations and service systems within a community? A second requirement is an analysis of the environment that surrounds the problem to be solved or the needs to be met. This may include inventorying the resources that are available for continuing education, the forces that favor it, and those that may block or resist a CE effort.

In an environment in which there is agreement that continuing education could be useful in dealing with a problem, it is most sensible for the continuing educator to build on a readiness for collaboration. This requires bringing together the relevant parties to explore the facts and to reconcile opposing viewpoints through reasoned discussion. The continuing educator then moves to achieve some agreement on the need to collaborate in order to deal with the problem.

The continuing educator may act as a guide or catalyst, a convener, a mediator, a consultant, or even a coordinator. He or she may work with committees, councils, or task forces. He or she may work toward an organizational structure that is convened only to initiate or support a particular activity or may move to a more permanent and formal structure. For example, when establishing a "mental health skills laboratory" in a metropolitan area under NIMH funding, the director of a university-based continuing education program instituted a formal advisory committee under the joint auspices of the university and the Community Mental Health Board. It included representatives from all the major mental health agencies in the community, all the professional groups (psychiatry, social work, psychiatric nursing, public health, and psychology), and members from different service fields (substance abuse, child welfare, geriatrics, education, community mental health, etc.), as well as representatives of ethnic minorities. The lab's co-director describes her perception of this type of arrangement in the following way:

It's a perfect arrangement for us. Our committee people know what is going on, what the needs are, and what will work. They act as a bridge to the agencies and their various constituents. That means our interests get communicated, our efforts are legitimated. Without them we would be just ourselves in isolation. With them we are a programmatic and organizational entity.

However, a second continuing educator argues that permanent boards and committees are limiting:

You start them up in order to extend your services. But you wind up restricting services. When you create and staff a policy board or committee, or even a task force, it has a way of taking on a life of its own. The committee begins to have its own ideas. I'd much rather work with ad hoc groups convened for a specific purpose such as planning a workshop, writing a grant, or trying to figure out how to put pressure on the legislature for more funds.

The choice of structure depends on the nature of the organizations, individuals, or groups a continuing educator is trying to build bridges between and the functions of those bridges.

Although virtually all the continuing educators we interviewed are oriented toward some type of cooperative planning structure, there are times when circumstances dictate a different strategy. We've observed that when there is considerable disagreement on either side of an issue, the educator may abandon all efforts to build a collaborative structure. Instead, she or he may band together whatever forces exist in the community or the organization that support a particular point of view in order to attempt to achieve victory over the opposition. If you can't join 'em, lick 'em.

This is what finally happened as a result of the initial failure described in the second illustration in this chapter. The continuing educator suggested to the casework supervisor that he organize a small committee to lobby the staff development cause within the hospital and to caucus within the state department of mental health. At first the committee tried to present its case clearly and "professionally." Response from the administration was polite but noncommittal. The committee then turned its attention to the state capitol. The continuing educator, who knew people at the state level, was quite helpful here. Several well-placed inquiries from state-level personnel to the administration of the hospital resulted in an allocation of funds and the establishment of a continuing education program for the hospital social work staff. Pressure and the implied threat of further coercion worked, whereas earlier efforts at rational persuasion did not.

Formulating Objectives, Means, and Strategies

The objective of intervention may be a new skill in the learner, a change in relationships among staff in an agency, or increased efficiency in mental health service delivery. The achievement of an objective requires a variety of means. The selection of appropriate instructional means requires paying attention to formats, teaching approaches, settings, and so on. But instructional schemes often must be complemented by changes in organizational readiness and administrative supports. These may require using other techniques, such as consultation, or changes in regulations and operating procedures. Strategy is the matching of an objective with the appropriate means to reach it.

The actual nature of the activity or program to be implemented reflects the continuing educator's perspective on what makes sound educational sense and the consumer's idea of the acceptable and the useful. The vest pocket CE program probably works so well because the format is acceptable to the physicians involved. The course structure is one with which they are familiar. The presence of a consultant with technical competence and the fraternal atmosphere that emerges from meeting at the homes of fellow physicians jibe with their notions of themselves as responsible adults and competent professionals. A similar effort involving nurses did not succeed. "Since most nurses are paid—or underpaid—by some organization," explains the nursing continuing educator, in retrospect, "they feel their employer should foot the bill and they should be learning on the organization's time."

The choice of the objectives and the program format requires a careful matching of the capacities of the CEP, its staff, and its resources with the capacities of the trainees or consumers to make effective use of the resultant activities. An effective match between provider and consumer takes into consideration technical qualifications, prestige and status, and anticipated level of accomplishment.

The technical qualifications of the continuing education staff refer both to subject matter and to the style or approach used in presentation. When the subject matter or content is off target or not related sufficiently to the interests or needs of the learners, they may rate the quality of their experience or the quality of the CE program as low. Whatever virtuosity the educator possesses and whatever the range of techniques and educational approaches used, these will be ineffective if they don't match the consumer's learning styles or perceptions of appropriateness. Games and simulations, for example, may be perfectly appropriate with one group but totally ineffective with another. Formal courses may make sense for some, whereas problem-solving seminars or independent learning experiences may be better for others.

The image of the continuing education program, its prestige or status, and the recognition accorded its instructional personnel, as well as the institution or profession under whose auspices the CE activity is offered, must match the image that the consumer group has of itself. If physicians will not submit to a training program conducted by lay practitioners in a self-help drug group, will paraprofessionals feel comfortable in a medical school? No less important is the level at which the training or educational activity is pitched. The continuing education staff may be aiming at basic structural changes within a particular service agency. The agency may be contracting only for an introductory workshop in a particular treatment modality.

In many of our interviews we noted instances in which consumers' expectations of an educational experience were quite different from what the provider intended. Often both parties seemed to be lulled into an early sense of security about the ability of each to satisfy the other. "When you've got a product to sell, and the buyer has a need but the services are limited," explains one educator, "you're likely to oversell or kid yourself into believing that what you have is what they really do need. The buyer compounds the error by kidding himself just as much." The initial relationships between provider and consumer sometimes resemble a courtship. The courtship, however, may be much too short—the intricacy of relationships having been explored insufficiently—and in many cases the marriage is a failure.

Implementation

Implementation and program management are where the planning process leads.[3] Program implementation requires an organizational complex that provides the auspices for the activity and a locus for its coordination and management of essential resources. The establishment and maintenance of such an organizational complex were discussed in Chapters 6, 7, and 9 of this volume. Resource acquisition and allocation were discussed in Chapters 6 and 8.

---

[3]The options and possibilities are too broad to discuss in this section. They are treated more fully in Armand Lauffer and Celeste Sturdevant, *Doing Continuing Education and Staff Development*, McGraw-Hill, New York, 1977.

Monitoring, Feedback, and Evaluation

No program development effort is complete without giving serious attention to monitoring, feedback, and evaluation.[4] These are continuous rather than one-time activities. Monitoring refers to checking on the relationships between means and ends in the planning or programming processes. If the means are unequal to the task, they must be adjusted. If the ends are unrealistic, they need revision. Feedback refers to a systematic way of gathering information to be evaluated so as to make monitoring possible. It may include inputs from consumers, instructional personnel, funders, and sponsors. Feedback requires a continuous system of interaction, whereas monitoring requires analysis of data inputs and decisions about modification, means, or ends.

Both monitoring and feedback are components of evaluation. Evaluation measures the efforts, inputs, and outputs of the planning or programming process. Was the original objective accomplished? To what extent? How was it modified and why? Will the procedures and methods used be effective or efficient? How might they have been modified? What are the next steps? What aspects of the problem that initiated action are still unresolved? Have new problems or new definitions of problems emerged? Have new needs been identified or new interests expressed? Was the initial perception of the problem as being rooted in the inadequacies of individual mental health workers correct, or is the problem now seen as rooted in the structure of service delivery or in the kinds of services being delivered?

Like the other stages in the program development process, evaluation includes analytic and interactional activities. It may require activating the original network of interested parties through which the continuing educator originally identified the problem. It is not sufficient for the CE planner alone to be satisfied that something went well or to be aware that something may have gone poorly. The other interested parties—those directly and indirectly affected by the problem or by the continuing educator's intervention—must also be involved in the evaluation of the program.

The evaluation process is very similar to problem definition or assessment. Evaluation of change, for example, may include assessing further need at the end of a training activity and contrasting findings with those of a pretraining assessment. Thus the planning process may seem to go in full circle from problem definition, through the

---

[4]Evaluation is treated more fully in Chapter 13.

development of a structure, design of objectives and instructional formats, implementation, and finally monitoring, feedback, and evaluation, only to return again to problem definition.

SOME GENERAL OBSERVATIONS
ON PROGRAM DEVELOPMENT FORCE

A number of continuing educators and staff developers might object to the way in which we have described the program development process. Some may insist that programming must begin with a rigorous period of study and problem definition. Others argue that it begins with the design of instructional objectives. Some educators come down heavily on the analytic or rational aspects of the process; others consider only the interactional and cooperative aspects. In our observation both sets of activities are necessary for effective program planning. We've also noted that planning efforts tend to be more successful when they are cooperative, continuous, concrete, and comprehensive.

Program designs are often more on target when they are cooperative and involve other relevant actors. Just bringing interested parties together, however, is not enough. Cooperative efforts require a considerable amount of time, a willingness to modify or shift goals, and skill in planning and democratic decision making.

When program planning is a continuous process, a CEP stands a better chance of sustained programmatic output and regular resource inflow. Ad hoc and unrelated ideas may result in periodic high energy inputs that skew the directions of program development according to the whims of the moment or the interests of the most vocal.

Concreteness in planning is essential if measurable goals are to be reached or if the means to achieving these goals are to be adjusted. Too many CE projects have fuzzy aims such as "increasing skill" or "improving service" without ever specifying what is meant by these terms. Objectives that are not specified in operational terms reduce the likelihood that progress will be monitored or accomplishments evaluated. The lack of concrete objectives is not the only problem we have observed. Although specifying objectives may be desirable in certain situations, it does not guarantee the development of a professional commitment to accomplishment.

In addition, too many plans pay little attention to housekeeping details such as registration procedures, room assignments, setups, creature comforts, finding someone to run the projectors, or having enough videotapes on hand. The result may be losses in efficiency and effectiveness as well as loss of potential consumers or resource providers for future activities.

There are significant benefits to both the CEP and the individual learner or organizational consumer when planning is comprehensive in its approach. Comprehensiveness implies an overview in both time and space. In planning an instructional activity, attention might be given to the individual learner's career line. This could include focusing on such characteristics as previous experience and educational preparation, current occupational needs and concerns, and future aspirations. Nevertheless, as noted in several of the vignettes, focal concern with the individuals' learning needs can be self-defeating if equivalent attention is not given to the factors in their environment that may support or obstruct the application of what they have learned.

SUGGESTIONS FOR FURTHER READING

Beal, George, et al.: *Social Action and Interaction in Program Planning*, Iowa State University Press, Ames, 1966.

Cross, Patricia, and John R. Valley: *Planning Non-traditional Programs*, Jossey-Bass, San Francisco, 1974.

Houle, Cyril O.: *The Design of Education*, Jossey-Bass, San Francisco, 1974.

McKinley, John, and Robert M. Smith: *Guide to Program Planning for Adult Education*, Seabury Press, New York, 1965.

U.S. Civil Service Commission, *Planning, Organizing, and Evaluating Training Programs*, Washington, D.C., 1971.

Chapter 11

Marketing
Continuing Education

Marketing is an approach to program development. It should not be confused with a more limited sales orientation that emphasizes finding customers for existing products. Marketing requires uncovering the needs or wants of a consumer population and then creating the goods or services to satisfy that population.

    A university educator is quite explicit about his use of marketing logic: "If you analyze the reasons for our success, it's because we developed the right product, backed it by the right promotion, and put it in the right place at the right price." We would add a fifth variable: the effective use of consumers and others as active partners in addressing the above-mentioned concerns.

THE RIGHT PRODUCT, THE RIGHT PROMOTION, THE RIGHT PLACE, THE RIGHT PRICE, AND THE RIGHT PARTNERS

The Right Product

At first glance a CE program's product seems relatively simple to identify. It might be a course, a workshop, a conference, or instructional materials such as a gamed simulation, a series of videotaped lectures, or a newsletter. It might also be a process that can be used to alter relationships among agency staff. Each of these products, however, may be redefined as one means toward building other products. A course, for example, may open opportunities to move up the career ladder, while the product may be the numbers of persons receiving completion certificates. A workshop might be the means of expanding an old skill or introducing a new one.

Designation of the product is intertwined with the program development process. When a continuing educator identifies an interest in a workshop on crisis intervention, the resulting workshop may be designated as the product. When mental health workers from several agencies in a local community conclude that something can be done about the problem of school dropouts and the university's CEP can contribute to that end, then the product may be a reduced dropout rate. The intervening course, workshop, or consultation is a means toward creation of that product. When a state hospital contracts with a school of social work to train the staff of two wards in milieu therapy so as to change the treatment processes on those wards, then the product might be the establishment of ward-based therapeutic communities.

The designation of products is also a function of the model of continuing education being followed. When a service is being provided to individuals (consumer choice model), the product is generally a course, clinic, workshop, booklet, or instructional document. When a consultation model is used (service to a service system), the product may be a process for giving help, a changed policy, program, or service. A change in behavior or individual performance may be the product of a CEP's training approach. Finally, new designs for programs, services, or resource allocation may be the products of a CE project oriented toward systems change.

These distinctions have important implications for the way in which continuing education programs perceive themselves and their products. They affect the image a CEP will project to the community, the way it identifies problems to work on, the design of its products, the way it allocates its staff and other resources, and, finally, the promotion of its products.

The Right Promotion

We have to stop playing the Wizard of Oz game. The Wizard made a lot of noise, but there was not much substance to it. You can't just bluster and thunder and put on a jolly good show and then expect that the product will take care of itself.

Dorothy's objective was quite modest. All she wanted was to get back to Kansas and Aunt Em. The Wizard had other ideas. Dorothy couldn't reach her objective until she realized that the Wizard had little to offer, that only she could get herself where she wanted to go. CE programs may find themselves trying out their own brand of wizardry if they offer what the consumer does not need or promise more than they can deliver.

Promotion that is unrelated to the product and to the program is dishonest. When it is unrelated to the needs or interests of the potential consumers or unreceptive to the target of change, it is ineffective. If the objective is a specific change in the service delivery pattern (e.g., the development of an outreach program by drug counselors), effective promotion will refer to that objective, not to the fact that the CEP is sponsoring a workshop on outreach procedures. A total CE effort may require consultation in addition to training activities. Misunderstandings about the CEP's approach and its objectives may occur if the contracting agency expects to get a two-day workshop and finds it has purchased obligatory consultation as well.

Promotion that does not mesh with the interests of the consumer is not likely to draw much response. However, when divergent interests complement each other, they are more easily accommodated. When they are in conflict, it is important that the conflict be understood so that later misunderstandings and recriminations can be avoided.

Although promotion is often aimed at increasing demand for the product, demand is not generally a variable directly under the CEP's control. It is more likely to be a function of the general social climate, the availability of funds to support participation, national and state licensing laws, service priorities, or changes in civil service regulations and criteria for advancement. Effective promotion may require an oblique strategy. A change in the civil service requirements, for example, may do much more than any number of beautifully designed brochures and talks at professional meetings to promote CE courses and workshops. Many continuing educators seem well aware of this. We found them to be active in lobbying for changes in civil service regulations, in the design of credentialing examinations, or in the writing of new legislation affecting training. Other continuing educators, however, limit their promotional efforts to brochures, pamphlets, flyers, advertisements, and other written matter.

Promotional opportunities exist everywhere: in a course or workshop currently being offered, at a meeting of a professional association, through an article in the press or a paper in a professional journal. Certainly no brochure or promotional piece can be expected to carry all the weight of promotion. Nor can promotion be effective or efficient if the supply of resources or consumers does not warrant the investment.

Advertisements that generate registration of 500 participants for a course that can absorb only 250 may in the long run boomerang. A promotional campaign that aims at recruiting 2,000 learners, when the potential consumer population and funds available to finance their participation might realistically produce no more than 1,000 registrants, is wasteful and inefficient. "The idea," as one CE director put it, "is neither to undersell nor overkill."

> We sold everybody a bill of goods. We got everyone to come to our workshops last summer, and we made a few dollars. But we couldn't produce at the level we seemed to be promising. We've been suffering from the reverberations all year. We've really lost a lot of our credibility and are having a hard time recovering.

Most promotional activities are directed outward from the continuing education program toward consumers, suppliers, and in some cases outside regulatory groups. The program's survival and its ability to get resources may require redirecting some promotional activities inward to the organization or institution that serves as the CEP's host. The following excerpt from one of our interviews with a university-based continuing educator demonstrates the relationship between internal and external promotion. Despite its length, it is presented almost in its entirety because of the usefulness and sophistication of the insights given:

> Limiting your promotions to external groups can be shortsighted. I'm a pretty good outside man; that's why we've grown as rapidly as we have—that and building a quality product in a quality program. We've got advisory groups in seven cities throughout the state. We run extension courses in fifteen locations. We run conferences and workshops in cooperation with local agencies. We've built our instructional program around the issues raised by practitioners and agency administrators. In short, we've got a reputation for being responsive.
>
> We don't take things on unless we think we can succeed. Even in

those instances where a program has been a flop, we have recouped our relationships with those for whom the program has proven a disservice. We readily admit our own shortcomings and are ruthless in our self-evaluations. We admit our mistakes not only to those people with whom we think we've failed but also to others. Promoting your operation doesn't mean selling something that you haven't got. It means building relationships.

But relationships have to be built on substance. Over the past five years I have published regularly, made presentations at conferences, and participated in several task forces within my profession that relate to training or continuing education. The result is that we have a solid reputation. Although funders don't necessarily seek us out exclusively, I have pretty much of an open door at several state and federal agencies. Sometimes they call me, but I can walk in unannounced in lots of places.

I don't visit potential funders just to ask for a handout. Sometimes I drop in for a chat when I'm in Washington or in the state capital. I try to be helpful whenever I can. I know that they know that it's part of my promotional approach, but they also know it's an honest approach. I make it a rule never to buy a cup of coffee for a funder.

On the other hand, I do not hesitate to share. One of the Department of Labor people is a nut on reprints. I think he's always wanted to be on the faculty of a university, and he overcompensates for being a bureaucrat by reading voraciously and by collecting and building his own training library. Anytime I find an article I think might interest him, I duplicate it and send it off. Incidentally, I do the same thing with agency administrators that we've had or hope to have relationships with. I also periodically write up a report on our activities for internal distribution to the faculty of the school. But I make sure several copies get placed appropriately around the country and around the state with little handwritten notes saying "Thought you'd be interested."

Still, on reflection, I find that I've fallen down on promoting the CEP internally. A couple of years ago we had a crucial vote within the faculty. It had to do with the kind of financial and faculty resources that we could command from the school. We lost because people thought the CEP was overreaching itself and expanding too rapidly. People felt we might drain too many scarce resources from other operations. They didn't see these as investments that could generate additional resources. They saw them only in terms of expenditures.

A couple of months later I had a similar blow when my dean tried to get university general funds to support a staff position for the CEP. No one in the university administration was familiar enough with the program to be ready to commit scarce funds to us. It was a shock to realize that I hadn't been working my own street.

As we met with continuing educators in many other settings, we uncovered a variety of promotional tactics for "working the street" internally that are apparently quite effective. A number of the more inventive and useful approaches are reported below.

Boosting the Faculty

When an instructor has done a particularly good job in teaching, I will send him a note of thanks with a copy to the dean. Sometimes I send a note or memo to that effect to the dean directly, with a copy to the faculty person. At the end of the year, when the dean asks all faculty for recommendations on promotions, I make sure to include information on those faculty I think have made the most important contributions to the program, and I point out how their efforts have helped the school in terms of teaching content in the M.S.W. program or improved relationships with social agencies. It's a little thing, but it does wonders for building support from both the faculty and the dean.

Keeping in Touch

I regularly meet with the department heads, telling them what we're up to and asking their advice on where we ought to go. When they have an idea, I see if I can help them use the staff development unit as an instrument for accomplishing their objectives—if it fits in with the agency's goals and with the unit's priorities.

Annual Report

I've developed what I think might be an interesting format for our annual report to the agency. I use only the left half of the page for the report. And next to each section of the report I have a box on the right side of the page. This is for comments and remarks by the staff and anybody else who might read the report.

We have a machine that perforates the page right down the middle. The comments can be clipped off and sent back to me as feedback. Within a couple of weeks of receiving this feedback, I summarize it and send it back to the whole staff in the form of a memo, thanking them for the suggestions. If some of the suggestions can be put into effect immediately, I inform them that we have already acted. Otherwise I indicate that they are being considered by the staff or by the CE committee.

Satisfied Customers Write In

The best promotional items I've ever had are letters from satisfied consumers. I don't just wait for them to come in accidentally. I try to generate them. I tell people honestly that our ability to continue to provide programs depends on their support, and that both the state association and national office would look more favorably on our expansion if they knew people cared about what we do. When they send letters to the president or executive secretary, the internal response is immediate.

Big Names Bring Prestige

Whether you like it or not, big names bring prestige to the agency. Although many of our CE offerings feature our own staff, we always make sure to bring in several people with international or national reputations or people who've recently published. I know we'd have a quality program even without them, but the big names do a lot to boost the egos of our own instructional staff and the total agency staff.

The Right Place

The location of a CE activity must be both accessible and desirable. Locating away from the work setting may be desirable if getting away or mixing with others in a neutral or stimulating environment is important. On the other hand, when a problem is located in the agency or the community, it may help to deal with that problem in its home setting. In selecting a location, the CE planner must consider its promotional value as well as its potential for supporting the achievement of learning objectives. "By locating the conference in New Orleans," an educator from a professional association explained, "we assured ourselves of full registration but empty sessions." The selection of a facility is no less important than its location:

> We picked what was undoubtedly one of the finest conference facilities in the country. It was accessible and fully equipped with everything one might desire. But its very opulence was counterproductive. People were so dazzled by the equipment and what they perceived as gimmickry that they focused more on that than on the substance of training.

Another educator explains:

> Retreats and conference facilities can be significant influences on the quality of learning and its transfer. But you can nullify all you gain if people can't get to or away from your site. We used a marvelous facility at a camp owned by one of our sister agencies one spring.
> We figured the setting created a marvelous atmosphere of openness and creativity. The workshop was five days long, but it only worked well for three of those days. It took participants a half a day to get there, and they spent the last day worrying about how they would get home. As it

turned out, one of our limousines broke down, and some people missed their planes. Others left three hours early for fear that they, too, would miss theirs. So much energy went into thinking about the travel arrangements that we lost fully three-fifths of the value of the program.

Some educators use different facilities for different kinds of offerings:

If we want to change attitudes, we bring people to a retreat facility where they can be removed from the influence of colleagues, friends, and their usual environment. If we want to impress them with scholarship, we bring them to the campus. The campus atmosphere reinforces the imparting of knowledge. If we're interested in skill training, we try to do it as close to the practice setting as possible, often in the agency. If we have people from several agencies, we may train them in a place that we think can serve as a model. People tend to apply the skills they have learned in a setting they can identify with.

When it comes to problem solving, we try to locate seminars as close as we can to the problem situation—an agency, a community facility in that particular neighborhood, etc. I don't have the data that these sites truly work, but I have a strong feeling that we've been making the right decisions.

The Right Price

Price represents the cost that a consumer must accept in order to obtain a service. In addition to financial costs, there are also psychic costs, energy costs, and community costs. The money factor, in fact, may be the least significant. Even "free" continuing education activities involve substantial costs.

If the price of attending the program is an admission of inadequacy or being treated like a child instead of an adult, the psychic costs may be great. The rewards must be compensatory. If the price of attending a course every Thursday night for thirteen week means not being able to participate in another activity, then the social and community costs may be too great. If participation in a series of weekend workshops is so draining or exhausting that the participants use most of Monday and Tuesday to recuperate, then the cost in energy expended may not be worth the benefits received.

The continuing educator must be prepared either to increase the rewards or reduce the costs relative to the benefits or rewards given or anticipated. A psychologist affiliated with a mental hospital staff training program explains:

In continuing education, as in everything else, you have to be able to give in order to get. But you can't expect people to give more than they're ready for. You have to build on their own motivation and on your own idea of what's good for them. You may feel that their earlier training was useless for their current work. But people have invested a lot of psychic energy and time in their professional capabilities even if you may think it's no more than trained inability.

If you ask them to throw away what they've got as the price of obtaining something new, the cost may be just too great. Sometimes it's a matter of moving incrementally, a sort of planned replacement buying. You purchase one piece of furniture at a time, not discarding your own, worn, and familiar pieces all at once. Maybe you don't even discard them, but you just shove them into a corner or store them in the attic.

The analogy is an apt one. We've noted that some CE promotional materials convey the notion that money is all that is needed for education. Payment of money upon enrollment, however, does not give the student the equivalent of a movie to enjoy or a steak to eat. The joy of learning may be immediate, but its application may be delayed and require other investments.

PARTICIPANTS AS PARTNERS AND AS PROVIDERS

The involvement of consumers and others in planning and conducting CE activities is often used as a complement to other marketing activities. Involvement facilitates product development, is integral to promotion, and ensures the selection of an appropriate place and the setting of an acceptable price.

In marketing terms, one can view participation as a vehicle for increasing either supply or demand. In practice, participation tends to be used more frequently to promote demand. In many sections of the country the involvement of consumers is used to build local demand for and receptivity to CE activities.

There are times, however, when demand or need exceeds supply. In these cases participation may very well increase supply or ensure a more adequate product. In a number of our interviews continuing educators spoke of how the participants is a course or workshop assumed much of the responsibility for their own learning through on-the-job application of what had been learned and by returning to the group for peer consultations.

Advisory Committees

Many continuing education programs utilize at least one formal advisory, program, or planning committee to ensure participation of relevant groups or populations. These committees may be local or statewide and generally relate to a specific project or set of activities.

An advisory body seldom is allocated the more well-defined functions of most policymaking boards and administrative committees. Nor does it command the same degree of authority. An advisory body may influence policy decisions, but it does not make them. It may review résumés and recommend applicants for staff jobs, but it does not control the final selection. It may express its preferences regarding program priorities, but it does not determine the final ordering of the CE program's activities. An advisory body generally does not have legal standing. Its influence and its value are only as great as that conferred on it by the continuing education program.

Advisory bodies, however, can be put to effective product development and promotion. They can foster two-way communications between the CEP and its publics; help legitimate planning objectives and priorities; provide information about the attitudes, needs, and opinions of potential consumer populations; serve as sounding boards for preliminary ideas; serve as political forces and as sources for community education; act as buffers against attacks and criticisms of the CEP and its activities; act as instruments for ventilating negative feelings and putting out fires; create bridges to specific constituencies; and supplement staff resources.

One of the local advisory committees we examined fostered two-way communications between a university-based CEP and its potential consumers in a rural community. It helped to legitimate and promote the CEP's offerings by putting a local stamp on them, by ensuring the relevance of the program content to be offered, and by assuring other local people that the resultant learning activities would be evaluated by people like themselves. This is a common strategy:

> When we were first starting our CEP, we established advisory committees throughout the state. We would go to the directors of the most prestigious mental health agencies or contract two or three people who were well regarded in the local community. They then suggested others to contact. We always tried to make sure there was some balance between types of agencies and fields of service. The result was rarely a cohesive group, but that wasn't our objective. We wanted to know what people thought, and we wanted each of them to know what each of the others thought so that the reasoning behind our providing one or another kind of learning activity would be based on some sound information. They would also have access to the same kind of information that we did. A bonus of this approach is a reduction of costs because of contributions of agency facilities and personnel for the CEP.

Another educator describes a process whereby representatives of various populations advised in the development of training materials:

The names of all our advisory committee people and their agency functions were listed on the inside front page of each learning module. You'd be amazed at how much legitimacy the names bring. The ivory tower image of a university product is dispelled immediately.

Committees can also be instruments for putting out fires or for giving feedback at appropriate moments so as to monitor and change CE activities that may not be directly on target:

By working through a planning committee that provided the official auspices for the conference, it was possible for us to be perceived as providing the manpower but not being in charge. The theme of the conference was controversial as hell. Thus it would not have been good for us to be seen as the sponsors. By setting up a planning group that would serve in an advisory capacity, we built a buffer against attack and criticism.

While several continuing educators promote the idea of a high-level advisory committee for the total CE program, others caution that such an advisory committee either may become too powerful and begin to see itself as a policy board or may serve the perfunctory role of rubber-stamping decisions. In either situation the committee is dysfunctional. Many educators prefer using a variety of committees and task forces according to need. Some can be relatively permanent, whereas others are purely ad hoc:

The care and feeding of committees requires a big investment of time. There's not much sense in establishing entities to which you will be accountable but which may not be accountable to anyone else. Better to build advisory committees whenever and wherever you need them, but with time-limited and content-limited objectives. If you need a committee to give you some legitimacy to move into an area where you haven't operated before, organize it for that purpose, but don't keep it going long after you've finished the job.

Another continuing educator disagrees, pointing out that it has been his strategy to build relatively permanent committees but to

float them free so that they have lives of their own. We've been responsible for establishing five training committees on different projects. Most of them now operate without any help from us. Just because the project funding period ended, the needs for education did not. One of our goals is always to build up local capacity. Our aim is to get local people to feel perfectly capable in planning their own programs and contracting with anybody they want to for service. Sometimes they'll approach us and ask us to run a course or workshop, but they might approach other universities if they think the other folks have got the goods.

A third speaks of a similar number of advisory committees that are called into being whenever the CEP needs their inputs:

The very fact that we've got so many of them is what gives us our freedom to maneuver. We can activate pressure on the university for new services when logical arguments by me from the inside have no impact at all. Having so many suggestions coming from different groupings makes it possible for us to make choices. We're not limited by having to respond to only one committee or one set of interests.

In many ways any discussion on marketing is really a discussion of program development. It includes both analysis and interaction. Problem identification and assessment of needs are required in product development. Structural relationships facilitate product development, promotion, and the selection of an appropriate place and the right price. They are also intertwined with goal and strategy selection. Implementation is akin to product testing and sales. It also is complemented by monitoring and evaluation: all of these processes discussed in the previous chapter.

SUGGESTIONS FOR FURTHER READING

Brown, David S.: "The Management of Advisory Committees: An Assignment for the '70's," *Public Administration Review*, vol. 32, no. 4, July/August 1972.

Cutlip, Scott M., and Allen H. Center: *Effective Public Relations*, 4th ed., Prentice-Hall, Englewood Cliffs, N.J., 1971.

Kotler, Philip: *Marketing for Non-profit Organizations*, Prentice-Hall, Englewood Cliffs, N.J., 1975.

Kotler, Philip, and Gerald Zaltman: "Social Marketing: An Approach to Planned Social Change," *Journal of Marketing*, vol. 35, no. 3, July 1971.

McCarthy, E. Jerome: *Basic Marketing: A Managerial Approach*, Richard D. Irwin, Homewood, Ill., 1968.

McGinniss, Joe: *The Selling of the President 1968*, Trident Press, New York, 1969.

Stern, Milton R.: *People, Programs, and Persuasion: Some Remarks about Promoting University Adult Education*, Notes and Essays, #33, Center for the Study of Liberal Education for Adults, Chicago, 1971.

Chapter 12

Assessment
in Continuing Education

Assessment is central to the program or product development processes in continuing education. It may be the basis upon which programming is developed. The very definition of a problem requires assessment of consumer needs and interests. Structure building requires an assessment of which relationships are possible and which might provide the greatest benefit. Formulating objectives requires an assessment of the payoffs of alternative strategies and of the capacities of the CEP to conduct different activities successfully.

Because the methods and techniques used in assesssment are often the same as those of evaluation and because both activities may take place concurrently, the two terms are sometimes used interchangeably. They are, however, conceptually distinct. Assessment focuses on examination of what is, what might or ought to be, and what is needed to achieve a desired state. Evaluation focuses on what happened, how it happened, and whether it should have happened.

NORMATIVE AND ANTICIPATORY APPROACHES
TO ASSESSMENT

In continuing education, assessment occurs when the consumer or the provider examines either an existing or a future situation and the availability of needed resources. Assessment of the present focuses on the current needs or interests of a consumer and the capacity of the CEP. Assessment of the future is intended to determine what a particular population or organization might want or might have to do at some future date and the anticipated capacity of the CEP to help it achieve those objectives. Future assessment can be either normative or anticipatory. The director of a school of nursing explains:

> When we build a training program, we try to define what we mean by a good nurse. Any such definition would include attitudes toward people, skill, an ongoing commitment to learning, and the capacity to learn. It also means the desire to stay ahead of the field. We knew five years ago that we would want more nurses to work in the public health arena on problems associated with early childhood, even though there weren't many people interested in this area at that time. Still, having decided it was valuable, we assessed where people were and then began training systematically, building interest at the same time we built skill and knowledge.

An approach described by the dean of a school of social work is somewhat different:

> We also have been training for work in early childhood, but not because of any predetermined image of what a social worker should be doing. We have a kind of market perspective, in which we try to anticipate what our people in all probability will be doing in the future. It was quite obvious back in '71 and '72 that new child-care legislation would create new demands for trained personnel. We just tried to figure out what those demands might be and then thought through what we might be able to do about them.

The first approach is normative; it begins with an image of a desired future state and uses training as one means to achieve it. The second approach is anticipatory; it attempts to predict a future state so as to prepare for it adequately. The normative approach requires building "interests" while at the same time building "skill and demand"; the anticipatory approach assumes their presence.

ASSESSING THE CEP'S CAPACITIES

Assessment is incomplete without examining the CEP's current and potential capacities to do the job. A number of educators try to avoid errors by staying away from anything they do not feel competent to handle. One staff development specialist says quite openly:

> I begin by looking at my staff resources and interests. Then I figure out what we can do. We're very strong on sensitivity approaches to problem solving, so if a problem doesn't fit our capabilities, we steer clear of it. I don't like to promise more than we can produce.

This attitude certainly limits the range of programs the CEP will undertake. Some educators, unfortunately, make the mistake of defining all the problems and issues before them in terms of their ability to deal with them. Taken to the extreme, this position may lead to correct but incomplete assessments focusing exclusively on the capacities of the CEP.

The reader may want to keep this point in mind while examining the following inventory of assessment tools. Several tools will be described: Delphi, force field analysis and the nominal group approach, functional job analysis, surveys, and consumer analysis. These tools were selected for inclusion for their relative technical sophistication and their usefulness in a variety of settings. The reader is cautioned, however, that no one of these tools can be expected to generate all the information needed. Several descriptive vignettes are included to help the reader who might otherwise be unfamiliar with the tools described.

ASSESSMENT TOOLS

Most assessment tools are useful in examining needs and interests; some are also useful in assessing resources and capabilities (see Chart 8, p. 171). After describing the tools, we will indicate how and where they might be stretched beyond their current, typical uses.

Delphi

The Delphi technique uses structured questionnaires to assess informed opinion about policy alternatives in some probable state of affairs. Its success depends upon the availability and involvement of the right group of respondents—those whose inputs will be diverse and carefully considered. Delphi is one of many "key informants" approaches. Persons normally selected as key informants include public officials, administrative and program personnel, private practitioners, representatives of professional or occupational groups, and educational specialists.

Until recently Delphi was known only to a limited number of practitioners in the field of technological forecasting. Since the early 1970s, however, a number of educators and others in the human service professions have made varied use of the tool. The associate director of the training division in a state department of mental health reports on some interesting variations in his use of Delphi:

> It didn't seem to make much sense to me to plan statewide training programs in substance abuse without getting some informed opinion on who needed the training most and who should be trained, on the context and format of such training, its location, length, and so on. There were some pretty basic questions—for example, should we focus on psychiatrists and other professionally trained mental health personnel? On lay care-givers? Ex-abusers? Teachers? GPs? Policy and other gatekeepers?
>
> In the past we would convene task forces to help us make policy decisions like these. But I wasn't happy with the work of these task forces. Sometimes the people whose opinion you really want are just not available for the task force. At other times task force members get bogged down in particulars or wind up agreeing on something just to agree. I wasn't ready to give up my use of task forces, but I needed some way to counteract "group think" and to focus task force deliberations. That's where Delphi was so ideal.
>
> Before convening regional task forces, I designed an exploratory Delphi questionnaire with eighteen issue statements and sent them to all those people who had agreed to serve, plus a number of others whose opinion I wanted to include. Each issue was stated in policy terms: "Training should be conducted in the home community or on the job rather than at state or regional centers," or "Users and ex-abusers should be trained to give help to their peers in trouble."
>
> I asked the respondents to rate each item on a five-point scale according to a number of dimensions. For example, I asked them to indicate whether a proposed policy was highly desirable, desirable, neutral, undesirable, or highly undesirable. I then asked them to rate each statement again in accordance with such criteria as estimate of cost, probability of attendance, and feasibility in terms of resources. I left space at the bottom for respondents to add as many as five additional statements, if they wanted to, or to comment on my eighteen.
>
> After summarizing the responses, my staff and I shared the results with each task force. We accounted for regional differences. That way

each task force could see how their thinking related to that of other regional planning groups. These preliminary inputs helped to cut down on some of the confusion that usually prevails at first meetings. Based on the first Delphi responses and the discussions reported by my staff at each of the regional meetings, I designed the second Delphi questionnaire.

On those items for which there was a great deal of consensus on desirability and feasibility, no further work was needed. We could just proceed with our planning. But on those items where there were big splits in opinion, or where people thought the idea was good but the feasibility poor, we needed to do a lot of probing. In some cases the clues came from the comments at the bottom of the first questionnaire. We then took what people said during the first task force meeting and put it into our second level of questionnaires. Following several more waves of questionnaires and task force meetings, we were able to arrive at some agreement on a statewide program with considerable variation at the local levels.

There are times when I'm tempted to use Delphi instead of task forces altogether. I have, in fact, in conference planning. Delphi is neater, it sharpens opinions and does not degenerate into group think where the least controversial policy is the one arrived at, or where some persons sway the rest by the sheer force of their personalities, status, or just plain stubbornness. With Delphi, the respondents can stay anonymous and are more apt to take risks and to be more honest about their thoughts and feelings.

The Delphi technique has been used by other continuing educators as well. As an assessment tool, it can be used independently or to complement committee work. But it is not a substitute for decision making or for face-to-face meetings. Decisions, even training decisions, are often made in a political context that requires convincing others, buying them off, or trading one reward for another. The Delphi can't make decisions. It can only inform them.

In general, Delphi is useful when one or more of the following conditions prevail: adequate information is unavailable and would take too long or be too costly to get by other means; the informed opinion of a panel of experts, including potential customers, may be as important as or more important than other hard data; the problems at hand or the tasks to be performed are so broad that more individuals are required to share opinions than can interact in any face-to-face interchange; disagreements among individuals are so severe as to preclude a communication process that is not both structured and referred; time is scarce or distances are great, and it is not feasible to bring people together for frequent group meetings; a supplemental group communication process helps to increase the efficiency and effectiveness of face-to-face meetings, as described in the vignette.

Delphi, however, is not an easy tool to use. It may fail if its designers do not know the issues well or if an appropriate panel cannot be convened. Some users of Delphi fail because of inadequate summarization and presentation of responses. Others fail when disagreements are glossed over, thereby discouraging dissenters and causing some to drop out. This results in an artificial consensus.

Force Field Analysis and the Nominal Group Approach

Unlike Delphi, force field analysis (FFA) and the nominal group approach (NGA) are problem-solving techniques that employ face-to-face contacts. They can be used in the assessment of either needs or interests within an agency staff. Force field analysis, in fact, is frequently used as a tool in agency development. It originated in the work of Kurt Lewin and is derived from the psychological notion that the individual or group exists within a "field" composed of him/itself and the psychological or social environment that influences the individual's or group's life space (field) at a given time.

FFA is a variant of a broader assessment approach sometimes referred to as the "community forum." It has an advantage over Delphi in that it involves all who may be directly affected by a problem and whose needs and interests must be addressed. It is relatively easy to arrange and inexpensive, and it allows the CE planner to spot persons who might later become leaders in program development. However, getting all the relevant participants together may be difficult. And FFA may foster unrealistic expectations. Despite these drawbacks, it has been proved useful in a variety of settings. Its utility for staff development is described by the psychiatric director of a state hospital:

> It fits our treatment orientation. We've built our therapeutic system around the notion that there are driving forces that exert pressures for change and restraining forces that resist change. So why not use the same idea to examine our needs to grow and develop as a staff?

In practice, FFA might be used by a CE consultant or planner with the total staff of an agency. First the staff is introduced to the underlying concepts or approach. Then the participants are divided into subgroups of five, six, or seven according to their discipline or by task. Subgroup members are then instructed to identify work-related problems that concern them and to describe all the forces that maintain the situation as a problem. Forces that might be activated or employed to reduce the problem are also examined. These driving and restraining forces are then sorted into three categories: those over which the group has control, those over which someone else within the organization has some control, and those over which neither have control.

The forces over which control can be exerted by the group are ranked in terms of potency and acceptability. Strategies for overcoming the problem are devised and implementation procedures are designed. Similar analysis is directed at those forces under someone else's control. During the process participants are helped to identify forces that are subject to influence through procedural, policy, or administrative changes and forces that require further training or education.

FFA is sometimes combined with the nominal group approach, in which each participant is asked to list his or her (or the staff's) needs and interests on a small card. The cards are then collected and grouped according to the "logic" they suggest to the group leader. The group discusses each card in turn, for purposes of clarification and explanation, and then compresses the contents of the cards into five or six items, which are ranked according to their priority. Following a general discussion, decisions are made about the content or objectives of a learning or training activity. These decisions are tested against such feasibility criteria as cost, readiness and motivation, acceptability, and instructional resources.

Like Delphi, NGA depends on the contributions of individuals. It reduces the likelihood that particularly verbal or powerful individuals will take over the direction of the deliberations early in the session. It does not work well when individual participants rebel against its highly structured and perhaps unfamiliar format, or when the group leader is either unwilling to hear what is said or unfair in his or her treatment of all the ideas that emerge.

Functional Job Analysis and Task Banks

Functional job analysis (FJA) begins with the assumption that all jobs are made up of specific tasks and that these tasks can be described. Once they are described, it is possible to (1) classify jobs according to complexity, (2) establish recruitment and selection criteria based on qualifications for performance of those tasks, (3) create a program of supervision designed to raise the level of performance, and (4) provide training for workers to prepare them for beginning-level work or for performance at advanced levels. FJA is most often used within the service agency arena.

The director of the mental health department of a Northwestern state describes his experience with this method:

> We had heard of the "task bank" designed by Sidney Fine and his associates at the Upjohn Foundation and decided to find out how we could use it. The Upjohn people had defined some 600 tasks performed by human service agency personnel—everyone from the typist and filing clerk through the caseworker and research director—and put them all on McBee cards so that one could hand-pull them out into a configuration that described somebody's job.
>
> After consulting with the foundation, we were able to develop our own task bank. It includes descriptions of the tasks currently being performed as well as those we expect to be assigned by the governor when the new legislative package is enacted into law. We put each task on a 3×5 card and grouped the cards into jobs people were performing now. We grouped a duplicate set into those jobs we figured they would be performing after the legislative changes. It really worked!
>
> For the first time ever we had clear job assignments instead of fuzzy job descriptions. We went a step further in designating criteria for beginning competence and for advanced skill. Now, if someone falls short of expectations, we know what to train for. And if staff members want to take on additional tasks or move to a new job, their knowledge and skill deficits are easy to identify. It's turned our whole training program around. No more hit or miss. Now we can identify an individual's strengths and needs, as well as those of a whole department.

Survey as Assessment

Although Delphi, FJA, FFA, and NGA are of interest because of their novelty and potency, the most commonly used tool of the continuing educator is still the survey. Unfortunately, we have found that many CE surveys are poorly conceived in design and execution. It seems as if people think they can use this instrument without technical knowledge. Improperly used, it can be an expensive, wasteful tool that yields trivial results. Even when properly designed, it can be expensive. For this reason many continuing educators seek expert consultation before embarking on an extensive survey.

Surveys are used to gather and disseminate information. In the following extract, the CE director of a school of social work at a Southern university describes a rather extensive survey of interests, needs, and available resources. Both the process and the findings were used to provide a foundation for the school's new continuing education program:

Chart 8 Usefulness of Assessment Tools in Relation to Orientation, Focus, and CE Model

Assessment tool	Orientation		Focus			CE model		
	Normative	Anticipatory	Needs and interests	Resources and capability	Consumer choice	Training	Consultation	Systems change
Delphi (key informants)	very useful	very useful	useful for needs	useful	useful if it predicts demand	useful to reflect policy	useful as part of consultation process	useful in practices and structure building
Force field analysis and nominal groups approach	very useful	somewhat useful	useful for interests	useful	very useful	useful in training but not for assessment	very useful	useful
Functional job analysis and task banks	useful	very useful	useful for needs of organization	useful	some but minimal usefulness	useful to the agency	very useful	very useful
Survey instruments	very useful	very useful	very useful	somewhat useful	very useful	somewhat useful	not very useful	somewhat useful
Consumer/provider analysis	useful	very useful	very useful	very useful	very useful	useful	useful	very useful

After an extensive assessment of training opportunities available to individuals and within service agencies, we searched for the differences between what was available and what people felt they needed and wanted. We contrasted the perceptions of staff at different levels within each organization and then contrasted these with the perceptions of other workers performing similar tasks in other agencies. The strengths and weaknesses of existing programs were identified. Respondents were also asked to describe their perceptions of the school and the role it might perform in helping agencies and individuals with their continuing education requirements. By the time we completed the survey, most of our respondents were just itching to get started. Apparently the survey not only yielded important data but served to motivate potential consumers as well.

In another survey aimed at assessing individual needs and interests, a psychologist on the faculty of a medical school in a rural state queried some 1,300 mental health workers and allied personnel:

We decided not to ask our respondents whether or not they wanted training. A "yes" answer wouldn't have told us much. People respond to a question on the basis of how it is phrased. We preferred to ask fairly open-ended questions like, "What are the most difficult mental health problems you encounter on your job which require your services?" Then we ask individuals what might be most helpful to them in dealing with such problems. If they specify training, we might expect this response to be a valid indication of interest.

The medical school's survey was oriented to practitioners' perceptions of their current needs. Similar surveys have also included questions relevant to the individual's future and anticipated career interests. The social work assessment focused on individual and organizational perceptions of interests versus available resources. It included projecting a role for the school's CEP. Like Delphi, FFA, NGA, and FJA, surveys can be used to assess current capability, needs, and interests and to project into the anticipated or desired future. Surveys appear to have utility for the CE practitioner in any of the practice arenas regardless of which practice model will be used.

Consumer/Provider Analysis

One of the problems we have observed in many assessments is their almost exclusive focus on the actual consumers of continuing education. Little regard is shown for those who don't attend CE activities, the *potential* consumer population. This often results in skewed and inaccurate information. We were impressed by one university-based continuing educator who developed a survey approach derived from marketing research:

> I was concerned with the fact that I knew which people were coming to our summer workshops but not why others stayed away. So I sat down over coffee with some of the guys at the business school, and we came up with a procedure that made a lot of sense.
>
> First, we examined the university's policies to find out just what the limit of its jurisdiction is and to identify those regulations or restrictions that might limit the CEP's activities. That still left a lot of things we could do, so we wrote them all down. We eliminated those items that were just too "way out" or for which we were obviously unprepared by temperament, training, or some other incapacity. Next we estimated the total potential consumer population for those services left. This was relatively simple. We know pretty well where we might draw consumers from. The state agency had figures on the numbers of psychiatrists, GPs, social workers, and nurses in mental health settings, school teachers and counselors, and so on. We used these. Then we took a look at who was actually coming to our offerings. We already had the data from previous assessments and evaluations. This made it possible to compare data on our actual versus the potential consumer populations.
>
> The next step was tricky. We had to ask ourselves, "why the differences in numbers and types?" Did location, training, availability of alternative training resources, types of work settings, or attitudes toward learning and advancement make a difference? Did some people just not know about us? Was our publicity pitched to a more narrow constituency? We had some ideas but no real answers to these questions. So the marketing boys helped us design a statewide survey.
>
> The findings led us to identify roadblocks in the way of certain groups—location, timing, money, perception by employers of our legitimacy. We then examined alternative strategies and their costs for overcoming these roadblocks if we wanted to move from serving only 7 percent to serving, say, 15, 25 or 50 percent. Then we calculated what it might cost and what the revenues might be if we continued offering our present services to larger percentages in three or five years. This step was relatively easy after gathering all the other data. But it assumed that a number of things would stay constant: types of offerings, consumer needs and interests, and opportunities and constraints within the university.
>
> For this reason we had to take our assessment one step further. We now examined the implications of changes in university policies or changes in our program direction. What began as a simple consumer analysis wound up as a total assessment of our present and future capabilities. We never went through so exhilarating or useful a procedure before!

Each of the tools discussed above complements one or more of the models of practice described in previous chapters: the consumer choice model, the training model, the consultation model, and the systems change model. The usefulness of each tool in relation to three broad sets of variables is summarized in Chart 8.

SUGGESTIONS FOR FURTHER READING

Avis, Warren E.: *Shared Participation: Finding Group Solutions to Personal Corporate and Community Problems*, Doubleday, New York, 1973.

Fine, Sidney A.: *Functional Job Analysis: How to Standardize Task Measurements*, W. E. Upjohn Institute for Employment Research, Kalamazoo, Mich., 1974.

Gestrelius, Kurt: *Job Analysis and Determination of Training Needs: Examples of Methods Applied to Teacher Trainers*, Gleerup Bökförlag, Stockholm, Sweden, 1972.

Lewin, Kurt: "Group Decision and Social Change," in H. Newcomb and E. L. Hartly (eds.), *Readings in Social Psychology*, Holt, New York, 1947.

Tripodi, Tony, Phillip Fellin, and Henry Meyer: *The Assessment of Social Research: Guidelines for Use of Research in Social Work and Social Science*, F. E. Peacock, Itasca, Ill., 1973.

Turoff, Murray: "The Design of a Policy Delphi," *Journal of Technological Forecasting and Social Change*, vol. 2, no. 2, 1970.

Warheit, George J., Roger A. Bell, and John J. Schwab: *Planning for Change: Needs Assessment Approaches*, HEW, NIMH, Washington, D.C., 1974.

Chapter 13

Program Evaluation

It's funny how people evaluate programs. Our participants loved the one project we considered our greatest failure to date.

The participants' criteria, we suspect, were different from the continuing educator's. So, perhaps, were those of the project's funders and the CEP's host institution. Evaluation is used by different groups for different purposes.

The underlying rationale for all program evaluation in CE is to secure information for future action. Findings can be used to improve the ongoing operations, to decide whether to terminate, modify, or restructure a program, to continue the program and possibly expand it, and to justify current investments in terms of future gains. These findings are often put to good use by continuing educators themselves, by consumers of a CEP's services, or by external sponsors of an evaluative effort. The sponsor may be the CEP's host institution or a project's funder (including its consumers).

WHAT TO EVALUATE AND WHAT TO LOOK FOR

If the objectives of a training program are to change the ways in which trainees perform a designated function, then one set of evaluative questions may be asked. If the aim is to change the way in which services are organized or delivered, then another set of questions may be more appropriate.

Decisions about what to evaluate and whom to involve in the evaluation flow logically from the CE model pursued. When operating on a consumer choice model, the questions raised will often relate to the individual learner's satisfaction with the activity and the extent to which CE activities met those expectations. When a training model is pursued, the evaluation's focus is on changed behavior of the individual learner. When systems change is the objective of a CE activity or project, the way in which services are organized and delivered after training may be contrasted with operations that preceded an instructional activity. When a consultation model of CE is used, evaluation may focus as much on process as on outcome.

One can distinguish between those approaches to program evaluation that emphasize examination of inputs, those concerned with outputs, and those that focus on program "throughputs" or efforts.

Program Efforts

Evaluations of program efforts are generally descriptive. They may include the number of courses or workshops, the number of participants in each, and the number of days or man-hours of participation; origins or work of the consumer population; or the nature of the training activity itself, its structure, content, and focus.

Reports on program efforts are generally expository in nature. They describe what actually happened, but they do not purport to measure the extent to which objectives were met or at what cost. Typical of a program effort–type evaluation would be the final report to a board of directors or policy committee.

Evaluation of Outputs

The evaluation of outputs places emphasis on results. Frequently these results are expressed as changes in knowledge, attitude, and skill by the learner. Output evaluation also focuses on the impact that CE or staff development activities may have on the ways in which services are organized and delivered or on their effect on client behavior. Output studies require a level of sophistication rarely available to continuing educators. Their cost may be prohibitive, rivaling and sometimes exceeding the cost of the educational activity itself. More modest approaches to evaluating program efforts are possible, however. They include "hip pocket" measures such as satisfaction quotients and consumer reports.

Evaluation of Inputs

If evaluations of outputs are concerned with results, input evaluations are concerned with the resources and processes used to accomplish those results. Programs and activities may be evaluated on the bases of the qualifications of faculty, the intellectual, educational, or status level of the student body, the student/instructor ratio, the originality of the training materials used, and so on. Universities and social agencies that are subject to review by accrediting bodies are accustomed to this type of evaluation.

When inputs are related to outputs, the emphasis may be on the relationship of cost to the program's outcomes. This is sometimes expressed in terms of efficiency. Evaluative studies that focus on efficiency are generally favored by those who must make difficult fiscal decisions based on the merits of competing programs. These persons include funders, legislators, university administrators, budget directors, and continuing educators who must compete for scarce resources or decide between competing pressures for program design and development.

Persons concerned with program efficiency want to know how much it would cost to achieve a certain outcome. They may ask questions regarding the relative costs of different techniques for recruitment and training, of different locations and formats, and of using staff with varying levels of expertise. They may focus on the efficiency of training different populations (e.g., training trainers versus training direct service personnel, or training higher-level professionals versus training paraprofessionals).

EVALUATION METHODS AND SOURCES OF DATA

Evaluation in continuing education may include everything from casual observations that are neither systematic nor based on scientific methods or statistical inference, to sophisticated experiments. Typically, continuing educators employ one or more of the following techniques: (1) nonobtrusive measures that are descriptive of program efforts, (2) instant or hip pocket evaluations that are generally directed toward an examination of program effectiveness defined in output terms, (3) subjective satisfaction measures that are also related to effectiveness, (4) standardized tests, (5) experimental designs that may examine either inputs or outputs in terms of effectiveness or efficiency, and (6) case studies that may focus on efforts in terms of effectiveness or efficiency.

Nonobtrusive Measures

Most continuing educators describe some of their program inputs and program efforts through use of nonobtrusive measures. These measures do not require participants to respond to interviews or fill out questionnaires. The most commonly used measures include reports on (1) numbers of courses, workshops, or conferences conducted, (2) facilities used, (3) costs, (4) numbers of persons with different backgrounds or in different occupational positions attending (reported either as absolute figures or as percentages of potential consumer populations), (5) the amount of staff time spent on individual programs and services, (6) categories of educational activities grouped around subject matter or the levels at which activities are directed (i.e., "beginning," "advanced," etc.), and (7) total number of participant-hours for selected activities.

These data are sometimes combined with such other information as (1) distances that people travel to attend an activity, (2) demographic characteristics of the consumer populations (e.g., sex, age, professional background and training, current work and job assignments), and (3) amount of other continuing education activities available to the same population.

The resulting information is not always useful or necessary. Yet it may continue to be collected ritualistically, as admitted by the director of a nursing school's CEP:

> Actually we do find it interesting to know where people are coming from and how much money we are spending per man-hour of training, but it doesn't help much in deciding what we should be doing or whom we should be attracing to our programs. Still, we would feel we weren't doing our job if we didn't keep collecting the information.

For others, however, similar data have proved useful in making decisions on program priorities, methods, or investments. Unfortunately, for our purposes we found little comparability between the data collected by different continuing education programs. Nor is there much comparability in their use of descriptive terms. A "work-shop" in one continuing education program may be labeled a "seminar" in another and a "course" in still another. Similarly, a "conference" may be called a "symposium" in one place and a "convocation" in another. Few standardized reporting systems exist.

Perhaps this is as it should be for the moment. CE activities are still so varied and changing that labels that may be appropriate one year no longer mean the same thing the next year. One CE planner argues in this vein:

> Sure, it would be helpful to know what other people are doing and what works and what doesn't, but I don't want to know too much yet. I am afraid that if we all used the same measures, we would all be doing pretty much the same thing. The moment you have a form to fill out or certain information that you have to retrieve each year, you begin planning your programs so that your reports look good.

Instant or Hip Pocket Evaluations

Some of the more informal evaluation procedures reflect common sense and informed hunches rather than hard data or rigorous investigation. These hip pocket evaluations are described by one of our interviewees as useful in getting throughput or output measures.

> There is no sense in spending lots of time or big money on program evaluations that give you all kinds of data you can't use. Although we do collect some standardized data, most of the time we collect only the information that we need. Our instruments tend to be informal, no more complex than a few questions written out on a slip of paper and kept in my "hip pocket."
>
> If we want to know whether people are enjoying a workshop and intend to return, we ask them. Or, if we want to find out whether people are employing some of the techniques we've taught them on the job, we spot-check by calling at random a number of our trainees or their supervisors. If they aren't, we try to find out why. This may require some more extensive investigation, but that's all right. It's better to spend the time and money on finding out what went wrong so you don't repeat your mistakes than trying to find out everything and throw out 90 percent of what you uncover.

One of the problems with this approach is that evaluations may be so idiosyncratic that the right questions are not always asked and many problems may remain undiscovered. An evaluators working under deadline may be subject to a number of dilemmas. They may be unable to use the more sophisticated long-range evaluation designs that they consider necessary. They may have to focus on short-term outcomes rather than long-term effects. They may be limited in the kinds of data they can collect, often depending on those that are available rather than using those that are more attuned to the needs of the evaluation design.

At times, evaluators may have to use data that were collected for other purposes, or data that may be unreliable, or data that measure only satisfaction rather than changed performance or learned behavior. They may have to substitute a case study for an experimental design, or use nonobtrusive measures when postparticipation questionnaires might have been preferred. They are sometimes pressured to do "instant evaluation," giving unsubstantiated impressions instead of statement of fact.

Subjective Satisfaction Measures

Subjective satisfaction measures comprise another evaluative approach to program efforts and outputs. They are used most frequently when either a consumer choice or a training model of CE is being pursued:

> We find that asking for feedback from students gives them a real chance to ventilate. Even though we can't always make use of the information we get, we are convinced that it is important for people to feel that we're concerned with their feelings.

But satisfaction measures can be used more purposefully. Another educator describes how he uses them as a component of the educational process:

> Instead of just getting a reaction to what we did or what they learned, at the end of each session we ask people: "Now that you've completed the course, what do you plan to take home to use?" A half a year later or so, we call or write them and say, "Six months ago you said that you were going to do this or that. Were you able to? Of those things that happened to you at the activity, what were most useful to you? What difficulties did you have in implementing what you learned, and why?" We try to keep the questions conversational and simple. We get the best results that way.

Many programs rely heavily on similar subjective satisfaction measures, although not without some ambivalence. "We don't know what else might work without an extraordinary expenditure of money," admits one CE planner. However, another contemptuously likens this approach to "Holiday Inn" questions, in which people are asked, "Was your room comfortable? Was the service adequate?" and so on. Still another educator calls it "getting your happiness quotient." He points out:

> These measures have their value, of course. But they sometimes tell you more about the person than about the program. We find that our trainees are reluctant to be critical. They come to our programs and they have a good time. They meet interesting people. They get "turned on" to new ideas. They are flattered by the attention they get from our instructors. They generally do believe that they are going to be able to make use of the information. How can they be critical? Even if they never use a thing they learn here, the experience was stimulating and exciting.
>
> It's no different if we ask their employers. If an administrator is going to spend a lot of money to send his staff to an expensive series of workshops, and the staff comes back excited and "turned on," he is going to be satisfied. If he had to justify sending them in the first place instead of spending money on something else, he can't very well admit he was wrong, especially if he sent his people to a status place like ours. It might be different if he had some alternative places to send his staff. But he doesn't. So you can pretty well bet he'll be satisfied.

Some investigators warn of the dangers of the "Dr. Fox Syndrome" described by a continuing educator associated with a medical society:

> We've had some razzle-dazzle conferences. Good facilities, charismatic lectures, good equipment, but insignificant content. On the other hand, we've had some programs where the content was thought-provoking, important, and useful, but the facilities were lousy or the speakers were dull. You can guess which programs the doctors were happiest with.

---

[1]The Dr. Fox Syndrome refers to an educational experiment at a Western medical school in which an actor was introduced to a group of practitioners as an expert in a subject area about which he actually had no substantive knowledge. He nevertheless gave a supposedly informational lecture, for which he had been carefully coached but which was full of nonsense and noninformation. His presentation, however, was lively and spotted with humor. He exuded considerable charisma. The participants in the course not only rated him highly effective as a teacher but indicated that they learned much from the presentation and would be able to apply what they had learned to their work. Some even claimed to have read some of Dr. Fox's professional articles.

Cautions aside, subjective satisfaction measures do and will continue to provide the largest source of feedback and evaluative data on CE activities for some time to come. The educators quoted identify at least five functions that they serve. First, they enable participants in a learning activity to ventilate and tell the educators how they felt about the activity, along with providing an opportunity to test their perceptions and reactions against those of others. Second, they can be used to help participants move from examining an experience to examining the implications of that experience, and thus to planning for changed behavior. Third, they can focus on specific aspects of a program such as transportation, location, or timing, or respond to a film or a simulation. The responses can then be used for planning changes in a program or for exploring new areas of program development. Fourth, satisfaction measures can be useful in program justification. Finally, there is the advantage of the relative low cost and simplicity with which satisfaction measures can be designed, conducted and used.

One caution should be noted. Some educators may use subjective satisfaction measures to deal with program inputs and then assume that responses to those questions give adequate information on program outputs. Our interviews yielded a considerable number of examples of such confusion.

Standardized Tests

Because standardized tests have been used frequently by other educators, some evaluators have attempted to apply them to training activities in CE. Some of these tests tend to measure those aspects of the individual that are relatively stable: personality, psychological type, intelligence, and so on. These are input measures. In evaluating education and training, however, one often attempts to find out what, if anything, has changed or how change took place. It is not very productive to invest much effort in using instruments designed to measure behavior under static conditions in hopes that they will also be capable of measuring change.

Tests of change in knowledge, attitude, and skill are more appropriate. They are integral to several state licensure and relicensure laws. They are relatively easy to design, yet some educators feel that these tests also are of minimal utility. They argue that such tests measure only changes that occur at the time of training but do not predict how the individual will behave in his or her home environment.

A more useful approach in using standard tests might be a "personal competency model.'' Although no one such model currently exists in a standardized form for any of the professions, several continuing educators have attempted to design their own variations. These are usually built along the lines of medical knowledge assessments or task banks, which were described in previous chapters.

Personal competency models can also be designed to measure growth and ability to learn, participate in a group, listen and understand what others have to say, say things clearly, openly, and un-self-consciously, and behave spontaneously. Similar approaches are used in T-groups and Tavistock conferences.

The use of such standardized tests is appropriate in relatively standardized educational programs. They would be too costly and unreliable if used for a single purpose or a one-shot event. They have the distinct advantage, however, of serving as both assessment and output evaluation tools.

Experimental Designs

Although experimental designs are not generally employed in continuing education, we have observed several experimental evaluations used to provide objective measures of learned skills or increased abilities. Experimental designs are of value when the learning of discrete tasks is the goal of the educational activity, but they are less valuable when a program has broad aims or a multiplicity of goals.

Experimental designs are costly. They usually require placing a lid on feedback and program improvement until after the evaluation is over, a restriction that is untenable to many program administrators. Moreover, only the most rigorous safeguards can protect against a Hawthorne effect, in which knowing that one is participating in an experiment may affect the outcome of the evaluation.

Case Studies

Case studies are used to describe program efforts. They are particularly useful for evaluating programs in which the staff has difficulty in specifying objectives, a difficulty not atypical for many new continuing educators. The case study can be used to pintpoint potential problems in the program's operations. For example, it might reveal that the effort to reach an intended target population is unsuccessful because of differences in status between that population and the staff of the CEP.

Case studies can be conducted by outsiders or by the actual participants in a learning or teaching experience, who are asked to keep diaries or log books from which daily insights are later retrieved.

Chart 9 summarizes our observations on how different evaluation methods are used and in what circumstances.

This chart is purely illustrative and should not be used as a prescriptive guide. The reader may utilize these and other methods for quite different purposes.

THE POLITICS OF EVALUATION: WHO, WHAT FOR, AND WHEN

Raising Fundamental Questions

When the evaluator is expected to examine only practices and techniques and not the values that underlie the continuing education program, he or she may face a peculiar dilemma—particularly if he or she has questions about these underlying values. How far can the evaluator go in raising fundamental questions? To what extent will his or her professional integrity be subject to challenge? Sharp disagreements over programmatic goals can reduce the evaluator's opportunities to communicate and gather data from staff members.

The evaluator may also face situations in which the goals of a particular program being evaluated are subject to shifts and changes. This makes it almost impossible to follow a particular design to its logical conclusion. Measurements and evaluation objectives may have to be changed. Evaluation techniques may have to be modified.

Undertaking an evaluation of the program does not imply an implicit commitment to the philosophy or goals of that program. The very fact that scientific and systematic evaluation is being conducted, however, may stamp the CE program with a legitimacy it does not deserve.

Bias is another problem. An evaluator who does not believe in a particular program might well be advised to steer clear of it for fear of prejudicing the outcomes of evaluation. Conversely, bias may be present if the evaluator believes strongly in a program that is being examined. Despite the logic of inquiry involved in program evaluation and presumption of scientific objectivity, the results of an evaluation are rarely value-free. Whatever the tools used, it is the social context in which the evaluator finds himself or herself that may be the greatest determinant of what he or she does.

Insiders as Evaluators

These biases may differ according to whether the evaluator is an insider or an outsider. An evaluator who is a member of the staff

Chart 9 How Evaluation Methods Are Used

Evaluation methods	General focus			Consumer choice	Relation to CE model used		
	Input	Throughput	Output		Training	Consultation	Systems change
Nonobstrusive measures	✓		✓	✓	✓	✓	✓
Hip pocket evaluation		✓	✓			✓	✓
Subjective satisfaction				✓			
Standardized tests	✓		✓		✓		
Experimental design			✓		✓		✓
Case studies		✓	✓			✓	✓

development or continuing education staff has the advantage of beginning with more detailed knowledge of the organization, program, and objectives of the CEP. He or she may be in a better position for relating to and getting the trust of those whose cooperation is needed. The concerns of this evaluator probably will be those of the CEP rather than the more theoretic concerns often characteristic of outside evaluators.

Outsiders, on the other hand, may be more objective. They may be more skilled and knowledgeable about evaluative approaches, and less subject to the effects of internal conflicts and to possible recrimination or political pressure in response to negative findings.

Evaluation Committees

The outcome of program evaluation is sometimes enhanced through the use of evaluation committees that determine what is to be evaluated; what tools, techniques or methods are to be used; when and where the evaluation is to take place and how deep it will go; and to whom it is to be reported. Several programs we visited utilized such committees. Their composition sometimes included instructional personnel, individual learners or organizational consumers, and the sponsors, funders, or organizations that provide the auspices for a continuing education program.

When, How, and for Whom to Evaluate

The continuing educator may have no choice over whether or not to evaluate. Evaluation may be required by funding bodies, by host institutions, by accrediting bodies, or by organizational consumers of CE services.

For evaluations to have maximal payoff, it is important for the evaluator to know not only what questions to ask but also who the major consumers of the findings will be. If these include the teaching staff of the CEP, one would expect a different set of questions than if they included the learners or the staff of an outside funding agency.

Generally, for findings to be useful in program planning, their implications for action should be clearly spelled out. Sometimes being too explicit may be counterproductive. For example, a state mental health agency acting as the funder may be concerned with the degree to which CE program objectives were met, whereas the administrative staff of the sponsoring school of social work may be concerned with those answers that spell out ways of improving the school's operations outside of the CEP. Giving the funder access to the latter information might not make much sense.

How Much to Invest in Evaluation

A heavy investment in formal evaluation is most likely to be justified under three sets of circumstances: (1) when the program itself is expensive, making the cost of the evaluation proportionate in relative terms, (2) when the program's potential impact is great but uncertain, and evaluation can be used to properly direct the program, and (3) when the program includes a number of relatively permanent activities so that improvements can be made the next time the activities are repeated.

In some of the more established CE programs, we have found evaluation to be an ongoing activity that feeds directly back into the programming and program development process. CE staff initially may have relied upon colleagues in the host organization and outside sources to help set up these procedures. Information gathered is used to gauge both the efficiency and effectiveness of CE operations and the accomplishment of program objectives, so that modifications in either means or objectives can be made whenever appropriate.

The Market Mechanism as Evaluation

Some evaluators we interviewed argued that sophisticated evaluation procedures are unnecessary in continuing education because the "market mechanism" determines whether a program is good or bad, effective or ineffective. If people come to CE activities or funders are willing to support them, the argument goes, "one can assume a certain extent of effectiveness."

This is a specious argument. Results of education cannot be measured in terms of the numbers of participants. The measurement of inputs does not supply answers to questions about outputs, nor does this drawing power of a program tell much about its effectiveness in accomplishing instructional objectives. Although consumers and funders may choose to attend or to support a program, the reasons for their choices may be unrelated to the CEP's objectives.

WHY EVALUATIONS FAIL

The reasons why some evaluation efforts in continuing education fail should be clear from the above. The objectives of an evaluation activity are sometimes confused. Such confusion may lead to using means and procedures appropriate as measures of inputs in order to get measures of outputs. Some evaluation efforts proceed as if the concern were with changing the individual learner, whereas the program is structured along a systems change model. Data gathering may be aborted or biased if the evaluator is either an insider or an outsider. Smug reliance on the market mechanism may preclude understanding of the program's efforts or efficiency. Different populations may interpret evaluative results differently, according to their own perspectives. Few human service continuing educators are knowledgeable about how to conduct or use evaluations. It is no wonder that program evaluation is often so inadequate and so half-hearted.

Most continuing educators do not have extensive research backgrounds. Those who come directly from clinical practice, in fact, may have backgrounds that are antithetical to research. This attitude is expressed by a psychiatrist, who confides:

> It may not be scientific, but I just "know" when something in a workshop has gone well and when it hasn't, on the basis of the kind of feeling that's been generated. It's like therapy. A good therapist knows when the relationship is good and when the patient is getting better. There is a magic you can't describe but you can feel. It's the same in training.

Perhaps it is the same, but in an age of accountability, "magic" is not enough.

We have found that most continuing educators approach evaluation with considerable ambivalence. This ambivalence stems from more than discomfort with the technical aspects. It also stems from the conviction that "it may be just too damned expensive in time and money, which we could be pouring into more and better training. And besides, with variable training populations, what you learn one time is not necessarily applicable to the next project." Program evaluation can be extraordinarily expensive, sometimes exceeding the actual cost of the educational activity itself. For others, despite considerable lip service to evaluation, their ambivalence stems from anxiety over being held accountable:

> Every federal and state grant we get now features evaluation and assessment. But the grants don't provide enough money to do them, and if they did it might cost more than the training itself. Besides, it puts us on the defensive, having to prove that we are doing the right thing the right way. We need room to feel our oats a little, to make some mistakes. We're new at this CE business. They should let us learn from our mistakes before they put the screws on.

Be that as it may, "putting the screws on" may result in fewer mistakes and require clearer focus by the continuing educator.

SUGGESTIONS FOR FURTHER READING

Isaac, Stephen, and William B. Michael: *Handbook on Research and Evaluation*, Knapp, San Diego, Calif., 1971.

National Institute of Mental Health: *Guidelines for Evaluation of Continuing Education Programs in Mental Health*, GPO, Washington, D.C., 1972.

Popham, W. James: *Evaluation in Education: Current Applications*, McCutchan, Berkeley, Calif., 1974.

Scriven, Michael: "Evaluating Education Programs," *Urban Review*, vol. 3, no. 4, February 1969.

————: "The Methodology of Evaluation," *Perspectives of Curriculum Evaluation*, American Educational Research Association, Monograph Series on Curriculum Evaluation, Rand McNally, Chicago, 1967.

Stake, Robert: "The Countenance of Educational Evaluation," *Teacher's College Record*, vol. 68, 1967.

Suchman, Edward: "Evaluating Educational Programs," *Urban Review*, vol. 3, no. 4, February 1969.

————: *Evaluative Research*, Russell Sage, New York, 1967.

Tripodi, Tony, Phillip Fellin, and Irwin Epstein: *Social Program Evaluation*, F. E. Peacock, Itasca, Ill., 1971.

Weiss, Carol H.: *Evaluation Research*, Prentice-Hall, Englewood Cliffs, N.J., 1972, pp. 1–9, 26–84.

Chapter 14

Continuing Education and the Continuing Educator

Although financial and other resources may be scarce at a given moment, virtually all continuing educators speak positively of the future. They point to a number of trends that support their prognoses. Changes in the human service professions, they say, will result in a greater demand for CE and staff development. New instructional formats and task analyses will make it possible to deliver services more effectively and efficiently. The use of CE as a change strategy is becoming better understood and acquiring more legitimacy. Continuing educators themselves are finding a common identity and increasing strength within their practice arenas.

CHANGES IN THE HUMAN SERVICES

The human services and the professions that provide these services have shifted their attention from preprofessional education—the one-time preparation for beginning practice—to ongoing and continuous education for changing practice. Several observers have spoken of the half-life of education in the various professions. Some estimate the half-life of medical knowledge to be five years. The half-life of social work knowledge may be even shorter. Social workers are responsive both to newly developed knowledge and to increased societal demand for the profession to perform new functions.

Human service professions are affected by new scientific discoveries and technological innovations. They are subject to fluctuations in the social environments surrounding their practice. These environments change so rapidly that earlier perceptions and established skills increasingly become passé in light of current concerns and conceptions.

The implications for education in the human services should be clear. A one-time infusion of knowledge and skill will no longer be acceptable, if indeed it ever was. Mental health professionals and allied personnel will be required to undergo ongoing and continuous education. Graduates of professional schools can expect major shifts in their occupational roles as new demands, new knowledge, and new techniques open up new opportunities and require modifications in professional practice.

In turn the public will demand increased accountability from the professions. Accountability processes will include specialized credentials apart from or in addition to professional schooling. They will include licensure, legal and professional certification, and recertification. Finally, recertification will require evidence of ongoing and continuing education under recognized and legitimated auspices—the university, the professional association, and the service agency.

These changes are complemented by changes in educational technology and new instructional approaches or formats. Together they extend CE activities to those populations that in previous years were not reached.

CHANGES IN INSTRUCTIONAL APPROACHES
AND IN MODELS OF PRACTICE

In an effort to be responsive to societal and organizational demands, CE programs will increasingly become oriented toward systems change and development. This trend is already evident in the priorities established by a number of federal agencies that fund "short-term" training or CE activities. NIMH, for example, will only give serious consideration to funding those CE projects that place emphasis on improving the development and delivery of mental health services.

This change in orientation is supported by a variety of newly developed instructional approaches and techniques. Although courses, workshops and seminars are perhaps still modal formats, they are being replaced by Tavistock conferences, T-groups or sensitivity training, the expanded use of professional conferences for CE purposes, and problem-solving sessions within an agency that combine consultation and training activities.

These approaches are complemented by such techniques and instructional methods as instructional games and simulations, force field analysis, and the use of organizational mirrors. New knowledge is also disseminated through new journals with innovative formats and through subject matter annuals composed of selected articles in a particular field, chosen to save the busy practitioner both time and money.

Instructional resource centers have been established at a number of universities, teaching hospitals, and state agencies in order to store and distribute materials and equipment and to consult with or instruct others on their uses. Consultation may be supplemented by short orientation sessions and workshops on the use of the center's resources. Many centers have print libraries, abstract files, electronic media libraries, museums, photographic exhibits, and audio-visual subcenters. A typical catalog of audio-visual equipment available in most university AV centers includes overhead projectors, record players, filmstrip viewers and projectors, cassette tape recorders, eight-millimeter film loop projectors, sixteen-millimeter film projectors, portable TV equipment for both shooting and showing, and a large array of films, slides, and tapes. AV centers have their own techniques or instructors who can help the user learn to make the most effective use of equipment and materials.

Increasingly, continuing educators may expect to find new facilities associated with libraries on the campus and in the larger community. In one Ohio city the public library has developed a media and resource center for mental health and other human service workers and has conducted workshops on using its resources in practice settings. Included are workshops on games, videotape recorders, and other instructional approaches using both hardware (equipment) and software (instructional methods).

In the future these facilities can be expected to incorporate other audio-visual services (sound recordings, video and motion pictures, photographic materials, graphic services, closed-circuit TV, broadcast television and radio facilities, etc.) as well as other special-purpose learning machines and computers.

New hospital and university buildings are almost invariably constructed with specially designed auditoriums that can either house large classes or be divided into smaller spaces. They frequently include jacks for film, video, and audio reception for individuals or small groups. It is often possible for two or more pictoral displays to occur simultaneously in the same room.

Some of these new teaching and learning rooms have elevated floors, interior climate control, accent lighting, and special acoustics. They may be connected with two-way computers for rapid processing of student responses, complete with feedback loops for reinforcement. By 1980 it should be common to have lectures given or films shown by one hospital telecast via satellite to another location. Thus students from different sections of the country can take the same course at the same time. Through computerized and programmed instruction and feedback, it may be possible to further individualize programs or to couple instruction with locally relevant discussion sections.

To service these new facilities, a number of materials production centers have already been established nationwide. The Joint Council on Educational Telecommunications predicts the development of more than five new centers by 1980. Many universities already have instructional centers that produce materials of various kinds. Although their staffs tend to be composed of media technologists, they have easy access to academic departments and subject matter specialists. They may also have adjunct writers, programmers, artists, illustrators, and others. As production centers develop more experience in creating, organizing, producing, testing, and disseminating instructional materials, these materials will become increasingly available for use in university CE programs, in social agencies, or by private groups.

Eventually such production centers might develop subdivisions related to materials development for independent learning, such as a subscription series and correspondence courses. They might include facilities for experimentation in which participants in CE activities could become the product designers as well as the product users.

Few continuing education programs can be expected to have sufficient financial or other resources to either develop instructional materials or build instructional centers for their exclusive use. Cooperation with other units at a university or with other CE programs in other parts of the United States and abroad is a highly practical means of expanding resources and opportunities and will inevitably become widespread.

COLLEAGUESHIP AND THE DEVELOPMENT OF A NEW OCCUPATIONAL IDENTITY

Like members of other groups within the human services, continuing educators and staff developers are finding an increasing amount in common with each other. A sense of colleagueship is strong between many continuing educators and is sought after by others. This development is not without its strains:

> It was difficult, at first, breaking away from my commitments to other psychiatrists. After all, we share a number of professional secrets. We know what we can't do and what we can, and we know how we look at clients and how we talk about them among ourselves. It's not something that we can share with people outside the fraternity, so to speak. It took a while before I could talk about these things to educators from other human service professions. I felt I was "finking out" on my former colleagues.
>
> But the more I began thinking of myself as a continuing educator, the more I realized I had to share some of my inside knowledge with other mental health continuing educators if I was going to plan my work effectively and help them do their jobs more effectively. What I found happening was that I slowly but surely shifted my perception of who my colleagues were. My former colleagues now became my clients. Sometimes I'm still not sure where I belong. I know I belong in both places, but it does create some internal tension.

Sometimes it builds other tensions as well. A nursing continuing educator at the university may be perceived by the nursing school faculty as one of their colleagues, but she may find that she has more in common with others in adult education or extension. At times she may be suspect to both, not privy to either group's inner councils. Therefore, the continuing educator must be attuned to the often contradictory signals she gets from both groups. It also means she has to work doubly hard to establish her credibility in order to develop or maintain a sense of trust.

Colleagues must be able to take one another's sentiments for granted, to communicate freely and openly among themselves, and to share confidences that could not be repeated to uninitiated ears. Colleagueship of this sort, although in its incipient stages, is not yet common to human service continuing educators. Too few know each other. They are located too far apart to have much opportunity for direct, personal interaction. It takes time to develop a shared cultural and political history, to find expression through a shared lore, shared secrets, jokes, and so on. But a shared history is emerging through common experiences exchanged in a variety of settings.

Announcements of national conferences (social work, psychology, psychiatry, nursing, etc.) show evidence of an increasing number of sessions devoted to the discussion of continuing education by continuing educators. Small groups of continuing educators in

New England and on the West Coast meet regularly on an informal basis. One group gets together to talk about their practices, share problems, and get informal consultation. Another group meets to exchange information about problems in service delivery in its area and to consider ways in which members might cooperate or collaborate on the creation of training programs to deal with those problems. Several national or regional networks of continuing educators have developed, some within a particular profession, others cutting across previous professional and occupational identities or personal histories.

What we are witnessing is the development of new occupational groupings within and across each of the human service professions. In time they may become recognized as separate sections, divisions, or specializations within each profession. Or they may unite as one separate occupational group:

> A few years back several of us were talking about a national association of continuing educators from all the mental health professions. We even considered affiliating with a national body like the Adult Education Association. But the idea was premature. We were still too tied to our former occupational identities.

However, well-established professional identities do not blur easily. A psychiatrist, a social worker, a social planner, and a sociologist may continue to identify first with their professions, second with their places of employment, and only third with their occupational roles as continuing educators or staff developers. Because of investments in an earlier professional image, they may view themselves more as practitioners or researchers than as continuing educators. Yet some will increasingly consider themselves primarily as continuing educators and thus identify more and more with each other. This will happen out of a sense of collective predicament, a sharing of common solutions, and will be supported through the development of common norms and expectations for professional behavior.

It is insufficient for continuing educators to claim a separate occupation or the mandate to perform certain functions. Both mandate and authority must be conferred by outside institutions such as regulating groups, employing agencies, professional associations, and individual consumers.

Although anyone can offer a course, workshops, or other learning experience, recognizable patterns are emerging. Professional associations, for example, have designated only certain types of CE as applicable to credentialing or certification. State laws often define continuing education in terms of specific content that must be offered by accredited institutions. The advent of the CEU as a basic unit in CE may do much to give university-based programs an edge over the private entrepreneur or consulting agency.

Moreover, despite considerable variability, a number of practice principles held in common by many continuing educators are very much in evidence. They relate to planning and program design, marketing, consumer involvement, and selection of content and format, among others. These were sketched out on the preceding pages. New principles and approaches to practice will continue to develop, paralleling the continued expansion of CE programs and activities.

SUGGESTIONS FOR FURTHER READING ON INSTRUCTIONAL APPROACHES AND MODELS OF PRACTICE

Blakely, R. J., and I. M. Lappin: *New Instructional Arrangements and Organizational Patterns for Continuing Education*, Syracuse University Press, Syracuse, N.Y., 1969.

Burke, W. Warner, and Richard Beckhard: *Conference Planning*, National Education Association, Washington, D.C., 1970.

Cantwell, Zita, and Hortense A. Doyle: *Instructional Technology: An Annotated Bibliography*, Scarecrow Press, Metuchen, N. J., 1974.

Carnegie Commission on Higher Communication: *The Fourth Revolution: Instructional Technology and Higher Education*, McGraw-Hill, New York, 1972.

Commission on Instructional Technology: *To Improve Learning: A Report to the President and Congress of the United States*, R. R. Bowker, New York, 1970.

Craign, Robert L., and Lester Bittel (eds.): *Training and Development Handbook*, American Management Association, New York, 1971.

Dermilye, D. W. (ed.): *The Expanded Campus*, Jossey-Bass, San Francisco, 1972.

Dressel, Paul S., and Mary Thompson: *Independent Study*, Jossey-Bass, San Francisco, 1973.

Engel, Herbert M.: *Handbook of Creative Learning Exercises*, Gulf, Houston, Tex., 1973.

Gosling, P., et al.: *The Use of Small Groups in Training*, Tavistock Institute for Human Relations, London, 1967.

Gould, S. B., and K. B. Cross (eds.): *Explorations in the Non-traditional Study*, Jossey-Bass, San Francisco, 1972.

Groombridge, Bryan (ed.): *Adult Education and Television*, National Institute of Adult Education for England and Wales, London, 1966.

Holtzman, W. H. (ed.): *Computer Assisted Instruction, Testing, and Guidance*, Harper & Row, New York, 1970.

Lauffer, Armand: *The Aim of the Game: A Primer on the Use and Design of Gamed Social Simulations*, Gamed Simulations, New York, 1973.

Levian, R. E.: *The Emerging Technology: Instructional Uses of a Computer in Higher Education*, McGraw-Hill, New York, 1972.

Mathieson, D. E.: *Correspondence Study: A Summary Review of Research and*

Development Literature, ERIC Clearinghouse of Adult Education, Syracuse, N.Y., 1971.

Mead, Margaret, and Paul Beyers: *The Small Conference: An Innovation in Communication*, Mouton Press, Paris, 1968.

National School Public Relations Association: *The Conference Planner*, National Education Association, Washington, D.C., 1967.

Niemi, John A. (ed.): *Mass Media and Adult Education*, Educational Technology Publications, Englewood Cliffs, N.J., 1971.

Noulenda, M.: *Annotated Bibliography of the Educational Implications of Cabled TV*, University of North Carolina, Greensboro, 1972.

———: *Annotated Bibliography on Video Cassettes in Education*, University of North Carolina, Greensboro, 1972.

Sattler, William, and N. E. Miller: *Discussions and Conferences*, Prentice-Hall, Englewood Cliffs, N.J., 1961.

Schein, Edgar, and Warren G. Bennis: *Personal and Organizational Change through Group Methods*, Wiley, New York, 1965.

Tracey, William R.: *Designing Training and Development Systems*, American Management Association, New York, 1971.

Wodaiski, John S.: "Use of Video Tape in Social Work," *Clinical Social Work Journal*, vol. 3, no. 2, 1975.

SUGGESTIONS FOR FURTHER READING ON OCCUPATIONS AND OCCUPATIONAL IDENTITY

Barber, Bernard: "Some Problems in the Sociology of the Professions," *Daedalus*, Fall, 1963.

Becker, Howard, and Anselm Strauss: "Careers, Personality, and Adult Socialization," *American Journal of Sociology*, vol. 62, November 1965.

Becker, Howard, Everett C. Hughes, Anselm Strauss, and Blance Geer: *Boys in White*, University of Chicago Press, Chicago, 1966.

Blau, Peter, et al.: "Occupational Choice: A Conceptual Framework," *Industrial Labor Relations Review*, vol. 9, no. 4, July 1956.

Frankel, Charles: "Social Values and Professional Values," *Journal of Education for Social Work*, vol. 5, no. 1, Spring 1969.

Friedson, Eliot: *The Professions and Their Prospects*, Sage, Beverly Hills, Calif., 1973.

Gartner, Alan: "Four Professions: How Different, How Alike," *Social Work*, vol. 20, no. 5, September 1975.

Henry, William E., John H. Sims, and S. Lee Spray: *The Fifth Profession*, Jossey-Bass, San Francisco, 1971.

Hughes, Everett C.: *Men and Their Work*. Free Press, Glencoe, Ill., 1958.

———: "The Professions," *Daedalus*, Fall 1963.

Kaplow, Theodore: *The Sociology of Work*, University of Minnesota Press, Minneapolis, 1954.

Miller, Albert C., and William H. Form: *Industrial Sociology*, Harper, New York, 1951.

Super, Donald E.: *The Psychology of Careers*, Harper, New York, 1957.

Wilensky, Harold L.: "Work, Careers, and Social Integration," *International Social Science Journal*, vol. 12, no. 4, Fall 1960.

Zinberg, Norman E.: "Psychiatry: A Professional Dilemma," *Daedalus*, Fall 1963.

Appendixes:
Resources for
Continuing
Educators

Information and Search Services

1. American Psychological Association
   1200 17th Street NW
   Washington, D.C. 20036
   More than 20,000 entries taken from an association publication, *Psychological Abstracts*, are stored in a computerized data bank. Any individual wishing to initiate a search through all or part of these records can do so through PASAR (Psychological Abstracts Search and Retrieval). Either natural language or index codes may be used. The full tapes are also available to information centers on lease and licensing through PATELL (Psychological Abstracts Tape Edition Lease or Licensing). Agencies and universities have access to the data through a service called PADAT (Psychological Abstracts Direct Access Terminal). Modest fees are charged.

2. The Center of Alcohol Studies
   Rutgers University
   New Brunswick, N.J. 08903
   Scientific literature on alcohol and alcoholism is collected, classified, abstracted, and noted in a *Master Catalog of Alcohol Literature* as well as the *Classified Abstract for the Archive of Alcohol Literature*. There are sixty CAAAL depositories in the United States, Canada, and several other countries. Retrospective

bibliographies, prepared on highly specific topics, are available in response to written requests. Visitors can use the center's special library. The center also publishes a *Quarterly Journal of Studies in Alcohol*, an *International Bibliography of Studies in Alcohol*, a *CAAAL Manual*, and the *Alcoholism and Treatment Digest*.

3 Clearinghouse for Federal Scientific and Technical Information
   National Bureau of Standards
   U.S. Department of Commerce
   Springfield, Va. 22151
   The clearinghouse serves as a focal point for the collection, announcement, and dissemination of unclassified United States government-sponsored research and development reports. A guide to its product services can be ordered from the Bureau of Standards at no cost.

4 DATRIX (Direct Access to Reference Information: A Xerox Service)
   300 North Zeeb Road
   University Microfilms
   Xerox Corporation
   Ann Arbor, Mich. 48106
   Approximately 90 percent of all completed and approved dissertations are added to the DATRIX data base, which goes back to 1938. Users can request a printed listing with cross-references to *Dissertation Abstracts*, a monthly service of University Microfilms library services. A simple order form can be used to request titles of all dissertations relevant to a particular interest, if they are to be found in the microfilm library.

5 ERIC (Educational Resources Information Center)
   Office of Education, Department of Health, Education and Welfare
   Washington, D.C. 20202
   ERIC has a network of twenty specialized centers or clearinghouses, each of which is responsible for a particular area of education. Clearinghouse outputs include monographs, state-of-the-art publications, and references on published articles and books on education and aspects of mental health. "How to Use ERIC," a publication available from the Government Printing Office, describes ERIC procedures in detail. ERIC also publishes *Research in Education, Pace Setters in Innovation, Manpower Research,* and *Inventory for Fiscal Years 1966, '67, '68, '69,* etc.
       The ERIC clearinghouses of greatest interest to continuing educators include:
   The Clearinghouse in Career Education (includes adult and continuing education): Northern Illinois University, College of Education, DeKalb, Ill. 60115.
   Educational Administration: Hendricks Hall, University of Oregon, Eugene, Oreg. 97403
   Educational Media and Technology: Institute for Communication Research, Stanford University, Stanford, Calif. 94305
   Higher Education: George Washington University, Washington, D.C. 20036
   Junior Colleges: University of California, 406 Hilliard Avenue, Los Angeles, Calif. 90024
   Social Science Education: Social Science Building, University of Colorado, 970 Aurora Avenue, Boulder, Colo. 80302
   Tests, Measurement, Evaluation: Educational Testing Service, Princeton, N.J. 08540

6   Mental Health Materials Center
Information Resources Center for Mental Health and Family Life Education
419 Park Avenue South
New York, N.Y. 10016
The center has two subscription services, a *Comprehensive Information Center*
service (IRC) and a *Selective Guide to Materials for Mental Health and Family
Life Education.* The IRC service is offered to national, state, or local agencies,
which pay a set fee per year and receive a *Selective Guide* consisting of about 180
individual annotated bulletins on mental health programs, copies of all special
publications issued by IRC, and answers by mail to questions about the selection
and use of publications and audio-visual aids appropriate to mental health and
family life education. Subscribers also get preferential treatment in applying for
places in seminars conducted by IRC. The *Selective Guide* is a regularly updated
listing of pamphlets, books, films, and other educational materials. Designed for
practitioners and lay persons, it may also be found useful to researchers.

7   National Clearinghouse for Drug Abuse Information (NCDAI)
National Institute of Mental Health
5600 Fishers Lane
Rockville, Md. 20852
Established for the collection and dissemination of drug-abuse information within
the federal government, NCDAI serves to coordinate information for eductional
and information-dissemination groups throughout the country. The clearinghouse
also disseminates information on pertinent films, records, plays, posters, etc.
It provides packets of informational materials, consultation to groups preparing
for seminars, lectures or other continuing education programs, and an updated
audio-visual catalog of films and other materials available for review, rental, loan or
purchase. It publishes an *Annotated Bibliography of Drug Dependence and Abuse*
and an *Annotated Directory of Drug Abuse Programs in the United States.* It
periodically prepares an updated *Guide to Federal Drug Abuse Programs.* Computer searches and printouts of relevant bibliographies are available to the inquirer
at no charge.

8   National Clearinghouse for Mental Health Information (NCMHI)
National Institute of Mental Health
5600 Fishers Lane
Rockville, Md. 20852
The clearinghouse stores almost 2,000 abstracts on its computer tapes on
psychological and social aspects of behavior, personality, cognition in higher
mental processes, etc. Special sections on the training of mental health personnel
may be of particular interest to continuing educators. It publishes a *Mental Health
Directory,* which contains information on more than 3,000 mental health facilities,
and a *Mental Health Digest,* which summarizes developments in the field.
     NCHMI is responsible for abstracting concepts from NIMH-supported pro-
jects as well as from general literature in mental health and for disseminating
research results in a rapid and effective manner. Interested parties can contact the
clearinghouse for current information and retrospective searches. In making a
request, the user should provide information on his or her role in addition to spelling
out concisely and objectively what he or she is looking for. A reply can be expected
within approximately two weeks.
     NCMHI recently published a four-part annotated bibliography on training
methods:

Part I: Background Theory and Research
Part II: Planning and Administration
Part III: Instructional Methods and Techniques
Part IV: Audio-visual Theory, Aids and Equipment

A related group of indexed and annotated bibliographies on mental health in-service training is available for use by "key professionals in community mental health," "allied professionals in community mental health," and "staff in residential institutions."

Additional Organizations with Information or Services of Interest to Human Services Continuing Educators and Staff Developers

Administration on Aging
U.S. Department of Health, Education
and Welfare
Washington, D.C. 20201

Adult Education Association of the
U.S.A.
810 18th Street NW
Washington, D.C. 20006

Al-Anon
Family Group Headquarters, Inc.
115 East 23rd Street
New York, N.Y. 10010

American Academy of Arts and
Sciences
280 Newton Street
Brookline Station
Boston, Mass. 02146

American Academy of Pediatrics
1801 Hinman Avenue
Evanston, Ill. 60204

American Association for Continuing
Higher Education
University of Oklahoma
1700 Asp
Norman, Okla. 73069

American Association for Extension
Education
Junior College Division
Black Hills State College
Spearfish, S.D. 57783

American Foundation for the Blind,
Inc.
15 West 16th Street
New York, N.Y. 10011

American Medical Association
535 North Dearborn Street
Chicago, Ill. 60610

American Mental Health Foundation
2 East 86th Street
New York, N.Y. 10028

American Nurses' Association
2420 Pershing Road
Kansas City, Mo. 64108

American Psychiatric Association
1700 18th Street NW
Washington, D.C. 20009

American Public Health Association
1015 18th Street NW
Washington, D.C. 20036

American Public Welfare Association
1313 East 60th Street
Chicago, Ill. 60637

American Social Health Association
1740 Broadway
New York, N.Y. 10019

American Society for Training and
Development
6414 Odana
Madison, Wis. 53705

Association for Childhood Education
3615 Wisconsin Avenue
Washington, D.C. 20016

Association for Educational
Communications and Technology
1201 16th Street NW
Washington, D.C. 20036

Association of American University
Presses
One Park Avenue
New York, N.Y. 10016

Child Study Association of America
50 Madison Avenue
New York, N.Y. 10010

Child Welfare League of America, Inc.
67 Irving Place
New York, N.Y. 10003

Council of National Organizations for
Adult Education
810 18th Street NW
Washington, D.C. 20006

Council on Social Work Education
345 East 46th Street
New York, N.Y. 10017

Educational Press Association of
America
Newhouse Communications Center
Syracuse University
Syracuse, N.Y. 13210

National Association of State
Universities and Land Grant
Colleges
One Dupont Circle
Washington, D.C. 20036

Extension Service
U.S. Department of Agriculture
Washington, D.C. 20250

Family Publications Center
Louisiana Association of Mental
Health
1528 Jackson Avenue
New Orleans, La. 70130

Family Service Association of America
44 East 23rd Street
New York, N.Y. 10010

Florence Crittenden Association of
America
201 North Wells Street
Chicago, Ill. 60608

Group for the Advancement of
Psychiatry
Western Psychiatric Institute
3811 O'Hara Street
Pittsburgh, Pa. 15213

The Hogg Foundation for Mental
Health
University of Texas
Austin, Tex. 78712

Interstate Clearinghouse on Mental
Health
c/o Council of State Governments
1313 East 60th Street
Chicago, Ill. 60637

Joint Information Service (of the
American Psychiatric
Association and the National
Association for Mental Health)
1700 18th Street NW
Washington, D.C. 20009

National Association for the Education
of Young Children
1834 Connecticut Avenue NW
Washington, D.C. 20009

National Association for Mental
Health
1800 North Kent Street
Rosslyn, Va. 22209

National Association for Public
Continuing and Adult Education
1201 16th Street NW
Washington, D.C. 20036

National Association for Retarded
Children, Inc.
2709 Avenue East
Arlington, Tex. 76011

National Association of Human
Service Technologies
1127 11th Street, Main Floor
Sacramento, Calif. 95814

National Association of Social
Workers
1425 H Street NW, Suite 600
Washington, D.C. 20005

National Conference on Social
Welfare
22 West Gay Street
Columbus, Ohio 43215

National Congress of Parents and
Teachers
700 North Rush Street
Chicago, Ill. 60611

National Council on Alcoholism
Two Park Avenue
New York, N.Y. 10016

National Council on Crime and
Delinquency
411 Hackensack Avenue
Hackensack, N.J. 07601

National Education Association
1201 16th Street NW
Washington, D.C. 20036

National Jewish Welfare Board
15 East 26th Street
New York, N.Y. 10010

National Society for the Study of
Education
5835 Kimbark Avenue
Chicago, Ill. 60637

National University Extension
Association
One Dupont Circle, Suite 360
Washington, D.C. 20036

NTL Institute
1815 North Fort Myer Drive
Arlington, Va. 22209

Office of Education
U.S. Department of Health, Education
and Welfare
Washington, D.C. 20202

Playschool Association, Inc.
120 West 57th Street
New York, N.Y. 10019

Rehabilitation Services Administration
Social and Rehabilitation Service
U.S. Department of Health, Education
and Welfare
Washington, D.C. 20201

Rutgers Center of Alcohol Studies
Rutgers University
New Brunswick, N.J. 08903

Salvation Army
120 West 14th Street
New York, N.Y. 10011

Science Research Associates, Inc.
259 East Erie Street
Chicago, Ill. 60611

Sex Information and Education
Council of the United States
(SIECUS)
1855 Broadway
New York, N.Y. 10023

Syracuse University Publications in
Continuing Education (SUPICE)
Syracuse University
224 Huntington Hall
Syracuse, N.Y. 13210

United Way of America
801 North Fairfax Street
Alexandria, Va. 22314

Addresses of Federal Regional Offices

Most federal regional offices include units with specialized agencies of importance to continuing educators. These agencies may gather information on manpower needs or may have funds available to support local, state, or regional training efforts. Some of these agencies are the Social and Rehabilitation Service, the National Institute of Mental Health, the Department of Labor, the Office of Child Development, and the Administration on Aging.

Region I

(Connecticut, Maine, Massachusetts,
    New Hampshire, Rhode Island,
    Vermont)
John F. Kennedy Federal Building
Government Center, Room 1512
Boston, Mass. 02203

Region II

(New Jersey, New York, Puerto Rico,
    Virgin Islands)

26 Federal Plaza, Room 3838
New York, N. Y. 10007

Region III

(District of Columbia, Delaware,
    Maryland, Pennsylvania,
    Virginia, West Virginia)
PO Box 13716
Philadelphia, Pa. 19101

Region IV

(Alabama, Florida, Georgia,
    Kentucky, Mississippi, North
    Carolina, South Carolina,
    Tennessee)
Room 404, 50 57th Street NE
Atlanta, Ga. 30323

Region V

(Illinois, Indiana, Michigan,
    Minnesota, Ohio, Wisconsin)
300 South Wacker Drive, Room 2904
Chicago, Ill. 60607

Region VI

(Arkansas, Louisiana, New Mexico,
    Oklahoma, Texas)
114 Commerce Street, Room 1008
Dallas, Tex. 75202

Region VII

(Iowa, Kansas, Missouri, Nebraska)

601 East 12th Street, Room 520
Kansas City, Mo. 64106

Region VIII

(Colorado, Montana, North Dakota,
    South Dakota, Utah, Wyoming)
Room 9017, Federal Office Building
19th and Stout Street, Room 11033
Denver, Colo. 80202

Region IX

(American Samoa, Arizona, California,
    Guam, Hawaii, Nevada, Wake
    Island)
Federal Office Building
50 Fulton Street, Room 416
San Francisco, Calif. 94102

Region X

(Alaska, Idaho, Oregon, Washington)
Arcade Building
1321 Second Avenue, Room 5030
Seattle, Wash. 98101

Directories and Special Publications

1 *Audio-Visual Center Catalogue*
   National Audio-Visual Center
   National Archives and Records
   Government Services Administration
   Washington, D.C. 20409
   Central information on availability of government motion pictures, filmstrips, audio and video tapes, and other AV materials. The center's services include information, sales, and distribution.

2 *Audio-Visual Instruction*
   Department of Audio-Visual Instruction
   National Education Association
   1201 16th Street NW
   Washington, D.C. 20036
   A list of documents that describe audio-visual materials and equipment.

3 *Directory of Education Information Centers*
   Division of Information Technology and Dissemination

Note: See also Appendix 1.

Bureau of Research
Office of Education
U.S. Department of HEW
Washington, D.C. 20202

or

Superintendent of Documents
U.S. Government Printing Office
Washington, D.C. 20402
Prepared by the Systems Development Corporation for the U.S. Office of Education, the directory lists a wide range of information centers offering services to
educators. Each entry includes the address, director, sponsor, services, users,
and holdings of the center. Although not exhaustive or comprehensive, the directory does list approximately 400 resources, many of which are of direct interest to
staff developers and continuing educators in the human services.

4 *Directory of Federally Supported Information Analysis Centers*
Clearinghouse for Federal Scientific and Technical Information
National Bureau of Standards
U.S. Department of Commerce
Springfield, Va. 22151
A guide to agencies ranging from ERIC clearinghouses to the Office of Economic
Opportunity Information Center. Entries list addresses, director, sponsor, year of
inception, missions, scope, services, staff, and qualified users. It contains an
index of subject areas, many of which are beyond the interest of most continuing
educators in the field of mental health. Nevertheless, it does an excellent job of
describing organizations that acquire, select, store, retrieve, evaluate, analyze,
and synthesize information and data in a variety of areas, many of which are
relevant to continuing education and to all the human services.

5 *Directory of Information Resources in the United States: Social Sciences*
Superintendent of Documents
U.S. Government Printing Office
Washington, D.C. 20402
Includes a listing of information resources that will accept and answer questions,
even though they may not be primarily in the business or information dissemina-
tion.

6 *Educational Directory*
Superintendent of Documents
U.S. Government Printing Office
Washington, D.C. 20402
A directory consisting of five volumes. The three that are pertinent include one
describing accredited institutions of higher education state by state, one listing
educational associations, and one listing educational agencies and personnel
within the federal government.

7 *The Educational Index*
H. W. Wilson Company
950 University Avenue
Bronx, N.Y. 10452
An index by subject matter and author relating to selected educational periodicals,
books, and pamphlets.

8 *Educational Recaps*
Educational Testing Service
Princeton, N. J. 48540
Brief descriptions of the latest developments in education, educational technology, programs, and related issues of interest.

9 *Educational Researcher*
American Educational Research Association
1126 16th Street NW
Washington, D.C. 20036
Publishes news of federal products and funding in educational research. Includes news of its own activities, of the professional activities of AERA members, and of foundations, institutions of higher education, federal agencies, and placement services as well as reviews of new publications.

10 *Education Pilot Report*
Educational Products Information Exchange Institute
386 Park Avenue South
New York, N.Y. 10016
Provides the consumer with advice, information, and evaluation of materials related to educational technology—hardware and software. It is considered the consumers union of the education field.

11 *Evaluation Comment*
Center for the Study of Evaluation
University of California at Los Angeles
145 Moorehall
Los Angeles, Calif.
Provides a forum for evaluators to discuss issues in the study of evaluation of educational programs.

12 *Research Reporter*
Center for Research and Development in Higher Education
1945 Center Street
Berkeley, Calif. 94720
A free quarterly publication disseminating the latest research findings on higher education.

Educational Film Libraries (Selected Listing)

Northeast

Boston University
Abraham Krasker Memorial Film
   Library
765 Commonwealth Avenue
Boston, Mass. 02215

Pennsylvania State University
Audio-Visual Aids Library
University Park, Pa.

Syracuse University Film Rental
   Library
1455 East Colvin Street
Syracuse, N.Y. 13210

South

Florida State University
Educational Media Center
Tallahassee, Fl. 32306

University of Kentucky
College of Education
Taylor Education Building
Lexington, Ky. 40506

University of South Carolina
Audio-Visual Division
School of General Studies
Columbia, S.C. 29208

University of Texas (in-state only)
Visual Instruction Bureau
Division of Extension
Austin, Tex. 78712

Midwest

University of Illinois
Visual Aids Service
704 South 6th Street
Champaign, Ill. 61820

Indiana University
Audio-Visual Center
Bloomington, Ind. 47401

Iowa State University
Visual Instruction Service
Pearson Hall 121
Ames, Iowa 50010

Michigan State University (in-state
      only)
Audiovisual Center
A-3 South Campus
East Lansing, Mich. 48823

University of Michigan
Audio-Visual Instruction Center
Frieze Building
Ann Arbor, Mich. 48106

University of Minnesota
Audio-Visual Extension Service
2037 University Avenue
Minneapolis, Minn. 55455

Southern Illinois University
Audio-Visual Service
Carbondale, Ill. 62901

University of Wisconsin
Bureau of Audio-Visual Instruction
Extension Division
1312 West Johnson Street
Madison, Wis. 53701

Rocky Mountain

University of Colorado
Bureau of Audio-Visual Instruction
Stadium 348
Boulder, Colo. 80302

University of Utah
Autio-Visual Bureau
Extension Division
Salt Lake City, Utah 84112

Pacific Coast

University of California at Berkeley
Extension Media Center
Berkeley, Calif. 94720

Oregon State University
Office of Audio-Visual Instruction
Oregon State System of Higher
      Education
Corvallis, Oreg. 97331

University of Southern California
School of Performing Arts
Division of Cinema
Film Distribution Section
University Park
Los Angeles, Calif. 90007

University of Washington
Audio-Visual Services
Ground Floor, Lewis Hall
Seattle, Wash. 98105

Washington State University
Audio-Visual Center
Pullman, Wash. 99163

Alaska

University of Alaska
Department of Audio-Visual
      Communications
College, Alaska 99735

Journals and Periodicals

Administration in Mental Health[1]
National Institute of Mental Health
5600 Fishers Lane
Rockville, Md. 20852

Adult Education
Adult Education Association of the
    U.S.A.
810 18th Street NW
Washington, D.C. 20006

Adult Leadership
Adult Education Association of the
    U.S.A.
810 18th Street NW
Washington, D.C. 20006

Alcoholism Treatment Digest
Rutgers Center for Alcohol Studies
Rutgers University
New Brunswick, N. J. 08903

American Journal of Orthopsychiatry
American Orthopsychiatric
    Association
1775 Broadway
New York, N.Y. 10019

American Journal of Psychiatry
American Psychiatric Association
1700 18th Street NW
Washington, D.C. 20009

[1]Published quarterly, this journal includes articles on a variety of topics and issues selected by the editors with the intention of advancing the practice or study of the process of administration in mental health settings. In addition to contents relating to both theory and practice, the quarterly publishes literature reviews, annotated

APA Monitor
American Psychological Association
1200 17th Street NW
Washington, D.C. 20036

Behavioral Science
Mental Health Institute
University of Michigan
Ann Arbor, Mich. 48104

Change Magazine
59 East 54th Street
New York, N.Y. 10022

Community Mental Health Journal
Behavioral Publications
72 Fifth Avenue
New York, N.Y. 10011

The Digest of Neurology and
    Psychiatry
Institute for Living
Retreat Avenue
Hartford, Conn. 06103

Educational Technology
Educational Technology Publications,
    Inc.
140 Sylvan Avenue
Englewood Cliffs, N. J. 07632

EDUCOM
Interuniversity Communications
    Council, Inc.
Box 364
Princeton, N. J. 08540

Harvard Educational Review
Longfellow Hall
13 Apian Way
Cambridge,

Hospital and Community Psychiatry
American Psychiatric Association
1700 18th Street NW
Washington, D.C. 20009

Journal of Education for Social Work
Council on Social Work Education
345 East 46th Street
New York, N.Y. 10017

Journal of Psychiatric Nursing and
    Mental Health Services
Charles B. Slack, Inc.
6900 Grove Road
Thorofare, N. J. 08086

Manpower
Superintendent of Documents
U.S. Government Printing Offiice
Washington, D.C. 20402

Memo to the Faculty
The Center for Research on Learning
    and Teaching
University of Michigan
Ann Arbor, Mich. 48104

Mental Health Digest
National Clearinghouse for Mental
    Health Information
National Institute of Mental Health
5600 Fishers Lane
Rockville, Md. 20852

Mental Hygiene
National Association for Mental
    Health
1800 North Kent Street
Rosslyn, Va. 22209

---

bibliographies, reports on original research, case studies, essays, descriptions or suggestions for training programs, etc. In the Winter of 1974 issue, for example, the journal's editor, Saul Feldman, proposed a graduate curriculum complete with course content and descriptions for educating the future mental health executive. Announcements on training programs and other happenings are included, as are book notes and abstracts. An article in the Winter 1972 issue discussed teaching mental health administration to psychiatric residents and fellows and described the training program at the Albert Einstein College of Medicine and the Maimonides Hospital and Medical Center. An article by Charles J. Austin in the fall 1973 issue discussed a national study of educational programs in health administration. A regular feature is a section entitled "On the Federal Scene," which discusses legislation, program reorganization, fiscal issues, involvement of NIMH and HIHW staff in matters relating to mental health administration, etc.

Michigan Manpower Quarterly Review
Board of Michigan Employment
   Security Commission
7310 Woodward Avenue
Detroit, Mich. 48202

Personnel Administration
Society for Personnel Administration
Suites 485–487, National Press Building
529 14th Street NW
Washington, D.C. 20004

Psychiatric News
American Psychiatric Association
1700 18th Street NW
Washington, D.C. 20009

Psychiatric Progress
Eli Lewley and Company
3 West 57th Street
New York, N.Y. 10019

Psychiatry Digest
Psychiatry Digest, Inc.
445 Central Avenue
Northfield, Ill. 60093

Schizophrenia Bulletin
Office of Communications
National Institute of Mental Health
5600 Fishers Lane
Rockville, Md. 20852

Social Work
National Association of Scoial Workers
1425 H Street NW
Washington, D.C. 20005

Social Work Education Reporter
Council on Social Work Education
345 East 46th Street
New York, N.Y. 10017

Training and Development Journal
American Society for Training and
   Development
Box 5307
Madison, Wis. 53705

Work Force
Vocations for Social Change, Inc.
Box 13
Canyon, Calif. 94516

Information Sources on Grant and Contract Possibilities

1 *Catalog of Federal Domestic Assistance (CFD)*
Published at the start of each fiscal year by the U.S. Government Printing Office, Washington, D.C. 20402. Generally in looseleaf with detailed information on all domestic programs; who is eligible, now to apply, known deadlines.

2 *Federal Register*
Published Monday through Friday every week by the U.S. Government Printing Office. Goes beyond the CFDA to inform reader on all new and changing federal programs and grant possibilities as they are announced.

3 *Federal Management Circular 74-7.*
Available from the Office of Management and Budget, Executive Office Building, 17th Street and Pennsylvania Avenue NW, Washington, D.C. 20006. Details uniform administrative standards for assistance to local and other governmental recipients.

4 *User's Guide to Funding Resources*
Published by Chilton Book Company, Human Resources Network, 2010 Chancellor Street, Philadelphia, Pa. 19103. Includes four books each of which can be purchased separately: "How to Get Money for Education, Fellowships and Scholarships," "How to Get Money for Youth, the Elderly, the Handicapped, Women and Civil Liberties," "How to Get Money for Conservation and Community

Development,'' and ''How to Get Money for Arts and Humanities, Drug Abuse and Health.''

5   *The Foundation Directory* (Edition 5, 1975)
Available from Columbia University Press, 136 South Broadway, Irvington, N.Y. 10533. Contains information on private foundations and community trusts, including name, address, financial data, range of grants, and names of trustees. Organized by state. Limited to foundations with assets of $1 million or grants of $500,000 or more.
   A companion volume, *The Foundation Grants Index*, describes all available grants of over $5000. The bimonthly *Foundation News* includes papers in which foundation people share information with other foundation people. Both publications are available from Columbia University Press.

6   *Program Planning and Proposal Writing*
Order from Grantsmanship Center, 1015 West Olympic Boulevard, Los Angeles, Calif. 90015. A how-to-do-it guide on proposal development, from setting of objectives through budgeting, staffing, and evaluation. See also the *Grantsmanship Center News*, which discusses public policies, gives tips on grantsmanship, reviews relevant publications and documents, and prints in-depth articles on both private and public funding sources. It is published eight times a year.

7   *Commerce Business Daily*
Published by the U.S. Commerce Department; order from the Superintendent of Documents, U.S. Government Printing Office. Lists all government contracts, grants, and bids as they are announced.

8   *Profiles of Involvement: Handbook of Corporate Social Responsibility*
Order from Human Resources Network, 2010 Chancellor Street, Philadelphia, Pa. 19103. Includes information on over 200 social responsibility programs sponsored by major corporations.

9   *LRC Newsbriefs*
Published by the Lutheran Resource Commission, Dupont Circle Building, 1346 Connecticut Avenue NW, Washington, D.C. 20036. Information is provided through a network of former government employees who serve as information gatherers and disseminators for a wide variety of programs and whose presentation of information is clearer than that of official documents.

Field Visit Sites

Eastern States

Organization	Person(s) Interviewed
Alcoholism Training Program Boston City Hospital Boston, Mass.	Robert Mannering Chaim Rosenberg
Community Training Resources Cambridge-Somerville Center Cambridge, Mass.	Patricia Pappernow
Continuing Education for Nurses and Mental Health Care Workers Teachers College Columbia University New York, N.Y.	Fanny Siegel

Note: Some sites are not listed on the request of persons interviewed.

Continuing Education Program   Louise Frey
Boston University School
  of Social Work
Boston, Mass.

Department of Psychiatry   Andrew Morrison
Tufts University
Boston, Mass.

Harvard Laboratory of   Marie Killery
Community Psychiatry   Robert Weiss
Cambridge, Mass.

Mental Health Services   Ann Twomey
Federal Region I
Boston, Mass.

Mental Health Skills Center   Sandra Fox
Washington School of Psychiatry
Washington, D.C.

Nathan Ackerman Family   Kitty LaPerriere
  Therapy Institute
New York, N.Y.

New Careers Project   Lydia Peters
Boston University Community
  Mental Health Program
Boston, Mass.

New York City Manpower   Ann Cunningham
  and Training Development
New York, N.Y.

Project Place   Zachary Klein
Boston, Mass.

School of Education   Simon Wittes
University of Massachusetts
Boston, Mass.

School of Nursing   Honora Farrell
Adelphi University   Elaine Goldman
Garden City, Long Island, N.Y.

School of Social Work and   Charles Cacace
  Social Planning
University of Maryland
Baltimore, Md.

Simmons School of Social Work   Francis Lewis
Boston, Mass.

United Community Services   Harold Demone
Boston, Mass.   Herbert Hoffman
                                      Walter Stern

University of Pennsylvania Hospital   Sidney Pulver
Philadelphia, Pa.

Washington School of Psychiatry	Jeannie Lee Adams
Washington, D.C.	John Ainslie
	Robert Kvarnes
	William Lillycrop
	Arthur Norman

Midwestern States

Organization	Person(s) Interviewed
Association of Clinical Pastoral Education Prairie View Community Mental Health Center Hayes, Kansas	Tom Counts
Center for Applied Behavioral Sciences The Menninger Foundation Topeka, Kans.	Herbert C. Klemme
Mental Health Skills Laboratory Community Mental Health Board Detroit, Mich.	George Mink
Ohio Academy of Family Physicians Cleveland, Ohio	James Hodges
Ohio Department of Mental Health and Mental Retardation Columbus, Ohio	Alan Cotzin M. D. McCullough Calvin Young
School of Applied Social Sciences Case-Western Reserve University Cleveland, Ohio	Lois G. Swack
School of Social and Community Services University of Missouri Columbia, Mo.	Charles Mitchell Dwight Reiman
School of Social Work Ohio State University Columbus, Ohio	Barry Weiss
School of Social Work University of Illinois, Chicago Circle Chicago, Illinois	Freda Engel

Western States

Organization	Person(s) Interviewed
California Center for Training Northern Region Berkeley, Calif.	Donald Brown Elias Katz Irving Shapiro

California Center for Training Southern Region Los Angeles, Calif.	Arnold Beiser Helen Olander
California Department of Health Training Division Sacramento, Calif.	Jack Hubbard
Continuing Education in Mental Health School of Medicine University of New Mexico Albuquerque, N.M.	Jerome Levy
Continuing Education in Mental Health Program Fort Logan Mental Health Center Denver, Colo.	Boris Gertz
Continuing Education in Nursing University of California San Francisco, Calif.	Darlene Anarude
College of Medicine University of Utah Salt Lake City, Utah	Steven Zlutnik
Los Angeles Center for Group Psychiatry Los Angeles, Calif.	Kathleen Morganstern
Los Angeles County Hospital Los Angeles, Calif.	Alexander Ragowski
Medical School University of Oregon Portland, Oreg.	Peter Maher
Physicians Education Project Portland, Oreg.	Robert Daugherty
School of Public Health University of California Berkeley, Calif.	Marc Pilisuk
School of Social Work University of California Los Angeles, Calif.	Virginia Mills
Suicide Prevention Center Los Angeles, Calif.	Norman Farberow
Western Interstate Commission on Higher Education (WICHE) Boulder, Colo.	Bernard Bloom Stanley Boucher Frank Dell'Apa Patricia McAtee Paul McCullough Louis Medina

224   APPENDIX 8

Southern States

Organization	Person(s) Interviewed
Adult Mental Health Services Department of Human Resources Raleigh, N.C.	William E. Thomas
Florida Board of Regents Tallahassee, Fla.	Michael Austin
Florida Mental Health Institute Tampa, Fla.	John Wright
Human Resources Training Institute East Carolina University Greenville, N.C.	William Byrd Richard Schmitt
Kentucky Mental Health Manpower Commission Louisville, Ky.	Earl Staton
Psychology Department Vanderbilt University Nashville, Tenn.	Martin Katahn Arthur Robbins
School of Medicine University of North Carolina Chapel Hill, N.C.	Noel A. Mazade
School of Nursing Vanderbilt University Nashville, Tenn.	Sally Archer Sally Sample
Southern Region Education Board (SREB) Atlanta, Ga.	Harold McPheeters

National Associations

Organization	Person(s) Interviewed
American Psychiatric Association Washington, D.C.	Hugh Carmichael Howard Kern
Council on Social Work Education New York, N.Y.	Deborah Miller
National Association of Social Workers Washington, D.C.	Leonard Stern
National Conference on Social Welfare Columbus, Ohio	Joe Hoffer
Nursing Continuing Education American Nurses' Association Kansas City, Mo.	Elizabeth Allen Elda Popiel

Index